THE STANDARD EDITION OF
THE COMPLETE PSYCHOLOGICAL WORKS
OF SIGMUND FREUD

*

VOLUME III

PHOTOGRAPHIE   des CHAMPS ÉLYSÉES

à Mr. le Dr. Freud. Souvenir de la Salpêtrière
1886. 24 fevrier

JEAN-MARTIN CHARCOT

THE STANDARD EDITION
OF THE COMPLETE PSYCHOLOGICAL WORKS OF

SIGMUND FREUD

Translated from the German under the General Editorship of

JAMES STRACHEY

In Collaboration with
ANNA FREUD

Assisted by
ALIX STRACHEY and ALAN TYSON

VOLUME III
(1893–1899)

Early Psycho-Analytic Publications

LONDON
THE HOGARTH PRESS
AND THE INSTITUTE OF PSYCHO-ANALYSIS

PUBLISHED BY
THE HOGARTH PRESS LIMITED

*

CLARKE, IRWIN AND CO. LTD.
TORONTO

This Edition first Published in
1962
Reprinted 1962

131. 3462
F 895 s
V 3

35543

TRANSLATION AND EDITORIAL MATTER
© JAMES STRACHEY 1962

PRINTED AND BOUND IN GREAT BRITAIN
BY BUTLER AND TANNER LTD., FROME

CONTENTS

VOLUME THREE

v

FRONTISPIECE Photograph of Jean-Martin Charcot, presented by him to Freud in Paris, 1886.

PREFACE TO FREUD'S SHORTER WRITINGS 1893–1906
(1906)

EDITOR'S NOTE

PREFACE TO *SAMMLUNG KLEINER SCHRIFTEN ZUR NEUROSENLEHRE AUS DEN JAHREN 1893–1906*

(*a*) GERMAN EDITIONS:
1906   *S.K.S.N.*, **1**, iii. (1911, 2nd ed.; 1920, 3rd ed.; 1922, 4th ed.)
1925   *G.S.*, **1**, 241–2.
1952   *G.W.*, **1**, 557–8.

The present translation of the preface, by James Strachey, seems to be the first into English.

The volume to which this is the preface was the first of Freud's five collected volumes of shorter papers, of which the others appeared in 1909, 1913, 1918 and 1922. The present volume of the *Standard Edition* includes the majority of the contents of this first collection. The first of the French papers, however, which compares organic and hysterical paralyses (1893*c*), has been included in Volume I of the *Standard Edition*, as belonging almost wholly to the pre-psycho-analytic epoch. Similarly, the last three of its items (the two from the Löwenfeld volumes, 1904*a* and 1906*a*, as well as the paper 'On Psychotherapy', 1905*a*), which are of a later date than the rest, will be found in Volume VII of the *Standard Edition*. Moreover, the 'Preliminary Communication' (1893*a*), which was reprinted in *Studies on Hysteria* (1895*d*), is included in Volume II of the *Standard Edition* and has not been repeated here. Its place is taken, however, by the recently discovered lecture (1893*h*), which was contemporary with the 'Preliminary Communication' and covers the same ground and of which there is a shorthand report corrected by Freud. The present volume further contains two papers which Freud omitted from his collection: the discussion on forgetting (1898*b*), which was afterwards developed into the first chapter of *The Psychopathology of Everyday Life* and the paper

3

on 'Screen Memories' (1899*a*). It also includes the list of abstracts of Freud's earlier works (1897*b*), which he himself drew up with an eye to his application for a professorship.

In view of the precedence given by Freud among these papers to his obituary of Charcot, it seems appropriate to preface the present volume of the *Standard Edition* with a reproduction of the signed photograph which Charcot presented to him on his departure from Paris in February, 1886.

PREFACE TO FREUD'S COLLECTION OF SHORTER WRITINGS ON THE THEORY OF THE NEUROSES FROM THE YEARS 1893-1906

IN response to many wishes that have reached me, I have decided to lay before my colleagues in collected form the minor works on the neuroses which I have published since 1893. They consist of fourteen short papers, mostly in the nature of preliminary communications, which have appeared in scientific proceedings or medical periodicals—three of them in French. The two last (XIII and XIV),[1] which give a very succinct account of my present position as regards both the aetiology and the treatment of the neuroses, are taken from L. Löwenfeld's well-known volumes, *Die psychischen Zwangserscheinungen* [Psychical Obsessional Symptoms], 1904, and the fourth edition of *Sexualleben und Nervenleiden* [Sexual Life and Nervous Illness], 1906, having been written by me at the request of their author, who is an acquaintance of mine. [See p. 121.]

The present collection serves as an introduction and supplement to my larger publications dealing with the same topics—*Studies on Hysteria* (with Dr. J. Breuer), 1895; *The Interpretation of Dreams*, 1900; *The Psychopathology of Everyday Life*, 1901 and 1904; *Jokes and their Relation to the Unconscious*, 1905; *Three Essays on the Theory of Sexuality*, 1905; *Fragment of an Analysis of a Case of Hysteria*, 1905. The fact that I have put my Obituary of J.-M. Charcot at the head of this collection of my short papers should be regarded not only as the repayment of a debt of gratitude, but also as an indication of the point at which my own work branches off from the master's.

No one who is familiar with the course of development of human knowledge will be surprised to learn that I have in the meantime gone beyond some of the opinions which are expressed here, and have seen my way to modifying others. Nevertheless, I have been able to retain the greater part of them

[1] [See Editor's Note above.]

5

unaltered and in fact have no need to withdraw anything as wholly erroneous or completely worthless.[1]

[1] [It may be remarked that when these papers were reprinted in the first German collected edition of Freud's works (*G.S.*, **1**) in 1925, he added a few critical footnotes: See, for instance, p. 168 below.]

CHARCOT
(1893)

EDITOR'S NOTE

CHARCOT

(a) GERMAN EDITIONS:
1893   *Wien. med. Wschr.*, **43** (37), 1513–20.
1906   *S.K.S.N.*, **1**, 1–13. (1911, 2nd ed.; 1920, 3rd ed.; 1922, 4th ed.)
1925   *G.S.*, **1**, 243–57.
1952   *G.W.*, **1**, 21–35.

(b) ENGLISH TRANSLATION:
'Charcot'
1924   *C.P.*, **1**, 9–23. (Tr. J. Bernays.)

Included (No. XXII) in Freud's own collection of abstracts of his early works (1897*b*). The present translation is based on that of 1924.

From October, 1885, to February, 1886, Freud worked at the Salpêtrière in Paris under Charcot.[1] This was the turning-point in his career, for it was during this period that his interest shifted from neuropathology to psychopathology—from physical science to psychology. Whatever other and deeper factors were concerned in the change, the immediate determinant was undoubtedly the personality of Charcot. As he wrote to his future wife soon after his arrival in Paris (November 24, 1885): 'I think I am changing a great deal. I will tell you in detail what is affecting me. Charcot, who is one of the greatest of physicians and a man whose common sense is touched by genius, is simply uprooting my aims and opinions. I sometimes come out of his lectures as though I were coming out of Notre Dame, with a new idea of perfection. But he exhausts me; when I come away from him I no longer have any desire to work at my own silly things; it is three whole days since I have done any work, and I have no feelings of guilt. My brain is sated,

[1] Jean-Martin Charcot (1825–93).

as if I had spent an evening at the theatre. Whether the seed will ever bear any fruit, I do not know; but what I do know is that no one else has ever affected me in the same way . . .' [1] This obituary, written only a few days after Charcot's death, is further evidence of the greatness of Freud's admiration for him, and to the end of his own life Freud never lost it. Sayings of Charcot's were constantly cropping up in Freud's writings, and in all his accounts of his own development the part played by Charcot was never forgotten.

Though the present is Freud's longest study on him, it can be supplemented from two or three other works: from Freud's official report to the authorities of the University of Vienna on the course of his studies in Paris (1956a [1886]), which is the source of some of the material in this obituary, from his 'History of the Psycho-Analytic Movement' (1914d), *Standard Ed.*, **14**, 13–14, from the *Autobiographical Study* (1925d), ibid., **20**, 12–14, as well as from the first volume of Ernest Jones's biography (1953, 202–5).[2]

[1] The letter is included in the recently published collection of Freud's correspondence (Freud, 1960a).

[2] Freud translated two of Charcot's books into German at their author's request: the third volume of his *Leçons sur les maladies du système nerveux* (1887), of which the German version was published before the second half of the French original (Freud, 1886f), and the *Leçons du mardi* (*1887–8*) (1888) (Freud, 1892–94). Freud added a number of footnotes to the latter volume, without Charcot's permission; and this seems to have led to trouble. See a passage near the end of Chapter VII of *The Psychopathology of Everyday Life* (1901b), *Standard Ed.*, **6**, 161. A second volume of the *Leçons du mardi*, dealing with the academic year 1888–9, was translated by Max Kahane (1895), an early follower of Freud's.

CHARCOT

On the 16th of August of this year, J.-M. Charcot died suddenly, without pain or illness, after a life of happiness and fame. In him, all too soon, the young science of neurology has lost its greatest leader, neurologists of every country have lost their master teacher and France has lost one of her foremost men. He was only sixty-eight years old; his physical strength and mental vigour, together with the hopes he so frankly expressed, seemed to promise him the long life which has been granted to not a few mental workers of this century. The nine imposing volumes of his *Œuvres complètes*, in which his pupils had collected his contributions to medicine and neuropathology, his *Leçons du mardi*, the yearly reports of his clinic at the Salpêtrière, and other works besides—all these publications will remain precious to science and to his pupils; but they cannot take the place of the man, who had still much more to give and to teach and whose person or whose writings no one has yet approached without learning something from them.

He took an honest, human delight in his own great success and used to enjoy talking of his beginnings and the road he had travelled. His scientific curiosity, he said, had been aroused early, when he was still a young *interne*,[1] by the mass of material presented by the facts of neuropathology, material which was not in the least understood at the time. In those days, whenever he went the rounds with his senior in one of the departments of the Salpêtrière (the institution for the care of women) amid all the wilderness of paralyses, spasms and convulsions for which forty years ago there was neither name nor understanding, he would say: '*Faudrait y retourner et y rester*',[2] and he kept his word. When he became *médecin des hôpitaux*,[3] he at once took steps to enter the Salpêtrière in one of the departments for nervous patients. Having got there, he stayed where he was instead of doing what French senior physicians are entitled to

[1] [The French equivalent of the English 'house-physician'.]
[2] ['I shall have to come back here and stop here.']
[3] [The French equivalent of an English senior physician.]

do—transferring in regular succession from one department to another and from hospital to hospital, and at the same time changing their speciality as well.

Thus his first impression and the resolution it led him to were decisive for the whole of his further development. His having a great number of chronic nervous patients at his disposal enabled him to make use of his own special gifts. He was not a reflective man, not a thinker: he had the nature of an artist—he was, as he himself said, a '*visuel*', a man who sees. Here is what he himself told us about his method of working. He used to look again and again at the things he did not understand, to deepen his impression of them day by day, till suddenly an understanding of them dawned on him.[1] In his mind's eye the apparent chaos presented by the continual repetition of the same symptoms then gave way to order: the new nosological pictures emerged, characterized by the constant combination of certain groups of symptoms. The complete and extreme cases, the 'types', could be brought into prominence with the help of a certain sort of schematic planning, and, with these types as a point of departure, the eye could travel over the long series of ill-defined cases—the '*formes frustes*' [2]—which, branching off from one or other characteristic feature of the type, melt away into indistinctness. He called this kind of intellectual work, in which he had no equal, 'practising nosography', and he took pride in it. He might be heard to say that the greatest satisfaction a man could have was to see something new—that is, to recognize it as new; and he remarked again and again on the difficulty and value of this kind of 'seeing'. He would ask why it was that in medicine people only see what they have already learned to see. He would say that it was wonderful how one was suddenly able to see new things —new states of illness—which must probably be as old as the human race; and that he had to confess to himself that he now saw a number of things which he had overlooked for thirty

[1] [Freud had remarked on this in his Paris Report (1956a [1886]) and quoted it again in a slightly different form in his history of the psycho-analytic movement (1914d), *Standard Ed.*, **14**, 22 and in his short message to *Le Disque Vert* (1924a), ibid., **19**, 290.]

[2] [The French word '*fruste*', with the meaning 'blurred', is primarily applied to 'rubbed' coins or medals. Cf. footnote 2, p. 81 below.]

years in his hospital wards. No physician needs to be told what a wealth of forms were acquired by neuropathology through him, and what increased precision and sureness of diagnosis were made possible by his observations. But the pupil who spent many hours with him going round the wards of the Salpêtrière —that museum of clinical facts, the names and peculiar characteristics of which were for the most part derived from him— would be reminded of Cuvier, whose statue, standing in front of the Jardin des Plantes,[1] shows that great comprehender and describer of the animal world surrounded by a multitude of animal forms; or else he would recall the myth of Adam, who, when God brought the creatures of Paradise before him to be distinguished and named, may have experienced to the fullest degree that intellectual enjoyment which Charcot praised so highly.

Charcot, indeed, never tired of defending the rights of purely clinical work, which consists in seeing and ordering things, against the encroachments of theoretical medicine. On one occasion there was a small group of us, all students from abroad, who, brought up on German academic physiology, were trying his patience with our doubts about his clinical innovations. 'But that can't be true,' one of us objected, 'it contradicts the Young-Helmholtz theory.' He did not reply 'So much the worse for the theory, clinical facts come first' or words to that effect; but he did say something which made a great impression on us: *'La théorie, c'est bon, mais ça n'empêche pas d'exister.'* [2]

For a whole number of years Charcot occupied the Chair of Pathological Anatomy in Paris, and he carried on his neuropathological studies and lectures, which quickly made him famous abroad as well as in France, on a voluntary basis and as a secondary occupation. It was a piece of good fortune for

---

[1] [The Paris zoological gardens.]

[2] ['Theory is good; but it doesn't prevent things from existing.' This was a favourite quotation of Freud's and he repeated it all through his life. (See, for instance, the 'Dora' case history (1905e), *Standard Ed.*, 7, 115, Lecture IX of the *Introductory Lectures* (1916–17) and the *Autobiographical Study* (1925d), *Standard Ed.*, 20, 13.) On the first occasion on which Freud told the story—in a footnote to his translation of Charcot's *Leçons du mardi* (1887–8) (Freud, 1892–4, 210)—he revealed the fact that the objector who provoked Charcot's repartee was Freud himself.]

neuropathology that the same man could undertake the discharge of two functions: on the one hand he created the nosological picture through clinical observation, and on the other he demonstrated that the same anatomical changes underlay the disease whether it appeared as a type or as a *forme fruste*. It is very generally recognized how successful this anatomical-clinical method of Charcot's was in the field of organic nervous diseases—in tabes, multiple sclerosis, amyotrophic lateral sclerosis, and so on. Years of patient waiting were often necessary before the presence of organic change could be proved in those chronic illnesses which are not directly fatal; and only in a hospital for incurables like the Salpêtrière was it possible to keep the patients under observation for such long periods of time.[1] Charcot made his first demonstration of this kind before he had charge of a department. While he was still a student he happened to engage a maid-servant who suffered from a peculiar tremor and could not find a situation on account of her clumsiness. Charcot recognized her condition as a *paralysie choréiforme*, a disease which had already been described by Duchenne, but whose basis was unknown. Charcot kept this interesting servant, although in the course of the years she cost him a small fortune in dishes and plates. When at last she died he was able to demonstrate from her case that *paralysie choréiforme* was the clinical expression of multiple cerebro-spinal sclerosis.

Pathological anatomy has to serve neuropathology in two ways. Besides demonstrating the presence of a morbid change, it must establish the localization of that change; and we all know that during the last two decades the second part of this task has aroused the greater interest of the two and has been more actively pursued. Charcot played a most distinguished part in this work, too, although the pioneer discoveries were not made by him. To begin with he followed in the footsteps of our fellow-countryman, Türck, who is said to have lived and carried on his researches in comparative isolation among us. When the two great innovations came—the Hitzig-Fritsch stimulation

---

[1] [Jones (1953, 231) refers to a case at the Salpêtrière entrusted by Charcot to Freud for an autopsy. It was the case of a woman who had been in the hospital since 1853, suffering from the effects of an embolism. Freud reported on the case in 1891*a*. Cf. pp. 241–2 below.]

experiments and Flechsig's findings on the development of the spinal cord—which ushered in a new epoch in our knowledge of the 'localization of nervous diseases', Charcot's lectures on localization played the largest and best part towards bringing the new theories into touch with the clinical work and making them fruitful for it. As regards in especial the relationship of the somatic muscular apparatus to the motor area of the human cerebrum, I may remind the reader of the long time during which the more exact nature and topography of this relationship was in question. (Was there a common representation of both extremities in the same areas? or was there a representation of the upper extremity in the anterior central convolution and of the lower extremity in the posterior one—that is, a vertical disposition?) At last, continued clinical observations and experiments in stimulation and extirpation on living subjects during surgical operations decided the question in favour of the view of Charcot and Pitres that the middle third of the central convolutions mainly serves the representation of the arm, while the upper third and the mesial portion serve that of the leg—that is to say, that in the motor area the disposition is a horizontal one.

An enumeration of Charcot's separate contributions would not enable us to establish his significance for neuropathology. For during the last two decades there have not been many themes of any importance in whose formulation and discussion the school of the Salpêtrière has not had an outstanding share; and the 'school of the Salpêtrière' was, of course, Charcot himself, who, with the wealth of his experience, the transparent clarity of his diction and the plasticity of his descriptions, could easily be recognized in every publication of the school. Among the circle of young men whom he thus gathered round him and made into participants in his researches, a few eventually rose to a consciousness of their own individuality and made a brilliant name for themselves. Now and then, even, it happened that one of them would come forward with an assertion which seemed to the master to be more clever than correct; and this he would argue against with plenty of sarcasm in his conversation and lectures, but without doing any damage to his affectionate relationship with his pupil. And in fact Charcot leaves behind him a host of pupils whose intellectual quality and whose achievements up to now are a guarantee that the study and practice of neuropathology in Paris will not so quickly slip down from the height to which Charcot has brought them.

In Vienna we have repeatedly had occasion to realize that the intellectual significance of an academic teacher is not necessarily combined with a direct personal influence on younger men which leads to the creation of a large and important school. If Charcot was so much more fortunate in this respect we must put it down to the personal qualities of the man—to the magic that emanated from his looks and from his voice, to the kindly openness which characterized his manner as soon as his relations with someone had overcome the stage of initial strangeness, to the willingness with which he put everything at the disposal of his pupils, and to his life-long loyalty to them. The hours he spent in his wards were hours of companionship and of an exchange of ideas with the whole of his medical staff. He never shut himself away from them there. The youngest newly-qualified physician walking the wards had a chance of seeing him at his work and might interrupt him at it; and the same freedom was enjoyed by students from abroad, who, in later years, were never lacking at his rounds. And, lastly, on the evenings when Madame Charcot was at home to a distinguished company, assisted by a highly-gifted daughter who was growing up in the likeness of her father, the pupils and medical assistants who were always present met the guests as part of the family.

In 1882 or 1883, the circumstances of Charcot's life and work took on their final form. People had come to realize that the activities of this man were a part of the assets of the nation's '*gloire*', which, after the unfortunate war of 1870–1, was all the more jealously guarded. The government, at the head of which was Charcot's old friend, Gambetta, created a Chair of Neuropathology for him in the Faculty of Medicine (so that he could give up the Chair of Pathological Anatomy) and also a clinic, with auxiliary scientific departments, at the Salpêtrière. '*Le service de M. Charcot*' now included, in addition to the old wards for chronic female patients, several clinical rooms where male patients, too, were received, a huge out-patient department— the '*consultation externe*'—, a histological laboratory, a museum, an electro-therapeutic department, an eye and ear department and a special photographic studio. All these things were so many means of keeping former assistants and pupils permanently at the clinic in secure posts. The two-storeyed, weathered-looking buildings and the courtyards which they enclosed reminded the stranger vividly of our *Allgemeines Krankenhaus*;[1] but no doubt the resemblance did not go far enough. 'It may not be beautiful here, perhaps,' Charcot would say when he showed a visitor his domain, 'but there is room for everything you want to do.'

Charcot was in the very prime of life when this abundance of facilities for teaching and research were placed at his disposal. He was a tireless worker, and always, I believe, the busiest in the whole institute. His private consultations, to which patients flocked 'from Samarkand and the Antilles',[2] could not keep him from his teaching activities or his researches. There is no doubt that this throng of people did not turn to him solely because he was a famous discoverer but quite as much because he was a great physician and friend of man, who could always find an answer to a problem and who, when the present state of science did not allow him to *know*, was able to make a good guess. He has often been blamed for his therapeutic method which, with its multiplicity of prescriptions, could not but offend a rationalistic conscience. But he was simply continuing the procedures which were customary at that time and place, without deceiving himself much about their efficacy. He was, however, not pessimistic in his therapeutic expectations, and repeatedly showed readiness to try new methods of treatment in his clinic: their short-lived success was to find its explanation elsewhere.

As a teacher, Charcot was positively fascinating. Each of his lectures was a little work of art in construction and composition; it was perfect in form and made such an impression that for the rest of the day one could not get the sound of what he had said out of one's ears or the thought of what he had demonstrated out of one's mind. He seldom demonstrated a single patient, but

---

[1] [The General Hospital in Vienna. In what follows, Freud probably had in mind the unsatisfactory laboratories at the Salpêtrière as compared with those he was accustomed to in Vienna. Cf. the 'Paris Report'.]

[2] [The quotation has not been traced.]

mostly a series of similar or contrasting cases which he compared
with one another. In the hall in which he gave his lectures there
hung a picture which showed 'citizen' Pinel having the chains
taken off the poor madmen in the Salpêtrière.[1] The Salpêtrière,
which had witnessed so many horrors during the Revolution,
had also been the scene of this most humane of all revolutions.
At such lectures Maître Charcot himself made a curious impression. He, who at other times bubbled over with vivacity and
cheerfulness and who always had a joke on his lips, now looked
serious and solemn under his little velvet cap; indeed, he even
seemed to have grown older. His voice sounded subdued. We
could almost understand how ill-disposed strangers could
reproach the whole lecture with being theatrical. Those who
spoke like this were doubtless accustomed to the formlessness of
German clinical lectures, or else forgot that Charcot gave only
one lecture in the week and could therefore prepare it carefully.

In this formal lecture, in which everything was prepared and
everything had to have its place, Charcot was no doubt following a deeply-rooted tradition; but he also felt the need to give
his audience a less elaborated picture of his activities. This
purpose was served by his out-patient clinic of which he took
personal charge in what were known as his '*Leçons du mardi*'.
There he took up cases which were completely unknown to
him; he exposed himself to all the chances of an examination,
all the errors of a first investigation; he would put aside his
authority on occasion and admit—in one case that he could
arrive at no diagnosis and in another that he had been deceived
by appearances; and he never appeared greater to his audience
than when, by giving the most detailed account of his processes
of thought and by showing the greatest frankness about his
doubts and hesitations, he had thus sought to narrow the gulf
between teacher and pupil. The publication of these improvised
lectures, given in the year 1887 and 1888, at first in French and
now in German as well, has also immeasurably widened the
circle of his admirers; and never before has a work on neuropathology had such a success with the medical public as this.

At about the time at which the clinic was established and

---

[1] [Philippe Pinel (1745–1826) was appointed as head physician at
the Salpêtrière in 1794, at the time of the French Revolution, and
initiated the humaner treatment of the insane.]

at which he gave up the Chair of Pathological Anatomy, a
change occurred in the direction of Charcot's scientific pursuits,
and to this we owe the finest of his work. He now pronounced
that the theory of organic nervous illnesses was for the time
being fairly complete, and he began to turn his attention almost
exclusively to hysteria, which thus all at once became the focus
of general interest. This, the most enigmatic of all nervous
diseases, for the evaluation of which medicine had not yet found
a serviceable angle of approach, had just then fallen into
thorough discredit; and this discredit extended not only to the
patients but to the physicians who concerned themselves with
the neurosis. It was held that in hysteria anything was possible,
and no credence was given to a hysteric about anything. The
first thing that Charcot's work did was to restore its dignity to
the topic. Little by little, people gave up the scornful smile
with which the patient could at that time feel certain of being
met. She was no longer necessarily a malingerer, for Charcot
had thrown the whole weight of his authority on the side of the
genuineness and objectivity of hysterical phenomena. Charcot
had repeated on a small scale the act of liberation in memory of
which Pinel's portrait hung in the lecture hall of the Salpêtrière.
Once the blind fear of being made a fool of by the unfortunate
patient had been given up—a fear which till then had stood in
the way of a serious study of the neurosis—the question could
arise as to what method of approach would lead most quickly to
a solution of the problem. A quite unbiassed observer might
have arrived at this conclusion: if I find someone in a state
which bears all the signs of a painful affect—weeping, scream-
ing and raging—the conclusion seems probable that a mental
process is going on in him of which those physical phenomena
are the appropriate expression. A healthy person, if he were
asked, would be in a position to say what impression it was that
was tormenting him; but the hysteric would answer that he
did not know. The problem would at once arise of how it is that
a hysterical patient is overcome by an affect about whose cause
he asserts that he knows nothing. If we keep to our conclusion
that a corresponding psychical process *must* be present, and if
nevertheless we believe the patient when he denies it; if we
bring together the many indications that the patient is behaving
as though he *does* know about it; and if we enter into the history

of the patient's life and find some occasion, some trauma, which
would appropriately evoke precisely those expressions of feeling
—then everything points to one solution: the patient is in a
special state of mind in which all his impressions or his recollections of them are no longer held together by an associative
chain, a state of mind in which it is possible for a recollection to
express its affect by means of somatic phenomena without the
group of the other mental processes, the ego, knowing about it
or being able to intervene to prevent it. If we had called to
mind the familiar psychological difference between sleep and
waking, the strangeness of our hypothesis might have seemed
less. No one should object that the theory of a splitting of
consciousness as a solution to the riddle of hysteria is much too
remote to impress an unbiassed and untrained observer. For,
by pronouncing possession by a demon to be the cause of
hysterical phenomena, the Middle Ages in fact chose this
solution; it would only have been a matter of exchanging the
religious terminology of that dark and superstitious age for the
scientific language of to-day.[1]

Charcot, however, did not follow this path towards an
explanation of hysteria, although he drew copiously upon the
surviving reports of witch trials and of possession, in order to
show that the manifestations of the neurosis were the same in
those days as they are now. He treated hysteria as just another
topic in neuropathology; he gave a complete description of its
phenomena, demonstrated that these had their own laws and
uniformities, and showed how to recognize the symptoms which
enable a diagnosis of hysteria to be made. The most painstaking
investigations, initiated by himself and his pupils, extended over
hysterical disturbances of sensibility in the skin and deeper
tissues, over the behaviour of the sense organs, and over the
peculiarities of hysterical contractures and paralyses, and of
trophic disturbances and changes in metabolism. The many
different forms of hysterical attack were described, and a
schematic plan was drawn up by depicting the typical configuration of the major hysterical attack ['*grande hystérie*'] as

[1] [Cf. some remarks to the same effect at the beginning of Freud's
paper, written some thirty years later, on 'A Seventeenth-Century
Demonological Neurosis' (1923*d*), *Standard Ed.* **19**, 72, where a reference
to Charcot will also be found.]

occurring in four stages, which made it possible to trace the
commonly observed 'minor' attacks [*petite hystérie*'] back to this
same typical configuration. The localization and frequency of
occurrence of the so-called 'hysterogenic zones' and their relationship to the attacks were also studied, and so on. Once all
this information about the manifestations of hysteria had been
arrived at, a number of surprising discoveries were made.
Hysteria in males, and especially in men of the working class,
was found far more often than had been expected; it was
convincingly shown that certain conditions which had been put
down to alcoholic intoxication or lead-poisoning were of a
hysterical nature; it was possible to subsume under hysteria a
whole number of affections which had hitherto not been understood and which had remained unclassified; and where the
neurosis had become joined with other disorders to form complex pictures, it was possible to separate out the part played by
hysteria. Most far-reaching of all were the investigations into
nervous illnesses which followed upon severe traumas—the
'traumatic neuroses'—views about which are still under discussion and in connection with which Charcot has successfully
put forward the arguments in favour of hysteria.

After the latest extensions of the concept of hysteria had so
often led to a rejection of aetiological diagnosis, it became
necessary to enter into the aetiology of hysteria itself. Charcot
put forward a simple formula for this: heredity was to be
regarded as the sole cause. Accordingly, hysteria was a form of
degeneracy, a member of the '*famille névropathique*'. All other
aetiological factors played the part of incidental causes, of
'*agents provocateurs*'.[1]

The construction of this great edifice was naturally not
achieved without violent opposition. But it was the sterile
opposition of an old generation who did not want to have their
views changed. The younger among the neuropathologists,
including those in Germany, accepted Charcot's teaching to
a greater or lesser degree. Charcot himself was completely
certain that his theories about hysteria would triumph. When
it was objected that the four stages of hysteria, hysteria in men,
and so on, were not observable outside France, he pointed out

[1] [Cf. Freud's detailed criticism of this view in 'Heredity and the
Aetiology of the Neuroses' (1896a), p. 143 ff. below.]

how long he himself had overlooked these things, and he said once more that hysteria was the same in all places and at every time. He was very sensitive about the accusation that the French were a far more neurotic nation than any other and that hysteria was a kind of national bad habit; and he was much pleased when a paper 'On a Case of Reflex Epilepsy', which dealt with a Prussian Grenadier, enabled him to make a long-range diagnosis of hysteria.

At one point in his work Charcot rose to a level higher even than that of his usual treatment of hysteria. The step he took assured him for all time, too, the fame of having been the first to explain hysteria. While he was engaged in the study of hysterical paralyses arising after traumas, he had the idea of artificially reproducing those paralyses, which he had earlier differentiated with care from organic ones. For this purpose he made use of hysterical patients whom he put into a state of somnambulism by hypnotizing them. He succeeded in proving, by an unbroken chain of argument, that these paralyses were the result of ideas which had dominated the patient's brain at moments of a special disposition. In this way, the mechanism of a hysterical phenomenon was explained for the first time. This incomparably fine piece of clinical research was afterwards taken up by his own pupil, Pierre Janet, as well as by Breuer and others, who developed from it a theory of neurosis which coincided with the mediaeval view—when once they had replaced the 'demon' of clerical phantasy by a psychological formula.

Charcot's concern with hypnotic phenomena in hysterical patients led to very great advances in this important field of hitherto neglected and despised facts, for the weight of his name put an end once and for all to any doubt about the reality of hypnotic manifestations. But the exclusively nosographical approach adopted at the School of the Salpêtrière was not suitable for a purely psychological subject. The restriction of the study of hypnosis to hysterical patients, the differentiation between major and minor hypnotism, the hypothesis of three stages of 'major hypnosis', and their characterization by somatic phenomena—all this sank in the estimation of Charcot's contemporaries when Liébeault's pupil, Bernheim, set about constructing the theory of hypnotism on a more comprehensive

psychological foundation and making suggestion the central
point of hypnosis. It is only the opponents of hypnotism who,
content to conceal their lack of personal experience behind an
appeal to authority, still cling to Charcot's assertions and who
like to take advantage of a pronouncement made by him in
his last years, in which he denied to hypnosis any value as a
therapeutic method.[1]

Furthermore, the aetiological theories supported by Charcot
in his doctrine of the '*famille névropathique*', which he made the
basis of his whole concept of nervous disorders, will no doubt
soon require sifting and emending. So greatly did Charcot over-
estimate heredity as a causative agent that he left no room for
the acquisition of nervous illness. To syphilis he merely allotted
a modest place among the '*agents provocateurs*'; nor did he make
a sufficiently sharp distinction between organic nervous affections and neuroses, either as regards their aetiology or in other
respects. It is inevitable that the advance of our science, as it
increases our knowledge, must at the same time lessen the value
of a number of things that Charcot taught us; but neither
changing times nor changing views can diminish the fame of
the man whom—in France and elsewhere—we are mourning
to-day.

VIENNA, August 1893.

[1] [It may be remarked that in the Introduction with which in 1888
Freud had prefaced his translation of Bernheim's *De la suggestion* he
had been decidedly critical of Bernheim's views. (See Freud, 1888–9.)
He repeated his criticisms still more forcibly thirty years later in his
Group Psychology (1921c), *Standard Ed.*, **18**, 89 and 128 *n.*]

ON THE PSYCHICAL MECHANISM OF HYSTERICAL PHENOMENA: A LECTURE
(1893)

ÜBER DEN PSYCHISCHEN MECHANISMUS HYSTERISCHER PHÄNOMENE

(a) German Edition:

1893   *Wien. med. Presse*, **34** (4), 121–6 and (5), 165–7.
(January 22 and 29.)

(b) English Translation:

'On the Psychical Mechanism of Hysterical Phenomena'
1956   *Int. J. Psycho-Anal.*, **37** (1), 8–13. (Tr. James Strachey.)

The German original seems never to have been reprinted. The present translation is a very slightly emended version of the one of 1956.

The German original is headed with the words 'By Dr. Josef Breuer and Dr. Sigm. Freud of Vienna'. But this is in fact a shorthand report of a lecture delivered by Freud and revised by him. Though it deals with the same subject-matter (and often in similar terms) as the famous 'Preliminary Communication' (1893*a*), which has its proper place in the *Standard Edition* in Volume II at the beginning of *Studies on Hysteria* (1895*d*), this lecture bears every mark of being the sole work of Freud.

The Breuer and Freud 'Preliminary Communication' was published in a Berlin periodical, the *Neurologisches Zentralblatt*, in two instalments on January 1 and 15, 1893. (It was immediately afterwards reprinted in Vienna in the *Wiener medizinische Blätter* of January 19 and 26.) The lecture which is printed here was delivered by Freud at a meeting of the Vienna Medical Club on January 11—that is to say, before the second instalment of the 'Preliminary Communication' had been published.

What is perhaps the most noticeable thing about the lecture is the preponderance of the traumatic factor among the causes assigned for hysteria. This is, of course, a proof of the strength of Charcot's influence upon Freud's ideas. The shift over to a realization of the part played by 'instinctual impulses' still lay in the future.

ON THE PSYCHICAL MECHANISM
OF HYSTERICAL PHENOMENA[1]

GENTLEMEN,—I am appearing before you to-day with the object of giving you a report on a work the first part of which has already been published in the *Zentralblatt für Neurologie* under the names of Josef Breuer and myself. As you may gather from the title of the work, it deals with the pathogenesis of hysterical symptoms and suggests that the immediate reasons for the development of hysterical symptoms are to be looked for in the sphere of psychical life.

But before I enter further into the contents of this joint work, I must explain the position it occupies and name the author and the discovery which, in substance at least, we have taken as our starting point, although our contribution has been developed quite independently.

As you know, Gentlemen, all the modern advances made in the understanding and knowledge of hysteria are derived from the work of Charcot. In the first half of the eighties, Charcot began to turn his attention to the 'major neurosis', as the French call hysteria. In a series of researches he has succeeded in proving the presence of regularity and law where the inadequate or half-hearted clinical observations of other people saw only malingering or a puzzling lack of conformity to rule. It may safely be said that everything new that has been learnt about hysteria in recent times goes back directly or indirectly to his suggestions. But among Charcot's numerous works, none, in my estimate, is of higher value than the one in which he taught us to understand the traumatic paralyses which appear in hysteria; and since it is precisely this work of which ours appears as a continuation, I hope you will allow me to lay this subject before you once again in some detail.

[1] A lecture delivered by Dr. Sigm. Freud at a meeting of the 'Wiener medizinischer Club' on January 11, 1893. Special shorthand report by the *Wiener medizinische Presse*, revised by the lecturer. [This footnote appeared in the original publication.]

We will take the case of a person who is subjected to a trauma without having been ill previously and perhaps without even having any hereditary taint. The trauma must fulfil certain conditions. It must be severe—that is, it must be of a kind involving the idea of mortal danger, of a threat to life. But it must not be severe in the sense of bringing psychical activity to an end. Otherwise it will not produce the result we expect from it. Thus, for instance, it must not involve concussion of the brain or any really serious injury. Moreover, the trauma must have a special relation to some part of the body. Let us suppose that a heavy billet of wood falls on a workman's shoulder. The blow knocks him down, but he soon realizes that nothing has happened and goes home with a slight contusion. After a few weeks, or after some months, he wakes up one morning and notices that the arm that was subjected to the trauma is hanging down limp and paralysed, though in the interval, in what might be called the incubation period, he has made perfectly good use of it. If the case is a typical one, it may happen that peculiar attacks set in—that, after an aura,[1] the subject suddenly collapses, raves, and becomes delirious; and, if he speaks in his delirium, what he says may show that the scene of his accident is being repeated in him, embellished, perhaps, with various imaginary pictures. What has been happening here? How is this phenomenon to be explained?

Charcot explains the process by reproducing it, by inducing the paralysis in a patient artificially. In order to bring this about, he needs a patient who is already in a hysterical state; he further requires the condition of hypnosis and the method of suggestion. He puts a patient of this kind into deep hypnosis and gives him a light blow on the arm. The arm drops; it is paralysed and shows precisely the same symptoms as occur in spontaneous traumatic paralysis. The blow may also be replaced by a direct verbal suggestion: 'Look! your arm is paralysed!' In this case too the paralysis exhibits the same characteristics.

Let us try to compare the two cases: on the one hand a trauma, on the other a traumatic suggestion. The final result, the paralysis, is exactly the same in both cases. If the trauma

[1][The premonitory sensations which precede an epileptic or hysterical attack.]

in the one case can be replaced in the other case by a verbal suggestion, it is plausible to suppose that an idea of this kind was responsible for the development of the paralysis in the case of the spontaneous traumatic paralysis as well. And in fact a number of patients report that at the moment of the trauma they actually had a feeling that their arm was smashed. If this were so, the trauma could really be completely equated with the verbal suggestion. But to complete the analogy a third factor is required. In order that the idea 'your arm is paralysed' should be able to provoke a paralysis in the patient, it was necessary for him to be in a state of hypnosis. But the workman was not in a state of hypnosis. Nevertheless, we may assume that he was in a special state of mind during the trauma; and Charcot is inclined to equate that affect with the artificially induced state of hypnosis. This being so, the traumatic spontaneous paralysis is completely explained and brought into line with the paralysis produced by suggestion; and the genesis of the symptom is unambiguously determined by the circumstances of the trauma.

Charcot has, moreover, repeated the same experiment in order to explain the contractures and pains which appear in traumatic hysteria; and in my opinion there is scarcely any point at which he has penetrated into the understanding of hysteria more deeply than here. But his analysis goes no further: we do not learn how other symptoms are generated, and above all we do not learn how hysterical symptoms come about in common, non-traumatic hysteria.

At about the same time, Gentlemen, at which Charcot was thus throwing light on hystero-traumatic paralyses, Dr. Breuer, between 1880 and 1882, undertook the medical care of a young lady who—with a non-traumatic aetiology—fell ill of a severe and complicated hysteria (accompanied by paralyses, contractures, disturbances of speech and vision, and psychical peculiarities of every kind), while she was nursing her sick father.[1] This case will retain an important place in the history of hysteria, since it was the first one in which a physician succeeded in elucidating all the symptoms of the hysterical state, in

[1] [This was, of course, Fräulein Anna O., of Case History I in *Studies on Hysteria* (1895d).]

learning the origin of each symptom and at the same time in finding a means of causing that symptom to disappear. We may say that it was the first case of hysteria to be made intelligible. Dr. Breuer kept back the conclusions which followed from this case till he could be certain that it did not stand alone. After I returned, in 1886, from a course of study under Charcot,[1] I began, with Breuer's constant co-operation, to make close observations on a fairly large number of hysterical patients and to examine them from this point of view; and I found that the behaviour of this first patient had in fact been typical and that the inferences which were justified by that case could be carried over to a considerable number of hysterical patients, if not to all.

Our material consisted of cases of common, that is of non-traumatic, hysteria. Our procedure was to take each separate symptom and enquire into the circumstances in which it had made its first appearance; and we endeavoured in this way to arrive at a clear idea of the precipitating cause which might perhaps have determined that symptom. Now you must not suppose that this is a simple job. If you question patients along these lines, you will as a rule receive no answer at all to begin with. In a small group of cases the patients have their reasons for not saying what they know. But in a greater number of cases the patients have no notion of the context of their symptoms. The method by which something can be learnt is an arduous one. It is as follows. The patients must be put under hypnosis and then questioned as to the origin of some particular symptom —as to when it first appeared and what they remember in that connection. While they are in this state, the memory, which was not at their disposal in a waking state, returns. We have learnt in this manner that, to put it roughly, there is an affectively coloured experience behind most, if not all, phenomena of hysteria; and further, that this experience is of such a kind that it at once makes the symptom to which it relates intelligible and shows accordingly that the symptom, once again, is un-ambiguously determined. If you will allow me to equate this affectively coloured experience with the major traumatic experience underlying traumatic hysteria, I can at once formu-late the first thesis at which we have arrived: '*There is a com-*

[1] [Freud spent the winter of 1885–6 in Paris working at the Sal-pêtrière.]

plete analogy between traumatic paralysis and common, non-traumatic hysteria.' The only difference is that in the former a major trauma has been operative, whereas in the latter there is seldom a *single* major event to be signalized, but rather a *series* of affective impressions—a whole story of suffering. But there is nothing forced in equating such a story, which appears as the determining factor in hysterical patients, with the accident which occurs in traumatic hysteria. For no one doubts any longer to-day that even in the case of the major mechanical trauma in traumatic hysteria what produces the result is not the mechanical factor but the affect of fright, the *psychical* trauma. The first thing that follows from all this, then, is that the pattern of traumatic hysteria, as it was laid down by Charcot for hysterical paralyses, applies quite generally to all hysterical phenomena, or at least to the great majority of them. In every case what we have to deal with is the operation of psychical traumas, which unambiguously determine the nature of the symptoms that arise.

I will now give you a few instances of this. First, here is an example of the occurrence of contractures. Throughout the whole period of her illness, Breuer's patient, whom I have already mentioned, exhibited a contracture of the right arm. It emerged under hypnosis that at a time before she had fallen ill she was subjected to the following trauma. She was sitting half-dozing at the bedside of her sick father; her right arm was hanging over the back of her chair and went to sleep. At this moment she had a terrifying hallucination; she tried to fend it off with her arm but was unable to do so. This gave her a violent fright, and for the time being the matter ended there. It was not until the outbreak of her hysteria that the contracture of the arm set in.[1] In another woman patient, I observed that her speech was interrupted by a peculiar 'clacking' with her tongue, which resembled the cry of a capercaillie.[2] I had been familiar with this symptom for months and regarded it as

---

[1] [For a fuller account of this see *Standard Ed.*, 2, 38-9.]

[2] [This was Frau Emmy von N., of Case History II in the *Studies.*— An ornithologist describes the capercaillie's cry as 'a ticking ending with a pop and a hiss' (Fisher, 1955, 3, 46).—This particular symptom is accounted for at greater length in *Standard Ed.*, 2, 54 and 58.]

a *tic*. It was only after I once happened to question her under hypnosis about its origin that I discovered that the noise had first appeared on two occasions. On each of these she had made a firm decision to keep absolutely quiet. This happened once when she was nursing a child of hers who was seriously ill. (Nursing sick people often plays a part in the aetiology of hysteria.) The child had fallen asleep and she was determined not to make any noise that might wake it. But fear that she might make a noise turned into actually making one—an instance of 'hysterical counter-will';[1] she pressed her lips together and made the clacking noise with her tongue. Many years later the same symptom had arisen a second time, once again when she had made a decision to be absolutely quiet, and it had persisted ever afterwards. A single precipitating cause is often not enough to fixate a symptom; but if this same symptom appears several times accompanied by a particular affect, it becomes fixated and chronic.

One of the commonest symptoms of hysteria is a combination of anorexia and vomiting. I know of a whole number of cases in which the occurrence of this symptom is explained quite simply. Thus in one patient vomiting persisted after she had read a humiliating letter just before a meal and had been violently sick after it. In other cases disgust at food could be quite definitely related to the fact that, owing to the institution of the 'common table', a person may be compelled to eat his meal with someone he detests. The disgust is then transferred from the person to the food. The woman with the *tic* whom I have just mentioned was particularly interesting in this respect. She ate uncommonly little and only under pressure. I learnt from her in hypnosis that a series of psychical traumas had eventually produced this symptom of disgust at food.[2] While she was still a child, her mother, who was very strict, insisted on her eating any meat she had left over at her midday meal two hours later, when it was cold and the fat was all congealed.

---

[1] [Freud had very recently published a paper discussing this phenomenon and this same example of it: 'A Case of Successful Treatment by Hypnotism' (1892–93).—Some comments on Freud's use of the term 'to fixate', which appears just below, will be found in an Editor's footnote towards the end of this same paper.]

[2] [Cf. *Standard Ed.*, **2**, 80–3.]

She did so with great disgust and retained the memory of it; so that later on, when she was no longer subjected to this punishment, she regularly felt disgust at mealtimes. Ten years later she used to sit at table with a relative who was tubercular and kept constantly spitting across the table into the spitoon during meals. A little while later she was obliged to share her meals with a relative who, as she knew, was suffering from a contagious disease. Breuer's patient, again, behaved for some time like someone suffering from hydrophobia. During hypnosis it turned out that she had once unexpectedly seen a dog drinking out of a tumbler of water of hers.[1]

Sleeplessness or disturbed sleep are also symptoms that are usually susceptible to the most precise explanation. Thus, for years on end a woman could never get to sleep till six in the morning. She had for a long time slept in the room adjoining her sick husband, who used to rise at six o'clock. After that hour she had been able to sleep in quiet; and she behaved in the same way once more many years later during a hysterical illness. Another case was that of a man. He was a hysterical patient who had slept very badly for the last twelve years. His sleeplessness, however, was of a quite special sort. In the summer he slept excellently, but in the winter very badly; and in November he slept quite particularly badly. He had no notion what this was due to. Enquiry revealed that in November twelve years earlier he had watched for many nights at the bedside of his son, who was ill with diphtheria.

Breuer's patient, to whom I have so often referred, offered an example of a disturbance of speech. For a long period of her illness she spoke only English and could neither speak nor understand German. This symptom was traced back to an event which had happened before the outbreak of her illness. While she was in a state of great anxiety, she had attempted to pray but could find no words. At last a few words of a child's prayer in English occurred to her. When she fell ill later on, only the English language was at her command.[2]

The determination of the symptom by the psychical trauma is not so transparent in every instance. There is often only what

---

[1] [This was in fact the first symptom ever to be removed by catharsis; and the procedure was initiated by the patient herself spontaneously. See ibid., 34–5.]   [2] [Cf. ibid., 38–9.]

may be described as a 'symbolic' relation between the determining cause and the hysterical symptom. This is especially true of pains. Thus one patient[1] suffered from piercing pains between her eyebrows. The reason was that once when she was a child her grandmother had given her an enquiring, 'piercing' look. The same patient suffered for a time from violent pains in her right heel, for which there was no explanation. These pains, it turned out, were connected with an idea that occurred to the patient when she made her first appearance in society. She was overcome with fear that she might not 'find herself on a right footing'. Symbolizations of this kind were employed by many patients for a whole number of so-called neuralgias and pains. It is as though there were an intention to express the mental state by means of a physical one; and linguistic usage affords a bridge by which this can be effected. In the case, however, of what are after all the typical symptoms of hysteria—such as hemi-anaesthesia, restriction of the visual field, epileptiform convulsions, etc.—a psychical mechanism of this sort cannot be demonstrated. On the other hand this can often be done in respect to the hysterogenic zones.

These examples, which I have chosen out of a number of observations, seem to offer proof that the phenomena of common hysteria can safely be regarded as being on the same pattern as those of traumatic hysteria, and that accordingly every hysteria can be looked upon as traumatic hysteria in the sense of implying a psychical trauma and that every hysterical phenomenon is determined by the nature of the trauma.

The further question which would then have to be answered is as to the nature of the causal connection between the determining factor which we have discovered during hypnosis and the phenomenon which persists subsequently as a chronic symptom. This connection might be of various kinds. It might be of the type that we should describe as a 'releasing' factor. For instance, if someone with a disposition to tuberculosis receives a blow on the knee as a result of which he develops a tubercular inflammation of the joint, the blow is a simple re-

---

[1] [This was Frau Cäcilie M., whose 'symbolic' symptoms are discussed at the end of Case History V in the *Studies*. Cf. ibid., 176–80.]

leasing cause. But this is not what happens in hysteria. There
is another kind of causation—namely, *direct* causation. We can
elucidate this from the picture of a foreign body, which continues to operate unceasingly as a stimulating cause of illness
until it is got rid of. *Cessante causa cessat effectus.*[1] Breuer's observation shows us that there is a connection of this latter kind
between the psychical trauma and the hysterical phenomenon.
For Breuer learnt from his first patient that the attempt at
discovering the determining cause of a symptom was at the
same time a therapeutic manœuvre. The moment at which the
physician finds out the occasion when the symptom first
appeared and the reason for its appearance is also the moment
at which the symptom vanishes. When, for instance, the symptom presented by the patient consists in pains, and when we
enquire from him under hypnosis as to their origin, he will
produce a series of memories in connection with them. If we
can succeed in eliciting a really vivid memory in him, and if
he sees things before him with all their original actuality, we
shall observe that he is completely dominated by some affect.
And if we then compel him to put this affect into words, we
shall find that, at the same time as he is producing this violent
affect, the phenomenon of his pains emerges very markedly
once again and that thenceforward the symptom, in its chronic
character, disappears. This is how events turned out in all the
instances I have quoted. And it was an interesting fact that the
memory of this particular event was to an extraordinary degree
more vivid than the memory of any others, and that the affect
accompanying it was as great, perhaps, as it had been when the
event actually occurred. It could only be supposed that the
psychical trauma does in fact continue to operate in the subject
and maintains the hysterical phenomenon, and that it comes to
an end as soon as the patient has spoken about it.

As I have just said, if, in accordance with our procedure, one
arrives at the psychical trauma by making enquiries from the
patient under hypnosis, one discovers that the memory concerned is quite unusually strong and has retained the whole of
its affect. The question now arises how it is that an event which
occurred so long ago—perhaps ten or twenty years—can persist
in exercising its power over the subject, how it is that these

[1] ['When the cause ceases the effect ceases.']

memories have not been subject to the processes of wearing away and forgetting.

With a view to answering this question, I should like to begin with a few remarks on the conditions which govern the wearing-away of the contents of our ideational life. We will start from a thesis that may be stated in the following terms. If a person experiences a psychical impression, something in his nervous system which we will for the moment call the sum of excitation[1] is increased. Now in every individual there exists a tendency to diminish this sum of excitation once more, in order to preserve his health.[2] The increase of the sum of excitation takes place along sensory paths, and its diminution along motor ones. So we may say that if anything impinges on someone he reacts in a motor fashion. We can now safely assert that it depends on this reaction how much of the initial psychical impression is left. Let us consider this in relation to a particular example. Let us suppose that a man is insulted, is given a blow or something of the kind. This psychical trauma is linked with an increase in the sum of excitation of his nervous system. There then instinctively arises an inclination to diminish this increased excitation immediately. He hits back, and then feels easier; he may perhaps have reacted adequately—that is, he may have got rid of as much as had been introduced into him. Now this reaction may take various forms. For quite slight increases in excitation, alterations in his own body may perhaps be enough: weeping, abusing, raging, and so on. The more intense the trauma, the greater is the adequate reaction. The most adequate reaction, however, is always a deed. But, as an English writer has wittily remarked, the man who first flung a word of abuse at his enemy instead of a spear was the founder of civilization.[3] Thus words are substitutes for deeds, and in some circumstances (e.g. in Confession) the only substitutes. Accordingly, alongside the adequate reaction there is one that is less adequate. If, however, there is no reaction what-

[1] [Cf. an Editor's footnote pp. 48-9 below.]

[2] [Here was a tentative statement of the 'principle of constancy'. See the Editor's Appendix to ' The Neuro-Psychoses of Defence ' (1894a), p. 65 below.]

[3] [The English writer has not been identified. A similar remark by Lichtenberg is quoted by Freud in his book on jokes (1905c), *Standard Ed.*, **8**, 102.]

ever to a psychical trauma, the memory of it retains the affect[1] which it originally had. So that if someone who has been insulted cannot avenge the insult either by a retaliatory blow or by a word of abuse, the possibility arises that the memory of the event may call up in him once more the affect which was originally present. An insult that has been repaid, even if only in words, is recollected quite differently from one that has had to be accepted; and linguistic usage characteristically describes an insult that has been suffered in silence as a 'mortification' ['*Kränkung*', literally, 'making ill']. Thus, if for any reason there can be no reaction to a psychical trauma, it retains its original affect, and when someone cannot get rid of the increase in stimulation by 'abreacting'[2] it, we have the possibility of the event in question remaining a psychical trauma. Incidentally, a healthy psychical mechanism has other methods of dealing with the affect of a psychical trauma even if motor reaction and reaction by words are denied to it—namely by working it over associatively and by producing contrasting ideas. Even if the person who has been insulted neither hits back nor replies with abuse, he can nevertheless reduce the affect attaching to the insult by calling up such contrasting ideas as those of his own worthiness, of his enemy's worthlessness, and so on. Whether a healthy man deals with an insult in one way or the other, he always succeeds in achieving the result that the affect which was originally strong in his memory eventually loses intensity and that finally the recollection, having lost its affect, falls a victim to forgetfulness and the process of wearing-away.[3]

Now we have found that in hysterical patients there are nothing but impressions which have not lost their affect and whose memory has remained vivid. It follows, therefore, that

[1] [This is printed '*Effect*' ('effect') in the original German here and again nineteen lines lower down. These are almost certainly misprints for '*Affect*'.]

[2] [The term was introduced in the 'Preliminary Communication' (1893*a*), *Standard Ed.*, **2**, 8.]

[3] [In Section 3 of Part III of his 'Project for a Scientific Psychology', written in 1895, soon after this, Freud gave a most elaborate account of the mechanism by which what he there termed an 'untamed' memory is turned into a 'tamed' one. (Freud, 1950*a*). Cf. also a footnote added in 1907 to the last chapter of *The Psychopathology of Everyday Life* (1901*b*), *Standard Ed.*, **6**, 274–5.]

these memories in hysterical patients, which have become pathogenic, occupy an exceptional position as regards the wearing-away process; and observation shows that, in the case of all the events which have become determinants of hysterical phenomena, we are dealing with psychical traumas which have not been completely abreacted, or completely dealt with. Thus we may assert that *hysterical patients suffer from incompletely abreacted psychical traumas.*

We find two groups of conditions under which memories become pathogenic.[1] In the first group the memories to which the hysterical phenomena can be traced back have for their content ideas which involved a trauma so great that the nervous system had not sufficient power to deal with it in any way, or ideas to which reaction was impossible for social reasons (this applies frequently to married life); or lastly the subject may simply refuse to react, may not *want* to react to the psychical trauma. In this last case the contents of the hysterical deliria often turn out to be the very circle of ideas which the patient in his normal state has rejected, inhibited and suppressed with all his might. (For instance, blasphemies and erotic ideas occur in the hysterical deliria of nuns.) But in a second group of cases the reason for the absence of a reaction lies not in the content of the psychical trauma but in other circumstances. For we very often find that the content and determinants of hysterical phenomena are events which are in themselves quite trivial, but which have acquired high significance from the fact that they occurred at specially important moments when the patient's predisposition was pathologically increased. For instance, the affect of fright may have arisen in the course of some other severe affect and may on that account have attained such great importance. States of this kind are of short duration and are, as one might say, out of communication with the rest of the subject's mental life. While he is in a state of auto-hypnosis such as this, he cannot get rid associatively of an idea that occurs to him, as he can in a waking state. After considerable experience with these phenomena, we think it probable that in every

[1] [These two groups were to lead to the main division between the views of Breuer and Freud. The first group implied Freud's notion of 'defence', which became the basis of all his later work, while he very soon rejected the Breuer hypothesis of 'hypnoid states'.]

hysteria we are dealing with a rudiment of
French] '*double conscience*', dual consciousness
dency to such a dissociation and with it t
abnormal states of consciousness, which we
'hypnoid', is the basic phenomenon of hysteri

Let us now consider the manner in whi
operates. It falls in with one of the dearest human wishes
—the wish to be able to do something over again. Someone
has experienced a psychical trauma without reacting to it
sufficiently. We get him to experience it a second time, but
under hypnosis; and we now compel him to complete his
reaction to it. He can then get rid of the idea's affect, which
was so to say 'strangulated', and when this is done the operation of the idea is brought to an end. Thus we cure—not
hysteria but some of its individual symptoms—by causing an
unaccomplished reaction to be completed.

You must not suppose, then, that very much has been gained
by this for the therapeutics of hysteria. Hysteria, like the
neuroses,[1] has its deeper causes; and it is those deeper causes
that set limits, which are often very appreciable, to the success
of our treatment.

[1] [At this period Freud often used the term 'neuroses' to denote
neurasthenia and what he was later to describe as anxiety neurosis.]

THE NEURO-PSYCHOSES OF DEFENCE
(1894)

EDITOR'S NOTE

DIE ABWEHR-NEUROPSYCHOSEN

(a) GERMAN EDITIONS:
1894   *Neurol. Zbl.*, **13** (10), 362–4, and (11), 402–9.
       (May 15 and June 1.)
1906   *S.K.S.N.*, **1**, 45–59. (1911, 2nd ed.; 1920, 3rd. ed.; 1922,
       4th ed.)
1925   *G.S.*, **1**, 290–305.
1952   *G.W.*, **1**, 59–74.

(b) ENGLISH TRANSLATIONS:
       'The Defense Neuro-Psychoses'
1909   *S.P.H.*, 121–32. (Tr. A. A. Brill.) (1912, 2nd ed.; 1920,
       3rd ed.)

       'The Defence Neuro-Psychoses'
1924   *C.P.*, **1**, 59–75.(Tr. J. Rickman.)

Included (No. XXIX) in Freud's own collection of abstracts
of his early works (1897*b*). The present translation, with a
changed title, is based on that of 1924.

When Freud finished this paper in January, 1894, a year had
elapsed since the appearance of his last psychopathological
work—the 'Preliminary Communication', written jointly with
Breuer. (The only exceptions were the paper on hysterical
paralyses, planned and drafted years earlier, and the Charcot
obituary.) And another year was to elapse before any more were
to appear. Yet the years 1893 and 1894 were far from idle. In
1893 Freud was still producing a quantity of neurological work,
while in 1894 he was preparing his contributions to *Studies on
Hysteria*. But throughout both these years, as we can see from his
letters to Fliess, he was deeply engaged in investigating what
had now completely ousted neurology from his focus of interest
—the problems of the neuroses. These problems fell into two
fairly distinct groups, concerned respectively with what were

43

later (p. 279 below) to become known as the 'actual neuroses' and the 'psychoneuroses'. Freud was not prepared to publish anything about the former—neurasthenia and states of anxiety —for another year, till the beginning of 1895. But on hysteria and obsessions he was already able to map out the ground, and the present paper was the result.[1]

Here, of course, he was still deeply indebted to Charcot and to Breuer; but nevertheless it is possible here to detect too a first emergence of much that was to become an essential part of Freud's own views. For instance, though the theory of defence was very shortly mentioned in the 'Preliminary Communication', it is extensively discussed for the first time here. The term 'defence' itself occurs here for the first time (p. 47) and so too do 'conversion' (p. 49) and 'flight into psychosis' (p. 59).[2] The importance of the part played by sexuality begins to emerge (p. 52); the question of the nature of the 'unconscious' is touched on (p. 53). Most important of all, perhaps, the whole fundamental theory of cathexis and its displaceability is raised in the second section, and the hypothesis on which Freud's scheme was based is clearly enunciated in the penultimate paragraph of the paper. A fuller discussion of the first emergence of Freud's fundamental theoretical views appears in the Editor's Appendix to this paper, p. 62 ff. below.

[1] A list of Freud's principal writings dealing with conversion hysteria will be found at the end of *Studies on Hysteria*, *Standard Ed.*, 2, 310–11. A similar list of his writings on obsessional neurosis is given in *Standard Ed.*, 10, 319–20.

[2] The actual phrase 'flight into illness' seems to have appeared first in a paper on hysterical attacks (1909*a*), *Standard Ed.*, 9, 231–2.

THE NEURO-PSYCHOSES OF DEFENCE

(AN ATTEMPT AT A PSYCHOLOGICAL THEORY
OF ACQUIRED HYSTERIA, OF MANY PHOBIAS AND
OBSESSIONS[1] AND OF CERTAIN HALLUCINATORY
PSYCHOSES)

AFTER making a detailed study of a number of nervous patients suffering from phobias and obsessions, I was led to attempt an explanation of those symptoms; and this enabled me afterwards to arrive successfully at the origin of pathological ideas of this sort in new and different cases. My explanation therefore seems to me to deserve publication and further examination. Simultaneously with this 'psychological theory of phobias and obsessions' my observation of patients resulted in a contribution to the theory of hysteria, or rather to a change in it, which appears to take into account an important characteristic that is common both to hysteria and to the neuroses I have just mentioned. Furthermore, I had occasion to gain insight into what is undoubtedly a form of mental disease, and I found at the same time that the point of view which I had tentatively adopted established an intelligible connection between these psychoses and the two neuroses under discussion. At the end of this paper I shall bring forward a working hypothesis which I have made use of in all three instances.

I

Let me begin with the change which seems to me to be called for in the theory of the hysterical neurosis.

Since the fine work done by Pierre Janet, Josef Breuer and others, it may be taken as generally recognized that the syndrome of hysteria, so far as it is as yet intelligible, justifies the

---

[1] [Cf. some remarks on the translation of the German term '*Zwangs-vorstellung*' (which Freud uses here for the first time) in the Editor's Note to 'Obsessions and Phobias', p. 72 below.]

45

assumption of there being a splitting of consciousness, accompanied by the formation of separate psychical groups.[1] Opinions
are less settled, however, about the origin of this splitting of
consciousness and about the part played by this characteristic in
the structure of the hysterical neurosis.

According to the theory of Janet (1892-4 and 1893), the
splitting of consciousness is a primary feature of the mental
change in hysteria. It is based on an innate weakness of the
capacity for psychical synthesis, on the narrowness of the 'field
of consciousness (*champ de la conscience*)' which, in the form of a
psychical stigma, is evidence of the degeneracy of hysterical
individuals.

In contradistinction to Janet's view, which seems to me to
admit of a great variety of objections, there is the view put
forward by Breuer in our joint communication (Breuer and
Freud, 1893). According to him, 'the basis and *sine quâ non* of
hysteria' is the occurrence of peculiar dream-like states of
consciousness with a restricted capacity for association, for
which he proposes the name 'hypnoid states'. In that case, the
splitting of consciousness is secondary and acquired; it comes
about because the ideas which emerge in hypnoid states are cut
off from associative communication with the rest of the content
of consciousness.[2]

I am now in a position to bring forward evidence of two
other extreme forms of hysteria in which it is impossible to
regard the splitting of consciousness as primary in Janet's sense.
In the first of these [two further] forms I was repeatedly able to
show that *the splitting of the content of consciousness is the result of an
act of will on the part of the patient*; that is to say, it is initiated by
an effort of will whose motive can be specified. By this I do not,
of course, mean that the patient intends to bring about a
splitting of his consciousness. His intention is a different one;

----

[1] [The concept of 'psychical groups' was much employed by Freud
at this period. See, for instance, the case history of Frau Emmy von N.
in *Studies on Hysteria* (1895*d*), *Standard Ed.*, **2**, 104. It is interesting to
note that elsewhere in the same work (ibid., 69 *n*.) he makes use of the
term 'complex' in apparently the same sense. Cf. some remarks on the
history of that term in the Editor's Note to 'Psycho-Analysis and the
Establishment of the Facts in Legal Proceedings' (1906*c*), *Standard Ed.*,
9, 100-2.]

[2] [*Standard Ed.*, **2**, 12.]

but, instead of attaining its aim, it produces a splitting of consciousness.

In the third form of hysteria, which we have demonstrated by means of a psychical analysis[1] of intelligent patients, the splitting of consciousness plays an insignificant part, or perhaps none at all. They are those cases in which what has happened is only that the reaction to traumatic stimuli has failed to occur, and which can also, accordingly, be resolved and cured by 'abreaction'.[2] These are the pure 'retention hysterias'.

As regards the connection with phobias and obsessions, I am only concerned with the second form of hysteria. For reasons which will soon be evident, I shall call this form '*defence* hysteria', using the name to distinguish it from *hypnoid* hysteria and *retention* hysteria.[3] I may also provisionally present my cases of defence hysteria as 'acquired' hysteria, since in them there was no question either of a grave hereditary taint or of an individual degenerative atrophy.

For these patients whom I analysed had enjoyed good mental health up to the moment at which *an occurrence of incompatibility took place in their ideational life*—that is to say, until their ego was faced with an experience, an idea or a feeling which aroused such a distressing affect that the subject decided to forget about it because he had no confidence in his power to resolve the contradiction between that incompatible idea and his ego by means of thought-activity.

In females incompatible ideas of this sort arise chiefly on the soil of sexual experience and sensation; and the patients can recollect as precisely as could be desired their efforts at defence, their intention of 'pushing the thing away', of not thinking of it, of suppressing it. I will give some examples, which I could

---

[1] [The term 'to analyse' had already appeared in the 'Preliminary Communication' (1893*a*), *Standard Ed.*, **2**, 7. This is the first appearance of 'psychical analysis'; 'clinico-psychological analysis' occurs on p. 53 ; 'hypnotic analysis' on p. 59; 'psychological analysis' on p. 75. 'Psycho-analysis' first appears in the French paper on the aetiology of the neuroses (1896*a*), p. 151 below.]

[2] Cf. our joint communication, ibid., **2**, 8–9.

[3] [Cf. *Studies on Hysteria* (1895*d*), *Standard Ed.*, **2**, 211 and 285–6. This is the first appearance of the term 'defence', though the concept had already occurred in the 'Preliminary Communication' (1893*a*), ibid., 10.]

easily multiply, from my own observation: the case of a girl, who blamed herself because, while she was nursing her sick father, she had thought about a young man who had made a slight erotic impression on her; the case of a governess who had fallen in love with her employer and had resolved to drive this inclination out of her mind because it seemed to her incompatible with her pride; and so on.[1]

I cannot, of course, maintain that an effort of will to thrust things of this kind out of one's thoughts is a pathological act; nor do I know whether and in what way intentional forgetting succeeds in those people who, under the same psychical influences, remain healthy. I only know that this kind of 'forgetting' did not succeed with the patients I analysed, but led to various pathological reactions which produced either hysteria or an obsession or a hallucinatory psychosis. The ability to bring about one of these states—which are all of them bound up with a splitting of consciousness—by means of an effort of will of this sort, is to be regarded as the manifestation of a pathological disposition, although such a disposition is not necessarily identical with individual or hereditary 'degeneracy'.

As regards the path which leads from the patient's effort of will to the onset of the neurotic symptom, I have formed an opinion which may be expressed, in current psychological abstractions, somewhat as follows. The task which the ego, in its defensive attitude, sets itself of treating the incompatible idea as '*non arrivée*' simply cannot be fulfilled by it. Both the memory-trace and the affect which is attached to the idea are there once and for all and cannot be eradicated. But it amounts to an approximate fulfilment of the task if the ego succeeds in *turning this powerful idea into a weak one*, in robbing it of the affect—the sum of excitation—with which it is loaded.[2] The weak idea will

---

[1] These examples are taken from a volume by Breuer and myself which is still in preparation and which deals in detail with the psychical mechanism of hysteria. [*Studies on Hysteria* was published in the year after the present paper. The first of the cases mentioned here is that of Fräulein Elisabeth von R. (*Standard Ed.*, 2, 135 ff.); the second is that of Miss Lucy R. (ibid., 107 ff.).]

[2] [This metaphor (in German '*behaftet*') is one of several (e.g. '*ausgestattet*' 'supplied' on p. 53 below) that were before long to give place to the familiar standard term '*besetzt*' (cathected). See the Editor's Appendix at the end of the present paper, p. 63 below.—This seems to

then have virtually no demands to make on the work of association. *But the sum of excitation which has been detached from it must be put to another use.*

Up to this point the processes in hysteria, and in phobias and obsessions are the same; from now on their paths diverge. In hysteria, the incompatible idea is rendered innocuous by its *sum of excitation* being *transformed into something somatic.* For this I should like to propose the name of *conversion.*[1]

The conversion may be either total or partial. It proceeds along the line of the motor or sensory innervation[2] which is related—whether intimately or more loosely—to the traumatic experience. By this means the ego succeeds in freeing itself from the contradiction [with which it is confronted]; but instead, it has burdened itself with a mnemic symbol[3] which finds a lodgement in consciousness, like a sort of parasite, either in the form of an unresolvable motor innervation or as a constantly recurring hallucinatory sensation, and which persists until a conversion in the opposite direction takes place. Consequently the memory-trace of the repressed[4] idea has, after all, not been dissolved; from now on, it forms the nucleus of a second psychical group.

I will only add a few more words to this view of the psychophysical processes in hysteria. When once such a nucleus for a

be the first published use by Freud of the term 'sum of excitation', though it had appeared in the shorthand report of his lecture of January 11, 1893 (Freud, 1893*h*, p. 36 above). It occurs in a posthumously published letter to Breuer of June 29, 1892 (Freud, 1941*a*) and in a draft of the 'Preliminary Communication' written in November of the same year (Freud, 1940*d*). The underlying concept is discussed in the last paragraph but one of the present paper and in the Editor's Appendix, p. 66 ff.]

[1] [This is the first appearance of the term. See some remarks by Freud on the origin of the concept in his 'History of the Psycho-Analytic Movement' (1914*d*), *Standard Ed.*, **14**, 8–9.]

[2] ['*Innervation.*' From 1911 onwards this word was misprinted '*Intervention*' in all the German editions.]

[3] [The term here first introduced was employed frequently by Freud in his early writings. The best explanation of it, however, is from a later work—the first of his *Five Lectures* (1910*a*), *Standard Ed.*, **11**, 16–17.]

[4] [The concept and the term 'repression' were already present in the 'Preliminary Communication' (1893*a*), *Standard Ed.*, **2**, 10.]

hysterical splitting-off has been formed at a 'traumatic moment',[1] it will be increased at other moments (which might be called 'auxiliary moments') whenever the arrival of a fresh impression of the same sort succeeds in breaking through the barrier erected by the will, in furnishing the weakened idea with fresh affect and in re-establishing for a time the associative link between the two psychical groups, until a further conversion sets up a defence. The distribution of excitation thus brought about in hysteria usually turns out to be an unstable one. The excitation which is forced into a wrong channel (into somatic innervation) now and then finds its way back to the idea from which it has been detached, and it then compels the subject either to work over the idea associatively or to get rid of it in hysterical attacks—as we see in the familiar contrast between attacks and chronic symptoms. The operation of Breuer's cathartic method lies in leading back the excitation in this way from the somatic to the psychical sphere deliberately, and in then forcibly bringing about a settlement of the contradiction by means of thought-activity and a discharge of the excitation by talking.

If the splitting of consciousness which occurs in acquired hysteria is based upon an act of will, then we have a surprisingly simple explanation of the remarkable fact that hypnosis regularly widens the restricted consciousness of a hysteric and allows access to the psychical group that has been split off. Indeed, we know it as a peculiarity of all states resembling sleep that they suspend the distribution of excitation on which the 'will' of the conscious personality is based.

Thus we see that the characteristic factor in hysteria is not the splitting of consciousness but *the capacity for conversion*, and we may adduce as an important part of the disposition to hysteria—a disposition which in other respects is still unknown —a psycho-physical aptitude for transposing very large sums of excitation into the somatic innervation.

This aptitude does not, in itself, exclude psychical health; and it only leads to hysteria in the event of there being a

---

[1] ['*Moment*', the German word used here (and in many parallel passages), is the masculine word meaning 'moment of time'. It has been mistaken for the neuter '*das Moment*' and rendered by the English 'factor' in some previous translations.]

psychical incompatibility or an accumulation of excitation. In taking this view, Breuer and I are coming closer to Oppenheim's[1] and Strümpell's[2] well-known definitions of hysteria, and are diverging from Janet, who assigns too great an importance to the splitting of consciousness in his characterization of hysteria.[3] The presentation given here may claim to have made intelligible the connection between conversion and the hysterical splitting of consciousness.

II

If someone with a disposition [to neurosis] lacks the aptitude for conversion, but if, nevertheless, in order to fend off an incompatible[4] idea, he sets about separating it from its affect,

[1] According to Oppenheim, hysteria is an intensified expression of emotion. The 'expression of emotion', however, represents the amount of psychical excitation which normally undergoes conversion. [This approach to the views of Oppenheim and Strümpell is probably attributable to Breuer, who quotes both these definitions with apparent approval in his contribution to Studies on Hysteria, Standard Ed., 2, 245. Two or three years later Freud dissociated himself from Oppenheim's remark in a letter to Fliess of December 6, 1896 (Freud, 1950a, Letter 52).]

[2] Strümpell maintains that in hysteria the disturbance lies in the psycho-physical sphere—in the region where the somatic and the mental are linked together.

[3] In the second section of his acute paper 'Quelques définitions . . .' Janet [1893] has himself dealt with the objection which argues that splitting of consciousness occurs in psychoses and in so-called 'psychasthenia' as well as in hysteria, but in my judgement he has not met it satisfactorily. It is in the main this objection which obliges him to describe hysteria as a form of degeneracy. But he has failed to produce any characteristic which sufficiently distinguishes the splitting of consciousness in hysteria from that in psychoses and similar states.

[4] ['Unverträglich (incompatible)' in the original publication of 1894. Misprinted 'unerträglich (intolerable)' in all the later German reprints. The same misprint seems to have occurred at three other points later in this paper, though in two of these the misprint (if it is one) has already been made in the original. The term is used a very great number of times in Freud's writings of this period—and invariably, except in these instances, as 'unverträglich'. The view that this was what Freud intended is confirmed by the fact that he himself translated the word into French as 'inconciliable' (see p. 72 below). Nevertheless in the Collected Papers version of the present paper it is translated 'unbearable' throughout. Though no doubt the two words roughly imply the same meaning, they

then *that affect is obliged to remain in the psychical sphere.* The idea, now weakened, is still left in consciousness, separated from all association. *But its affect, which has become free, attaches itself to other ideas which are not in themselves incompatible; and, thanks to this 'false connection', those ideas turn into obsessional ideas.*[1] This, in a few words, is the psychological theory of obsessions and phobias mentioned at the beginning of this paper.

I will now indicate which of the various elements put forward in this theory can be directly demonstrated and which have been filled in by me. What can be directly demonstrated, apart from the end-product of the process—the obsession—, is in the first place the source of the affect which is now in a false connection. In all the cases I have analysed it was the subject's *sexual life* that had given rise to a distressing affect of precisely the same quality as that attaching to his obsession. Theoretically, it is not impossible that this affect should sometimes arise in other fields; I can only report that so far I have not come across any other origin. Moreover, it is easy to see that it is precisely sexual life which brings with it the most copious occasions for the emergence of incompatible ideas.

Furthermore, the most unambiguous statements by the patients give proof of the effort of will, the attempt at defence, upon which the theory lays emphasis; and at least in a number of cases the patients themselves inform us that their phobia or obsession made its first appearance after the effort of will had apparently succeeded in its aim. 'Something very disagreeable happened to me once and I tried very hard to put it away from me and not to think about it any more. I succeeded at last; but

---

give rather different pictures of the psychological situation, a difference which it seems desirable to preserve. It must however be noted that *'unerträglich'* reappears twice ten years later, in a paper first printed in a book by Löwenfeld (Freud 1906a), *Standard Ed.*, **7**, 276, again possibly as a misprint.]

[1] [A long discussion of 'false connections' will be found in a footnote to the case of Frau Emmy von N. in *Studies on Hysteria, Standard Ed.*, **2**, 67–70. See also ibid., 302–3. The term reappears in the 'Rat Man' case history (1909d), *Standard Ed.*, **10**, 175–6, where an account of displacement of affect is given very much like the present one.—The divergent vicissitudes of the idea and the affect attached to it foreshadow the account of repression in the metapsychological papers (1915d), ibid., **14**, 152–3.]

then I got this other thing, which I have not been able to get rid of since.' It was with these words that a woman patient confirmed the chief points of the theory I have developed here.

Not everyone who suffers from obsessions is as clear as this about their origin. As a rule, when one draws a patient's attention to the original idea of a sexual kind, the answer is: 'It can't come from that. I didn't think at all much about that. For a moment I was frightened, but I turned my mind away from it and I haven't been troubled by it since.' In this frequent objection we have evidence that the obsession represents a substitute or surrogate for the incompatible sexual idea and has taken its place in consciousness.

Between the patient's effort of will, which succeeds in repressing the unacceptable sexual idea, and the emergence of the obsessional idea, which, though having little intensity in itself, is now supplied [p. 48, *n.* 2] with an incomprehensibly strong affect, yawns the gap which the theory here developed seeks to fill. The separation of the sexual idea from its affect and the attachment of the latter to another, suitable but not incompatible idea—these are processes which occur without consciousness. Their existence can only be presumed, but cannot be proved by any clinico-psychological analysis [cf. p. 47, *n.* 1]. Perhaps it would be more correct to say that these processes are not of a psychical nature at all, that they are physical processes whose psychical consequences present themselves as if what is expressed by the terms 'separation of the idea from its affect' and 'false connection' of the latter had really taken place.[1]

Alongside of the cases which show a sequence between an incompatible sexual idea and an obsessional idea, we find a number of other cases in which obsessional ideas and sexual ideas of a distressing character are present simultaneously. To call the latter 'sexual obsessional ideas' will not do very well, for they lack one essential feature of obsessional ideas: they turn out to be fully justified, whereas the distressing character of ordinary obsessional ideas is a problem for both doctor and patient. So far as I have been able to see my way in cases of this kind, what is happening is that a perpetual defence is going

[1] [Here we have a first hint at innumerable later discussions by Freud as to the nature of the unconscious. Cf. below, p. 170, *n.* 3.]

on against sexual ideas that are continually coming up afresh—a piece of work, that is to say, which has not yet come to completion.

So long as the patients are aware of the sexual origin of their obsessions, they often keep them secret. If they do complain about them, they usually express their astonishment that they should be subject to the affect in question—that they should feel anxiety, or have certain impulses, and so on. To the experienced physician, on the contrary, the affect seems justified and comprehensible; what *he* finds noticeable is only that an affect of that kind should be linked with an idea which does not merit it. The affect of the obsession appears to him, in other words, as being *dislodged* or *transposed*;[1] and if he has accepted what has been said in these pages, he will be able, in a number of cases of obsessions, to attempt to *re-translate them into sexual terms*.

To provide this secondary connection for the liberated affect, any idea can be made use of which is either able, from its nature, to be united with an affect of the *quality* in question, or which has certain relations to the incompatible idea which make it seem as though it could serve as a surrogate for it. Thus, for example, liberated anxiety, whose sexual origin must not be remembered by the patient, will seize upon the common primary phobias of mankind about animals, thunderstorms, darkness and so on, or upon things which are unmistakably associated in one way or another with what is sexual—such as micturition, defaecation, or dirtying and contagion generally.

The ego gains much less advantage from choosing *transposition* of affect as a method of defence than from choosing the hysterical *conversion* of psychical excitation into somatic innervation. The affect from which the ego has suffered remains as it was before, unaltered and undiminished, the only difference being that the incompatible idea is kept down and shut out from recollection.[2] The repressed ideas, as in the other case, form the

---

[1] ['*Disloziert*' and '*transponiert*'. The word ordinarily used by Freud to describe this process—'*Verschiebung*', regularly translated 'displacement' —does not appear in this passage, though it occurs later in this paper, p. 60, and had been used by Freud as early as in his preface to his translation of Bernheim's *De la suggestion* (Freud, 1888–9).]

[2] [Freud elaborated this point in his metapsychological paper on 'Repression' (1915*d*), *Standard Ed.*, 14, 155–7.]

nucleus of a second psychical group, which, I believe, is accessible even without the help of hypnosis. If phobias and obsessions are unaccompanied by the striking symptoms which characterize the formation of an independent psychical group in hysteria, this is doubtless because in their case the whole alteration has remained in the psychical sphere and the relationship between psychical excitation and somatic innervation has undergone no change.

To illustrate what has been said about obsessions, I will give a few examples which are, I imagine, of a typical kind:

(1) A girl suffered from obsessional self-reproaches. If she read something in the papers about coiners, the thought would occur to her that she, too, had made counterfeit money; if a murder had been committed by an unknown person, she would ask herself anxiously whether it was not she who had done the deed. At the same time she was perfectly conscious of the absurdity of these obsessional reproaches. For a time, this sense of guilt gained such an ascendancy over her that her powers of criticism were stifled and she accused herself to her relatives and her doctor of having really committed all these crimes. (This was an example of a psychosis through simple intensification—an '*Überwältigungspsychose*' [a psychosis in which the ego is overwhelmed].[1]) Close questioning then revealed the source from which her sense of guilt arose. Stimulated by a chance voluptuous sensation, she had allowed herself to be led astray by a woman friend into masturbating, and had practised it for years, fully conscious of her wrong-doing and to the accompaniment of the most violent, but, as usual, ineffective self-reproaches. An excessive indulgence after going to a ball had produced the intensification that led to the psychosis.

[1] [Literally, 'psychosis of overwhelming'. The 'overwhelming' of the patient's ego in different forms of defence-neurosis is discussed at several points by Freud in a paper sent to Fliess on January 1, 1896 (Freud, 1950a, Draft K). The actual term '*Überwältigungspsychose*' occurs in a letter a year later, on January 11, 1897 (ibid., Letter 55). An allusion to the overwhelming of the ego will also be found in Freud's contribution to *Studies on Hysteria* (1895d), *Standard Ed.*, 2, 263–4. But the idea recurs in much later writings of Freud's; see, for instance, *The Ego and the Id* (1923b), *Standard Ed.*, 19, 57.]

After a few months of treatment and the strictest surveillance, the girl recovered.[1]

(2) Another girl suffered from the dread of being overcome by the need to urinate, and of being unable to avoid wetting herself, ever since a need of this kind had in fact once obliged her to leave a concert hall during the performance. By degrees this phobia had made her completely incapable of enjoying herself or of going into society. She only felt well if she knew that there was a W.C. near at hand which she could reach unobtrusively. There was no question of any organic complaint which might justify this mistrust in her power to control her bladder; when she was at home, in quiet conditions, or at night, the need to urinate did not arise. A detailed examination showed that the need had occurred first in the following circumstances. In the concert hall a gentleman to whom she was not indifferent had taken a seat not far from her. She began to think about him and to imagine herself sitting beside him as his wife. During this erotic reverie she had the bodily sensation which is to be compared with an erection in a man, and which in her case—I do not know if this is always so—ended with a slight need to urinate. She now became greatly frightened by the sexual sensation (to which she was normally accustomed) because she had resolved within herself to combat this particular liking, as well as any other she might feel; and next moment the affect had become transferred on to the accompanying need to urinate and compelled her after an agonizing struggle to leave the hall. In her ordinary life she was so prudish that she had an intense horror of everything to do with sex and could not contemplate the thought of ever marrying. On the other hand, she was so hyperaesthetic sexually that during every erotic reverie, in which she readily indulged, the same voluptuous sensation appeared. The erection was each time accompanied by the need to urinate, though without its making any impression on her until the scene in the concert hall. The treatment led to an almost complete control over her phobia.[2]

---

[1] [This case is reported again very briefly in 'Obsessions and Phobias' (1895c), below, p. 76.]

[2] [This case, too, is mentioned in 'Obsessions and Phobias', below, p. 77. It is also referred to by Freud in a letter to Fliess written on February 7, 1894, very soon after the completion of this paper: 'You

(3) A young married woman who, in five years of marriage, had had only one child, complained to me of an obsessional impulse to throw herself out of the window or from the balcony, and also of a fear, which seized her when she saw a sharp knife, of stabbing her child with it. She admitted that marital intercourse seldom occurred, and only subject to precautions against conception, but she did not miss it, she said, as hers was not a sensual nature. At this point I ventured to tell her that at the sight of a man she had erotic ideas and that she had there-fore lost confidence in herself and regarded herself as a depraved person, capable of anything. The translation back of the obses-sional idea into sexual terms was successful. In tears, she at once confessed the long-concealed poverty of her marriage; and later she told me also of distressing ideas of an unmodified sexual character, such as the often-recurring sensation of something forcing itself under her skirt.

I have turned observations of this kind to account in my therapeutic work by leading back the attention of patients with phobias and obsessions to the repressed sexual ideas in spite of all their protestations, and, wherever possible, by stop-ping up the sources from which those ideas sprang. I cannot, of course, assert that *all* phobias and obsessions arise in the manner I have shown here. In the first place, my experience of them includes only a limited number compared with the frequency of these neuroses; and in the second place, I myself am aware that such 'psychasthenic' symptoms, as Janet terms them, are not all equivalent.[1] There are, for instance, purely hysterical

are right. The connection between obsessional neurosis and sexuality is not always so obvious. I can assure you it was not so easy to find either in my Case 2 (Need to urinate). If anyone less mono-ideistic than I am had looked for it, he would have overlooked it. Yet in this case, which I have got to know thoroughly in the course of several months' treat-ment by feeding-up, sexuality dominated positively the whole scene.' (Freud, 1950a, Letter 16.) Freud used at this period sometimes to combine the cathartic method with the Weir Mitchell treatment. See *Studies on Hysteria, Standard Ed.*, 2, 267.]

[1] The group of typical phobias, of which agoraphobia is a model, cannot be traced back to the psychical mechanism described above; on the contrary, the mechanism of agoraphobia differs from that of obsessions proper, and of the phobias that are reducible to them, in one

phobias. Nevertheless, I think that it will be possible to show the presence of the mechanism of transposition of affect in the great majority of phobias and obsessions, and I would therefore urge that these neuroses, which are found in an isolated state as often as in combination with hysteria or neurasthenia, should not be thrown into a heap along with common neurasthenia, for the basic symptoms of which there is no ground at all to assume a *psychical* mechanism.

III

In both the instances considered so far, defence against the incompatible idea was effected by separating it from its affect; the idea itself remained in consciousness, even though weakened and isolated. There is, however, a much more energetic and successful kind of defence. Here, the ego rejects the incompatible[1] idea together with its affect and behaves as if the idea had never occurred to the ego at all. *But from the moment at which this has been successfully done the subject is in a psychosis, which can only be classified as 'hallucinatory confusion'.* A single example may serve to illustrate this statement:

A girl had given her first impulsive affection to a man, and firmly believed that he returned her love. In fact, she was wrong; the young man had a different motive for visiting the house. Disappointments were not wanting. At first she defended herself against them by effecting a hysterical conversion of the experiences in question and thus preserved her belief that one day he would come and ask her hand. But at the same time she felt unhappy and ill, because the conversion was incomplete and because she was continually being met by fresh painful impressions. Finally, in a state of great tension, she awaited his arrival on a particular day, the day of a family celebration. But the day wore on and he did not appear. When all the trains by which he could arrive had come and gone, she passed into a state of hallucinatory confusion: he had arrived, she heard his

decisive point. There is no repressed idea from which the anxiety affect might have been separated off. The anxiety of these phobias has another origin. [See the Editor's Appendix to 'Obsessions and Phobias', p. 83 f. below.]

[1] ['Intolerable' in all the German editions, but see footnote 4, p. 51 above.]

voice in the garden, she hurried down in her nightdress to receive him. From that time on she lived for two months in a happy dream, whose content was that he was there, always at her side, and that everything was as it had been before (before the time of the disappointments which she had so laboriously fended off). Her hysteria and her depression of spirits were overcome. During her illness she was silent about the whole latter period of doubt and suffering; she was happy so long as she was left undisturbed, and she broke out in fury only when some rule of conduct insisted on by those around her hindered her in something which seemed to her to follow quite logically from her blissful dream. This psychosis, which had been un-intelligible at the time, was explained ten years later with the help of a hypnotic analysis [cf. p. 47 n. 1].

The fact to which I now wish to call attention is that the content of a hallucinatory psychosis of this sort *consists precisely in the accentuation of the idea* which was threatened by the pre-cipitating cause of the onset of the illness. One is therefore justi-fied in saying that the ego has fended off the incompatible[1] idea through a flight into psychosis.[2] The process by which this has been achieved once more eludes the subject's self-perception, as it eludes psychologico-clinical analysis. It must be regarded as the expression of a pathological disposition of a fairly high degree and it may be described more or less as follows. The ego breaks away from the incompatible[3] idea; but the latter is inseparably connected with a piece of reality, so that, in so far as the ego achieves this result, it, too, has detached itself wholly or in part from reality.[4] In my opinion this latter event is the condition under which the subject's ideas receive the

[1] ['Intolerable' in all the German editions, but see footnote 4, p. 51 above.]

[2] [This notion, in the more generalized form of a 'flight into illness', became widely used and accepted. See Freud's *Autobiographical Study* (1925*d*), *Standard Ed.*, 20, 54, and p. 44 *n.* 2 above.]

[3] ['Intolerable' in all the German editions except the original publica-tion, which reads 'incompatible'. See footnote 4, p. 51 above.]

[4] [Freud was here touching on a problem that was to occupy him much towards the end of his life. See, for instance, 'Neurosis and Psychosis' (1924*b*), 'The Loss of Reality in Neurosis and Psychosis' (1924*e*), 'Fetishism' (1927*e*) and the posthumous fragment 'Splitting of the Ego in the Process of Defence' (1940*e* [1938]).]

vividness of hallucinations; and thus when the defence has been successfully carried out he finds himself in a state of hallucinatory confusion.

I have only very few analyses of psychoses of this sort at my disposal. But I think we have to do here with a type of psychical illness which is very frequently employed. For no insane asylum is without what must be regarded as analogous examples—the mother who has fallen ill from the loss of her baby, and now rocks a piece of wood unceasingly in her arms, or the jilted bride who, arrayed in her wedding-dress, has for years been waiting for her bridegroom.

It is perhaps not superfluous to point out that the three methods of defence here described, and, along with them, the three forms of illness to which those methods lead, may be combined in the same person. The simultaneous appearance of phobias and hysterical symptoms which is so often observed in practice is one of the factors which render it difficult to separate hysteria clearly from other neuroses and which make it necessary to set up the category of 'mixed neuroses'. It is true that hallucinatory confusion is not often compatible with a persistance of hysteria, nor, as a rule, of obsessions. On the other hand, it is not rare for a psychosis of defence episodically to break through the course of a hysterical or mixed neurosis.

I should like, finally, to dwell for a moment on the working hypothesis which I have made use of in this exposition of the neuroses of defence. I refer to the concept that in mental functions something is to be distinguished—a quota of affect or sum of excitation—which possesses all the characteristics of a quantity (though we have no means of measuring it), which is capable of increase, diminution, displacement and discharge, and which is spread over the memory-traces of ideas somewhat as an electric charge is spread over the surface of a body.[1]

This hypothesis, which, incidentally, already underlies our theory of 'abreaction' in our 'Preliminary Communication'

---

[1] [Some comments on this paragraph will be found in the appendix which follows this paper.]

(1893*a*), can be applied in the same sense as physicists apply the hypothesis of a flow of electric fluid. It is provisionally justified by its utility in co-ordinating and explaining a great variety of psychical states.

VIENNA, *end of January* 1894.

APPENDIX

THE EMERGENCE OF FREUD'S FUNDAMENTAL HYPOTHESES

WITH this first paper on the neuro-psychoses of defence Freud gave public expression, if not directly, at least by implication, to many of the most fundamental of the theoretical notions on which all his later work rested. It will be recalled that the paper was written in January, 1894—a year after the publication of the 'Preliminary Communication' and a year before the completion of the main portion of the *Studies on Hysteria* and of Breuer's theoretical contribution to that volume. At the time of writing this paper, therefore, Freud was deeply involved in his first series of psychological investigations. From these a number of clinical inferences were beginning to emerge, and behind them some more general hypotheses which would lend coherence to the clinical findings. But it was not for another six months after the publication of *Studies on Hysteria*—in the autumn of 1895—that Freud made a first attempt at a systematic exposition of his theoretical views; and that attempt (the 'Project for a Scientific Psychology') was left uncompleted and unpublished by its author. It first saw the light of day in 1950, more than half a century later. In the meantime the curious student of Freud's theoretical views had to pick up what he could from the discontinuous and sometimes obscure accounts given by Freud at various later points in his career. Moreover, his one extended discussion of his theories in later years—the metapsychological papers of 1915—have survived only in a truncated form: seven of the twelve papers having completely disappeared.[1]

In his 'History of the Psycho-Analytic Movement' (1914*d*) Freud declared that 'the theory of repression', or defence, to give it its alternative name, 'is the corner-stone on which the whole structure of psycho-analysis rests' (*Standard Ed.*, **14**, 16). The term 'defence' actually occurs for the first time in the

---

[1] See *Standard Ed.*, **14**, 105–7.

present paper (p. 47), and it is here that the theory receives its earliest effective consideration, though a bare sentence or two had been devoted to it in the 'Preliminary Communication' (*Standard Ed.*, **2**, 10) and in the 'Lecture' (p. 38 above).[1]

This clinical hypothesis of defence, however, was itself necessarily based on more general assumptions, one of which is specified in the penultimate paragraph of this paper (p. 60 above). This assumption may conveniently be named (though the name derives from a somewhat later date) the theory of 'cathexis' (*'Besetzung'*).[2] There is perhaps no other passage in Freud's published writings in which he so explicitly recognizes the necessity for this most fundamental of all his hypotheses: 'that in mental functions something is to be distinguished—a quota of affect or sum of excitation—which possesses all the characteristics of a quantity . . ., which is capable of increase, diminution, displacement and discharge. . . .' The notion of a 'displaceable quantity' had, of course, been implicit in all his earlier theoretical discussions. As he himself points out in this same passage, it underlay the theory of abreaction; it was the necessary basis of the principle of constancy (which will be discussed in a moment); it was implied whenever Freud made use of such phrases as 'loaded with a sum of excitation' (p. 48 above), 'provided with a quota of affect' (1893*c*), 'supplied with energy' (1895*b*) —predecessors of what was soon to become the standard term 'cathected'. Already, in his preface to his first translation of Bernheim (1888–9), he had spoken of 'displacements of excitability in the nervous system'.

---

[1] A still earlier hint at the theory may be traced in Section (5) of an unpublished draft of the 'Preliminary Communication' dated 'End of November 1892' (Breuer and Freud, 1940*d*).

[2] Freud's first use of the term in this sense seems to have been in the *Studies on Hysteria* (1895*d*), *Standard Ed.*, **2**, 89, and 152, which was published about a year later than the present paper. The German word is one in ordinary use, and, among many other senses, might have some such meaning as 'occupation' or 'filling'. Freud, who disliked unnecessary technical terms, was unhappy when in 1922 the present editor, in the supposed interests of clarity, introduced the invented word 'cathexis' (from the Greek κατέχειν, catechein, to occupy) as a translation. He may perhaps have become reconciled to it in the end, since it is to be found in his original manuscript of his *Encyclopaedia Britannica* article (1926*f*), *Standard Ed.*, **20**, 266.

This last example, however, reminds us of the presence of a further complication. Rather more than eighteen months after writing the present paper Freud sent to Fliess the remarkable fragment known as the 'Project' which has already been mentioned above. Here for the first and last time we find the hypothesis of cathexis fully discussed. But this full discussion brings clearly to light something that is only too easily forgotten. Throughout this period Freud appears to have regarded these cathectic processes as *material* events. In his 'Project' two basic assumptions were laid down. The first was the validity of the recent histological discovery that the nervous system consisted of chains of neurones; the second was the idea that excitation of the neurones was to be regarded as 'a quantity, subject to the general laws of motion'. By combining these two assumptions 'we arrive at the idea of a "cathected" neurone filled with a certain quantity, though at other times it may be empty' ('Project', Part I, Section 2). But though cathexis was thus defined primarily as a neurological event, the situation was not quite so simple. Till very recently Freud's interest had been centred on neurology, and now that his thoughts were being more and more diverted to psychology his first endeavour was naturally to reconcile his two interests. He believed it should be possible to state the facts of psychology in neurological terms, and his efforts to do so culminated precisely in the 'Project'. The attempt failed; the 'Project' was abandoned; and in the years that followed little more was heard of a neurological basis of psychological events except (as we shall see below, p. 108 f.) in connection with the problem of the 'actual neuroses'. Nevertheless, this repulse did not involve any wholesale revolution. The fact was, no doubt, that the formulations and hypotheses which Freud put forward in neurological terms had actually been constructed with more than half an eye to psychological events; and when the time came for dropping the neurology it turned out that the greater part of the theoretical material could be understood as applying, and indeed applying more cogently, to purely mental phenomena.

These considerations apply to the concept of 'cathexis', which possessed an entirely non-physical meaning in all Freud's later writings, including the theoretical seventh chapter of *The Inter-*

pretation of Dreams (1900a).[1] They apply also to the further hypothesis, which makes use of the concept of cathexis, and which was later known as the 'principle of constancy'. This too began as an apparently physiological hypothesis. It is stated in the ' Project' (Part I, Section 1) as 'the principle of neuronic inertia, which asserts that neurones tend to divest themselves of quantity'. It was stated twenty-five years later in psychological terms in *Beyond the Pleasure Principle* (1920g) as follows: 'The mental apparatus endeavours to keep the quantity of excitation present in it as low as possible or at least to keep it constant.' (*Standard Ed.*, **18**, 9.) This principle is not stated explicitly in the present paper, though it is implied at several points. It had already been mentioned in the lecture on the 'Preliminary Communication' (1893h, p. 36 above), though not in the 'Preliminary Communication' itself, and in the French paper on hysterical paralyses (1893c). It was also very clearly stated in a posthumously published draft of the 'Preliminary Communication' (1940d), dated 'End of November, 1892', and was referred to, earlier still, in a letter from Freud to Breuer dated June 29, 1892 (1941a), as well as, by implication, in one of Freud's footnotes to his translation of a volume of Charcot's *Leçons du mardi* (Freud, 1892–94, 107). In later years the principle was repeatedly discussed: for instance, by Breuer in his theoretical contribution to *Studies on Hysteria* (1895d), *Standard Ed.*, **2**, 197–8, and by Freud in 'Instincts and their Vicissitudes' (1915c), ibid., **14**, 119–21, and in *Beyond the Pleasure Principle* (1920g), ibid., **18**, 9 ff., 26 ff. and 55 f., where he first gave it the new name of 'Nirvana principle'.

The pleasure principle, no less fundamental in Freud's psychological armoury than the constancy principle, is equally

---

[1] It must be remarked that, though the theory of cathexis as a displaceable quantity was already explicit at the time of the present paper, further vitally important elaborations of the theory were still to be made: in particular the notion that cathectic energy occurs in two forms, bound and free. This additional hypothesis, with its corollary of the distinction between the primary and secondary mental processes, possibly adumbrated by Breuer in *Studies on Hysteria* (1895), *Standard Ed.*, **2**, 194 n., was included by Freud in his 'Project', but was first fully and publicly announced in Chapter VII of *The Interpretation of Dreams* (1900a). It may be hinted at in the second paper on anxiety neurosis (1895f), p. 132 below.

present, though once more only by implication, in this paper. To begin with he regarded the two principles as intimately connected and perhaps identical. In the 'Project' (Part I, Section 8) he wrote: 'Since we have certain knowledge of a trend in psychical life towards avoiding unpleasure, we are tempted to identify that trend with the primary trend towards inertia. In that case *unpleasure* would coincide with a rise in the level of quantity . . . *Pleasure* would be the sensation of discharge.' It was not until very much later, in 'The Economic Problem of Masochism' (1924c), that Freud demonstrated the necessity for distinguishing between the two principles, ibid., **19**, 159–61. The course of his changing views on this question is followed in detail in an Editor's footnote to the metapsychological paper on 'Instincts and their Vicissitudes' (1915c), ibid., **14**, 121 n.[1]

The further question may be asked of how far these fundamental hypotheses were peculiar to Freud and how far they were derived from other influences. Many possible sources have been suggested—Helmholtz, Herbart, Fechner, Meynert, among others. This, however, is not the place for entering into such a wide-ranging question. It is enough to say that it has been exhaustively examined by Ernest Jones in the first volume of his Freud biography (1953, 405–15).

A few words may be directed to a point that arises particularly out of the penultimate paragraph of this paper—the apparent equating there of the terms 'quota of affect (*Affektbetrag*)' and 'sum of excitation (*Erregungssumme*)'. Is Freud using the words as synonyms? The account that Freud gives of affects in Lecture XXV of his *Introductory Lectures* (1916–17) and his use of the word in Section III of his paper on *The Unconscious* (1915e), as well as numerous other passages, show that as a rule he meant by 'affect' much the same as what we mean by 'feeling' or 'emotion'. 'Excitation', on the other hand, is one of several terms that he seems to use to describe the unknown

[1] Freud's first long discussion of the pleasure principle occurs under the name of the 'unpleasure principle' in *The Interpretation of Dreams* (1900a), *Standard Ed.*, **5**, 600 ff.; he took the hypothesis up again (this time under its now familiar name) in his paper on the two principles of mental functioning (1911b), where he showed how the pleasure principle becomes modified into the reality principle, *Standard Ed.*, **12**, 219.

energy of 'cathexis'. In the 'Project', as we have seen, he simply calls this 'quantity'. Elsewhere he uses such terms as 'psychical intensity'[1] or 'instinctual energy'. 'Sum of excitation' itself goes back to his mention of the principle of constancy in his letter to Breuer of June, 1892. Thus the two terms would appear *not* to be synonyms. This view is confirmed by a passage in Breuer's theoretical chapter of *Studies on Hysteria* in which he gives reasons for supposing that affects 'go along with an increase in excitation', implying that they are two different things (*Standard Ed.*, **2**, 201–3). All this would seem quite straightforward if it were not for a passage in the metapsychological paper on 'Repression' (1915*d*), ibid., **14**, 152 ff. This is the passage in which Freud shows that the 'psychical representative' of an instinct consists of two elements which have quite different vicissitudes under repression. One of these elements is the idea or group of ideas cathected, the other is the instinctual energy cathecting it. 'For this other element of the psychical representative the term *quota of affect* has been generally adopted.'[2] A few sentences later, and at several other points, he refers to this element as 'the quantitative factor', but then, a little later still, he once more speaks of it as the 'quota of affect'. At first sight it looks as though Freud was here treating affect and psychical energy as synonymous notions. But this cannot, after all, be the case, since in the very same passage he mentions as a possible instinctual vicissitude 'the transformation into affects . . . of the psychical energies of instincts' (*Standard Ed.*, **14**, 153).

The explanation of the apparent ambiguity seems to lie in Freud's underlying view of the nature of affects. This is perhaps most clearly stated in the third section of the paper on 'The Unconscious' (1915*e*), *Standard Ed.*, **14**, 178, where Freud declares that affects 'correspond to processes of discharge, the final manifestations of which are perceived as feelings'. Similarly in Lecture XXV of the *Introductory Lectures* he enquires what an affect is 'in the dynamic sense' and goes on: 'An affect includes in the first place particular motor innervations or discharges

[1] See for instance pp. 130 and 308 below.
[2] In a much later passage, in his paper on 'Fetishism' (1927*e*), which refers back to this discussion in 'Repression', he writes once again of the differentiation 'between the vicissitude of the *idea* as distinct from that of the *affect*' (*Standard Ed.*, **21**, 153).

and secondly certain feelings; the latter are of two kinds—
perceptions of the motor actions that have occurred and the
direct feelings of pleasure and unpleasure which, as we say, give
the affect its key-note.' And, lastly, in the paper on 'Repression' from which we started, he writes that the quota of affect
'corresponds to the instinct in so far as the latter . . . finds
expression, proportionate to its quantity, in processes which are
sensed as affects.'

Thus it is probably correct to suppose that Freud was regarding the 'quota of affect' as a particular manifestation of the
'sum of excitation'. It is no doubt true that affect was what was
usually involved in the cases of hysteria and obsessional neurosis with which Freud was chiefly concerned in early days.
For that reason he tended at that time to describe the 'displaceable quantity' as a quota of affect rather than in more
general terms as an excitation; and this habit would seem to
have persisted even in the metapsychological papers where a
more precise differentiation might have contributed to the
clarity of his argument.

OBSESSIONS AND PHOBIAS

THEIR PSYCHICAL MECHANISM AND THEIR AETIOLOGY

(1895 [1894])

EDITOR'S NOTE

OBSESSIONS ET PHOBIES
(Leur mécanisme psychique et leur étiologie)

(a) French Editions:

1895 Rev. neurol., **3** (2), 33–8. (January 30.)
1906 S.K.S.N., **1**, 86–93. (1911, 2nd ed.; 1920, 3rd ed.; 1922, 4th ed.)
1925 G.S., **1**, 334–42.
1952 G.W., **1**, 345–53.

(b) English Translation:
'Obsessions and Phobias'
1924 C.P., **1**, 128–37. (Tr. M. Meyer.)

Included (No. XXX) in Freud's own collection of abstracts of his early works (1897b). The original is in French. The present translation is a considerably revised version of the one published in 1924. A German translation, by A. Schiff, under the title 'Zwangsvorstellungen und Phobien', was published in the *Wien. klin. Rundsch.*, **9** (17), 262-3 and (18), 276-8, on April 28 and May 5, 1895.

Though this paper was published a fortnight later than the first paper on anxiety neurosis (1895b), it was written earlier; for there is a reference here (p. 81) to the one on anxiety neurosis as something that Freud hopes to write in the future, and in that paper there is a reference back to this one (p. 97 n. below).

The earlier part of this paper is little more than a repetition of Section II of the first paper on 'The Neuro-Psychoses of Defence' (1894a), dealing with obsessions. The later part, concerned with phobias, is discussed in the Editor's Appendix below (pp. 83–4).

This is one of three papers which Freud wrote in French at

71

about this period; the first (1893c), dealing with the distinction
between organic and hysterical paralyses, will be found in the
first volume of the *Standard Edition*, and the remaining one
below, on p. 143 ff. In one or two cases the French terms
selected by Freud himself as renderings of the German ones are
of interest to the English translator. Thus he always translates
'*Zwangsvorstellung*' by the French '*obsession*'. This ought to set at
rest any uneasy feeling that the proper English version should
be 'compulsive idea' or something of the sort.[1] Actually there
seems to have been no German equivalent to the French and
English word until Krafft-Ebing introduced '*Zwangsvorstellung*'
in 1867 (cf. Löwenfeld, 1904, 8). The English 'obsession' in the
sense of a fixed idea, goes back at least to the seventeenth century. Similarly Freud translates '*Zwangsneurose*' by the French
'*névrose d'obsessions*'. The German '*Angstneurose*' he renders
'*névrose d'angoisse*'; in one place at least, however (on p. 75), he
renders *Angst* by '*anxiété*', a French word with much the same
connotation as the English 'anxiety'. (See p. 116 f. below.)
Another word which Freud uses very frequently indeed in his
writings at this period is '*unverträglich*' as applied to the ideas
repressed in hysteria or got rid of in other ways in obsessional
neurosis. There has been a good deal of unwillingness to accept
this word as meaning 'incompatible'. There is another German
word with only a single letter fewer, '*unerträglich*', which means
'intolerable'. This latter word appears a few times, probably
as a misprint, in the German editions (cf. p. 51, *n.* 4 above), and
'intolerable' was adopted as the uniform translation in the
greater part of the first volume of the *Collected Papers* of 1924.
Doubts about the sense intended by Freud seem to be settled
by the French equivalent which he has chosen—'*inconciliable*'.

It may be added that in Volume I of the *Gesammelte Werke*
(published in 1952), at the beginning of the first of these French
papers (which is the one included in Volume I of the *Standard
Edition*) the following footnote appears: 'In the three articles
in French, the original text has been revised and corrected as
regards misprints and errors in French, though strict respect has
been paid to the meaning.' The majority of the changes thus

---

[1] The sense may, of course, sometimes call for the term to be translated 'obsessional idea', and sometimes require the special introduction
of the notion of compulsion.

made are purely verbal and have consequently not affected the English translation. In some cases, however, in this paper and in the one below (p. 143 ff.), the changes may perhaps be thought to have gone further, though in two of these (pp. 145 and 153) the 1952 version actually goes back to the one found in the original periodical publication. In reaching a decision in the doubtful cases it has to be borne in mind that Freud himself most probably read through both the 1906 *and* the 1925 reprints, since he added new footnotes to the latter (cf. p. 6 *n.* above). The 1906 versions are the ones we have usually adopted in the text. In every instance the alternative is given in a footnote.[1]

[1] As a further point of interest to the translator, it may be remarked that throughout this paper Freud uses the French '*état émotif*' as a rendering of the German '*Affekt*'. Compare the last paragraph on p. 75 with the first paragraph on p. 52. See also his own abstract of the French paper, p. 250 below.

OBSESSIONS AND PHOBIAS
THEIR PSYCHICAL MECHANISM AND THEIR AETIOLOGY

I SHALL begin by challenging two assertions which are often found repeated in regard to the syndromes 'obsessions' and 'phobias'. It must be said, first, that they cannot be included under neurasthenia proper, since the patients afflicted with these symptoms are no more often neurasthenics than not; and secondly, that we are not justified in regarding them as the effect of mental degeneracy, because they are found in persons no more degenerate than the majority of neurotics in general, because they sometimes improve, and sometimes, indeed, we even succeed in curing them.[1]

Obsessions and phobias are separate neuroses, with a special mechanism and aetiology which I have succeeded in demonstrating in a certain number of cases, and which, I hope, will prove similar in a good number of fresh cases.

As regards classification of the subject, I propose in the first place to exclude a group of intense obsessions which are nothing but memories, unaltered images of important events. As an example, I may cite Pascal's obsession: he always thought he saw an abyss on his left hand 'after he had nearly been thrown into the Seine in his coach'. Such obsessions and phobias, which might be called *traumatic*, are allied to the symptoms of hysteria.

Apart from this group we must distinguish: (*a*) true obsessions; (*b*) phobias. The essential difference between them is the following:

Two constituents are found in every obsession: (1) an idea that forces itself upon the patient; (2) an associated emotional state. Now in the group of phobias this emotional state is always one of 'anxiety', while in true obsessions other emotional states, such as doubt, remorse, or anger, may occur just as well

[1] I am very glad to find that the authors of the most recent work on this subject express opinions very similar to mine. Cf. Gélineau (1894), and Hack Tuke (1894).

74

as anxiety.[1] I will first attempt to explain the really remarkable psychological mechanism of true obsessions, a mechanism quite different from that of the phobias.

I

In many true obsessions it is quite plain that the emotional state is the principal thing, since that state persists unchanged while the idea associated with it varies. The girl in Case 1 quoted below, for example, felt remorse in some degree for all sorts of reasons—for having stolen, for having ill-treated her sisters, for having made counterfeit money, etc. People who doubt have many doubts at the same time or in succession. It is the emotional state which remains constant in them; the idea changes. In other cases the idea, too, seems fixated, as in Case 4, of the girl who pursued the servants in the house with an incomprehensible hatred, though constantly changing the individual object.

Now a careful psychological analysis[2] of these cases shows that *the emotional state, as such, is always justified*. The girl in Case 1, who suffered from remorse, had good reasons for it; the women in Case 3 who doubted their powers of resistance to temptation knew very well why. The girl in Case 4, who detested servants, had good reasons for complaining, etc. Only, and it is in these two characteristics that the pathological mark lies, (1) *the emotional state persists indefinitely*, and (2) the associated idea is *no longer the appropriate original one, related to the aetiology of the obsession, but is one which replaces it, a substitute for it.*

The proof of this is the fact that we can always find in the previous history of the patient, *at the beginning of the obsession*, the original idea that has been replaced. The replaced ideas all have common attributes; they correspond to really distressing experiences in the subject's sexual life which he is striving to forget. He succeeds merely in replacing the incompatible idea by another ill-adapted for being associated with the emotional state, which for its part remains unchanged. It is this *mésalliance*[3] between the emotional state and the associated idea that accounts for the absurdity so characteristic of obsessions.

[1] [The first 'anxiety' in this sentence stands for '*angoisse*' in the original, and the second for '*anxiété*'.]   [2] [Cf. p. 47, *n.* 1.]
[3] [Elsewhere Freud uses the term 'false connection'. Cf. above, p. 52.]

I will now bring forward my observations and conclude with an attempt at a theoretical explanation.

Case 1. A girl reproached herself for things which she knew were absurd: for having stolen, for having made counterfeit money, for being involved in a conspiracy, etc., according to what she happened to have been reading during the day.

Reinstatement of the replaced idea: She reproached herself with the masturbation she had been practising in secret without being able to renounce it. She was cured by careful surveillance which prevented her from masturbating.[1]

Case 2. A young man, a medical student, suffered from an analogous obsession. He reproached himself for all sorts of immoral acts: for having killed his cousin, for having violated his sister, for having set fire to a house, etc. He got to the point of having to turn round in the street to see whether he had not killed the last passer-by.

Reinstatement: He had been much affected by reading in a quasi-medical book that masturbation, to which he was addicted, destroyed one's morale.

Case 3. Several women complained of an obsessional impulse to throw themselves out of the window, to stab their children with knives, scissors, etc.

Reinstatement: Obsessions based on typical temptations. These were women who, not being at all satisfied in marriage, had to struggle against the desires and voluptuous ideas that constantly troubled them at the sight of other men.

Case 4. A girl who was perfectly sane and very intelligent displayed an uncontrollable hatred against the servants in the house. It had been started in connection with an impertinent servant, and had been transferred from servant to servant, to an extent that made housekeeping impossible. The feeling was a mixture of hate and disgust. She gave as a reason for it that the coarseness of these girls spoilt her idea of love.

Reinstatement: This girl had been an involuntary witness of a love-scene in which her mother had taken part. She had hidden her face, had stopped up her ears, and had done her utmost to forget it, as it disgusted her and would have made it impossible

---

[1] [Freud had reported this case at greater length in his first paper on 'The Neuro-Psychoses of Defence' (1894a), pp. 55–6 above.]

for her to remain with her mother, whom she loved tenderly. She succeeded in her efforts; but her anger at her idea of love having been defiled persisted within her, and this emotional state soon linked itself to the idea of a person who could take her mother's place.

Case 5. A girl had become almost completely isolated on account of an obsessional fear of incontinence of urine. She could no longer leave her room or receive visitors without having urinated a number of times. When she was at home or entirely alone the fear did not trouble her.

Reinstatement: It was an obsession based on temptation or mistrust. She did not mistrust her bladder, but her resistance to erotic impulses. The origin of the obsession shows this clearly. Once, at the theatre, on seeing a man who attracted her, she had felt an erotic desire, accompanied (as spontaneous pollutions in women always are) by a desire to urinate. She was obliged to leave the theatre, and from that moment on she was a prey to the fear of having the same sensation, but the desire to urinate had replaced the erotic one. She was completely cured.[1]

Although the cases I have enumerated show varying degrees of complexity, they have this in common: the original (incompatible) idea has been replaced by another idea, the substituted idea. In the cases which I now append, the original idea has been replaced, but not by another idea; it has been replaced by acts or impulses which originally served as measures of *relief* or as *protective* procedures, and are now grotesquely associated with an emotional state which does not fit them, but which has persisted unchanged, and which has remained as justifiable as it was at its origin.

Case 6. *Obsessional arithmomania.*—A woman found herself obliged to count the boards in the floor, the steps in the staircase, etc.—acts which she performed in a ridiculous state of anxiety.

Reinstatement: She had begun the counting in order to distract her mind from obsessional ideas (of temptation). She had

[1] [This case, too, was reported in the earlier paper (p. 56 above), but in somewhat different terms.]

succeeded in doing so, but the impulse to count had replaced the original obsession.

Case 7. Obsessional brooding and speculating.—A woman suffered from attacks of this obsession which ceased only when she was ill, and then gave place to hypochondriacal fears. The theme of her worry was always a part or function of her body; for example, respiration: 'Why must I breathe? Suppose I didn't want to breathe?' etc.

Reinstatement: At the very beginning she had suffered from the fear of becoming insane, a hypochondriacal phobia common enough among women who are not satisfied by their husbands, as she was not. *To assure herself that she was not going mad,* that she was still in possession of her mental faculties, she had begun to ask herself questions and concern herself with serious problems. This calmed her at first, but with time the habit of speculation replaced the phobia. For more than fifteen years, periods of fear (pathophobia) and of obsessive speculating had alternated in her.

Case 8. Folie du doute.—Several cases showed the typical symptoms of this obsession but were explained very simply. These persons had suffered or were still suffering from various obsessions, and the knowledge that the obsessions had disturbed all their acts and had many times interrupted their train of thought provoked a legitimate doubt about the reliability of their memory. The confidence of each one of us is shaken, and we all of us have to re-read a letter or repeat a calculation if our attention has been distracted several times during the performance of the act. Doubt is a quite logical result when obsessions are present.

Case 9. Folie du doute. (Hesitation.)—The girl in Case 4 had become extremely slow in the performance of all her everyday actions, particularly in her toilet. She took hours to tie her shoe-laces or to clean her finger-nails. By way of explanation she said she could not make her toilet while the obsessional ideas were occupying her, nor immediately afterwards. As a result, she had become accustomed to wait a definite length of time after each return of the obsessional idea.

Case 10. Folie du doute. (Fear of scraps of paper.)—A young woman had suffered from scruples after having written a letter; at the same time she collected all the pieces of paper she saw.

She explained this by confessing to a love which she had formerly refused to admit. As a result of constantly repeating her lover's name, she was seized with a fear that the name might have slipped off the end of her pen, that she might have written it upon some scrap of paper in a pensive moment.[1]

Case 11. *Mysophobia.* [*Fear of dirt.*]—A woman kept washing her hands constantly and touched door-handles only with her elbow.

Reinstatement: It was the case of Lady Macbeth. The washing was symbolic, designed to replace by physical purity the moral purity which she regretted having lost. She tormented herself with remorse for conjugal infidelity, the memory of which she had resolved to banish from her mind.[2] In addition, she used to wash her genitals.

As regards the theory of this process of substitution, I will content myself with answering three questions that arise here.

(1) How can the substitution come about?

It seems to be the expression of a special inherited mental disposition. At any rate, 'similar heredity'[3] is often enough found in obsessional cases, as in hysteria. Thus the patient in Case 2 told me that his father had suffered from similar symptoms. He once introduced me to a first cousin who had obsessions and a *tic convulsif*, and to his sister's daughter, aged eleven, who already gave evidence of obsessions (probably of remorse).

(2) What is the motive for the substitution?

I think it may be regarded as an act of defence (*Abwehr*) of the ego against the incompatible idea. Among my patients there are some who remember a deliberate effort to banish the

---

[1] Cf. the German popular song:
> Auf jedes weisse Blatt Papier möcht' ich es schreiben:
> Dein ist mein Herz und soll es ewig, ewig bleiben.

> [On each blank piece of paper I will write it plain:
> My heart is thine and ever ever shall remain.]

The German couplet, with a slight variation, occurs in 'Ungeduld', one of the poems in Wilhelm Müller's cycle *Die schöne Müllerin*, set to music by Schubert.]

[2] [This point, including the reference to Lady Macbeth, was mentioned afterwards by Breuer in his contribution to *Studies on Hysteria* (1895*d*), *Standard Ed.*, 2, 245 *n*.]

[3] [See the discussion of this below, on pp. 144-5.]

distressing idea or recollection from the field of consciousness. (See Cases 3, 4, 11.) In other cases the expulsion of the incompatible idea is brought about in an unconscious manner which has left no trace in the patient's memory.

(3) Why does the emotional state that is associated with the obsessional idea persist indefinitely instead of vanishing like other states of our ego?

This question may be answered by reference to the theory of the genesis of hysterical symptoms developed by Breuer and myself.[1] Here I will only remark that, by the very fact of the substitution, the disappearance of the emotional state is rendered impossible.

II

In addition to these two groups of true obsessions there is the class of 'phobias', which must now be considered. I have already mentioned the great difference between obsessions and phobias: that in the latter the emotion is always one of anxiety, fear. I might add that obsessions are varied and more specialized, phobias are more monotonous and typical. But this distinction is not of capital importance.

Among the phobias, also, two groups may be differentiated, according to the nature of the object feared: (1) common phobias, an exaggerated fear of things that everyone detests or fears to some extent: such as night, solitude, death, illnesses, dangers in general, snakes, etc.; (2) contingent phobias, the fear of special conditions that inspire no fear in the normal man; for example, agoraphobia and the other phobias of locomotion. It is interesting to note that these phobias have not the obsessive feature that characterizes true obsessions and the common phobias. The emotional state appears in their instance only under special conditions which the patient carefully avoids.

The mechanism of phobias is entirely different from that of obsessions. Substitution is no longer the predominant feature in the former; psychological analysis reveals no incompatible, replaced idea in them. Nothing is ever found but *the emotional state*

---

[1] 'On the Psychical Mechanism of Hysterical Phenomena' (1893a) [the 'Preliminary Communication' to *Studies on Hysteria* (1895d), *Standard Ed.*, 2, 3].

of anxiety which, by a kind of selective process, brings up all the ideas adapted to become the subject of a phobia. In the case of agoraphobia, etc., we often find *the recollection of an anxiety attack*; and what the patient actually fears is the occurrence of such an attack under the special conditions in which he believes he cannot escape it.

The anxiety belonging to this emotional state, which underlies all phobias, is not derived from any memory; we may well wonder what the source of this powerful condition of the nervous system can be.

I hope to be able to demonstrate, on another occasion, that there is reason to distinguish a special neurosis, the 'anxiety neurosis',[1] of which the chief symptom is this emotional state. I shall then enumerate its various symptoms and insist on the necessity for differentiating this neurosis from neurasthenia, with which it is now confused. *Phobias, then, are a part of the anxiety neurosis*, and are almost always accompanied by other symptoms of the same group.

The anxiety neurosis, too, has a sexual origin as far as I can see, but it does not attach itself to ideas taken from sexual life; properly speaking, it has no psychical mechanism. Its specific cause is the accumulation of sexual tension, produced by abstinence or by unconsummated[2] sexual excitation (using the term as a general formula for the effects of coitus reservatus,[3] of relative impotence in the husband, of excitation without satisfaction in engaged couples, of enforced abstinence, etc.).

It is under such conditions, extremely frequent in modern society, especially among women, that anxiety neurosis (of which phobias are a psychical manifestation) develops.

In conclusion I may point out that combinations of a phobia

[1] [The first paper on anxiety neurosis (1895*b*) had in fact been published a fortnight before the present one. See below p. 87.]

[2] [The French word in the original is *'fruste'*. This word means 'worn', 'rubbed', as applied especially to coins, and is often used by Freud in the phrase *'forme fruste'* (e.g. in the Charcot obituary, 1893*f*, this volume, above, p. 12). It is here evidently confused with the quite different French word *'frustrée'*, meaning 'frustrated'. This too is often used by Freud in a German form *'frustrane'* (e.g. in the first paper on anxiety neurosis, p. 101 below).]

[3] [*'Réservé'* in all the earlier French editions. In 1952 only, this is changed to *'interrompu'*. Cf. Editor's Note above, pp. 72–3.]

and an obsession proper may co-exist, and that indeed this is a very frequent occurrence. We may find that a phobia had developed at the beginning of the disease as a symptom of anxiety neurosis. The idea which constitutes the phobia and which is associated with the state of fear may be replaced by another idea or rather by the *protective procedure* that seemed to relieve the fear. Case 7[1] (obsessive speculating) presents a neat example of this group: *a phobia along with a true substitutive obsession.*

[1] [In all the French editions this is wrongly given as '6'.]

APPENDIX

FREUD'S VIEWS ON PHOBIAS

Freud's earliest approach to the problem of phobias was in his first paper on the neuro-psychoses of defence (1894*a*); he dealt with it rather more fully a year later in the second section of the present paper and alluded to it again in the first paper on anxiety neurosis (1895*b*) which he wrote very shortly afterwards. In all these early discussions of phobias it is not hard to detect some uncertainty; indeed, in a further brief reference to the question in the second paper on anxiety neurosis (1895*f*) Freud speaks of the mechanism of phobias as 'obscure' (p. 134). In the earliest of these papers he had attributed the same mechanism to 'the great majority of phobias and obsessions' (p. 58), while excepting the 'purely hysterical phobias' (p. 57) and 'the group of typical phobias of which agoraphobia is a model' (p. 57, footnote 1). This latter distinction, making its first appearance in a footnote, was to prove the crucial one, for it implied a distinction between phobias having a psychical basis and those (the 'typical' ones) without any. This distinction thus linked up with that between what were later to be known as the psychoneuroses and the 'actual neuroses' (see below, p. 279, *n*. 1). In these early papers, however, the distinction was not consistently drawn. Thus, in the present paper, it seems to be made not between two different groups of phobias (as in the earlier one) but between the (psychically based) 'obsessions' on the one side and the (non-psychically based) 'phobias' on the other, the latter being declared to be 'a part of the anxiety neurosis' (pp. 80–1). Here, however, the picture is confused by the further division of phobias into two groups according to the nature of their objects (p. 80), and moreover by the segregation (as in the first paper) of another class of phobias 'which might be called traumatic' and which are 'allied to the symptoms of hysteria' (p. 74). Further, in the paper on anxiety neurosis the main distinction was not between obsessions and phobias, as it is here, but once again between phobias belonging to obsessional neurosis and

83

those belonging to anxiety neurosis (pp. 96–7): though once again the distinction was between the presence or absence of a psychical basis. In these papers, therefore, there remained undetermined links between phobias, hysteria, obsessions, and anxiety neurosis.

Apart from a very few scattered allusions, the subject of phobias seems not to have been discussed by Freud after the present group of papers for nearly fifteen years. Then, in the case history of 'Little Hans' (1909b), the first step was taken towards clearing up these obscurities by the introduction of a fresh clinical entity—'anxiety hysteria' (*Standard Ed.*, **10**, 15–16). Freud there observed that phobias 'should only be regarded as syndromes which may form part of various neuroses and that we need not rank them as an independent pathological process'; and he went on to propose the name of 'anxiety hysteria' for one particular type of phobia whose mechanism resembled that of hysteria. It was in this case history and in the later one of the 'Wolf Man' (1918b [1914]) that Freud gave his fullest clinical account of phobias—both of them, of course, occurring in children. A little later, in his metapsychological papers on 'Repression' and 'The Unconscious' (1915d and e), he entered into a detailed discussion of the metapsychology of the mechanism that produces phobias, whether related to hysteria or to obsessional neurosis (ibid., **14**, 155–7 and 181–5). There remained, however, the problem, going back to the earliest of the present set of papers, of the 'typical' phobias of anxiety neurosis. Here, as we have seen, the whole question of the 'actual neuroses' was involved; and this was not to be fully elucidated until later still, in *Inhibitions, Symptoms and Anxiety* (1926d), of which the core is a reconsideration of the phobias of 'Little Hans' and the 'Wolf Man'.

ON THE GROUNDS FOR DETACHING A PARTICULAR SYNDROME FROM NEURASTHENIA UNDER THE DESCRIPTION 'ANXIETY NEUROSIS'

(1895 [1894])

EDITOR'S NOTE

ÜBER DIE BERECHTIGUNG, VON DER NEURAS-
THENIE EINEN BESTIMMTEN SYMPTOMEN-
KOMPLEX ALS 'ANGSTNEUROSE' ABZUTRENNEN

(a) German Editions:

1895   *Neurol. Zbl.*, **14** (2), 50–66. (January 15.)
1906   *S.K.S.N.*, **1**, 60–85. (1911, 2nd ed.; 1920, 3rd ed.; 1922,
      4th ed.)
1925   *G.S.*, **1**, 306–33.
1952   *G.W.*, **1**, 315–42.

(b) English Translations:

    'On the Right to Separate from Neurasthenia a Definite
    Symptom-Complex as "Anxiety Neurosis"'
1909   *S.P.H.*, 133–54. (Tr. A. A. Brill.) (1912, 2nd ed.; 1920,
      3rd ed.)

    'The Justification for Detaching from Neurasthenia a
    Particular Syndrome: the Anxiety-Neurosis'
1924   *C.P.*, **1**, 76–106. (Tr. J. Rickman.)

Included (No. XXXII) in Freud's own collection of abstracts of his early works (1897b). The present translation, with a new title, is based on that of 1924.

This paper may be regarded as the first stretch of a trail that led, with more than one bifurcation and more than one sharp turning, through the whole of Freud's writings. But, as may be seen from the list of works dealing with anxiety[1] printed as an appendix to *Inhibitions, Symptoms and Anxiety* (1926d) (*Standard Ed.*, **20**, 175), this is not, strictly speaking, the beginning of the trail. It was preceded by several exploratory starts in the form of drafts submitted by Freud to Wilhelm Fliess (particularly in

[1] Some notes on the English translation of the German word '*Angst*' are given in an Editor's Appendix below (p. 116 f.).

Drafts A, B and E). Thus, in Section II of Draft B dated February 8, 1893 (Freud, 1950a), some of the main points of the present paper are already summarized. In particular, the need to 'detach' anxiety neurosis from neurasthenia is insisted upon and many of the symptoms are enumerated much as they are here. On the other hand, this Draft contains no indication of the deeper aetiology of the neurosis as it is proposed in the present paper—the accumulation of sexual excitation which is unable to find discharge in the psychical field. For this we have to turn to Draft E, where the theory is stated fully and perhaps even more clearly than it is below. Unluckily Draft E is not dated. The editors of the Fliess correspondence assign it for no very convincing reason to June, 1894; but in any case it must evidently have been written before, and not very long before, this paper. Some of the obscurities here have light thrown upon them by this Draft and also by Draft G (also undated, but certainly contemporary with the present work), which includes a remarkable diagram depicting Freud's ideas on the mechanism of the sexual process.

It is also advisable to bear in mind in reading these early papers that Freud was at the time deeply involved in an attempt to state the data of psychology in neurological terms— an attempt which culminated in his abortive 'Project for a Scientific Psychology' (1950a, written in the autumn of 1895, a few months after these Drafts, but, like them, only posthumously published) and which thereafter foundered completely. (Cf. above, p. 64.) He had not yet wholly adopted the hypothesis of there being unconscious mental processes (as is seen from a sentence in his earlier paper on 'The Neuro-Psychoses of Defence', p. 53 above). Thus in the present paper he distinguishes between 'somatic sexual excitation' on the one hand and 'sexual libido, or psychical desire' on the other (p. 107). 'Libido' is regarded as something exclusively 'psychical' though, again, no clear distinction seems yet to have been made between 'psychical' and 'conscious'. It is interesting to notice that in the abstract of this paper which Freud himself wrote only a couple of years later (1897b), p. 251 below, he evidently already accepts the view of libido as something potentially unconscious and writes: 'Neurotic anxiety is transformed sexual libido.'

But in whatever terms he expressed this theory, it was one which he held till very late in life, though with a number of qualifying complications. For a long series of changing opinions lay ahead, some account of which will be found in the Editor's Introduction (in Vol. XX of the *Standard Edition*) to the last of his major works on the subject, *Inhibitions, Symptoms and Anxiety* (1926*d*). But in the meantime he was faced by an immediate controversy with a sceptical acquaintance, the psychiatrist Löwenfeld of Munich, and the paper which follows this one was the result.

ON THE GROUNDS FOR DETACHING A PARTICULAR SYNDROME FROM NEURASTHENIA UNDER THE DESCRIPTION 'ANXIETY NEUROSIS'

[INTRODUCTION]

IT is difficult to make any statement of general validity about neurasthenia, so long as we use that name to cover all the things which Beard[1] has included under it. In my opinion, it can be nothing but a gain to neuropathology if we make an attempt to separate from neurasthenia proper all those neurotic disturbances in which, on the one hand, the symptoms are more firmly linked to one another than to the typical symptoms of neurasthenia (such as intracranial pressure, spinal irritation, and dyspepsia with flatulence and constipation); and which, on the other hand, exhibit essential differences in their aetiology and mechanism from the typical neurasthenic neurosis. If we accept this plan, we shall soon obtain a fairly uniform picture of neurasthenia. We shall then be in a position to differentiate from genuine neurasthenia more sharply than has hitherto been possible various pseudo-neurasthenias (such as the clinical picture of the organically determined nasal reflex neurosis,[2] the nervous disorders of the cachexias and arterio-sclerosis, the preliminary stages of general paralysis of the insane, and of some psychoses). Further, it will be possible—as Möbius has proposed—to eliminate some of the *status nervosi* [nervous conditions] of hereditarily degenerate individuals; and we shall also discover reasons why a number of neuroses which are to-day described as neurasthenia—in particular, neuroses of an intermittent or periodical nature—ought rather to be included under melancholia. But the most marked change of all will be introduced if

[1] [G. M. Beard (1839–83), the American neurologist, was regarded as the principal exponent of neurasthenia. Cf. Beard, 1881 and 1884.]

[2] [This was a clinical entity proposed by Fliess (1892 and 1893) and impressed by him upon Freud (cf. Freud, 1950a, Draft C).]

we decide to detach from neurasthenia the syndrome which I propose to describe in the following pages and which satisfies especially fully the conditions set out above. The symptoms of this syndrome are clinically much more closely related to one another than to those of genuine neurasthenia (that is, they frequently appear together and they replace one another in the course of the illness); and both the aetiology and the mechanism of this neurosis are fundamentally different from the aetiology and mechanism of genuine neurasthenia as it will be left after this separation has been effected.

I call this syndrome 'anxiety neurosis',[1] because all its components can be grouped round the chief symptom of anxiety, because each one of them has a definite relationship to anxiety. I thought that this view of the symptoms of anxiety neurosis had originated with me, until an interesting paper by E. Hecker (1893) came into my hands, in which I found the same interpretation expounded with all the clarity and completeness that could be desired.[2] Nevertheless, although Hecker recognizes certain symptoms as equivalents or rudiments of an anxiety attack, he does not separate them from the domain of neurasthenia, as I propose to do. But this is evidently due to his not having taken into account the difference between the aetiological determinants in the two cases. When this latter difference is recognized there is no longer any necessity for designating anxiety symptoms by the same name as genuine neurasthenic ones; for the principal purpose of giving what is otherwise an arbitrary name is to make it easier to lay down general statements.

---

[1] ['*Angstneurose.*' This was the first time Freud used the word in German in a published work. (He had already used it in French, p. 81 above.) He had been using the term at least as early as February 8, 1893, in his letters to Fliess (cf. Freud, 1950*a*, Draft B). According to Löwenfeld, 1904, 479, both the concept and the term are due to Freud. An attempt had been made a little time earlier by Wernicke (1894) to distinguish an anxiety *psychosis*.]

[2] Anxiety is actually brought forward as one of the principal symptoms of neurasthenia in a work by Kaan (1893).

I

THE CLINICAL SYMPTOMATOLOGY OF ANXIETY NEUROSIS

What I call 'anxiety neurosis' may be observed in a completely developed form or in a rudimentary one, in isolation or combined with other neuroses. It is of course the cases which are in some degree complete and at the same time isolated which give particular support to the impression that anxiety neurosis is a clinical entity. In other cases, where the syndrome corresponds to a 'mixed neurosis', we are faced with the task of picking out and separating those symptoms which belong, not to neurasthenia or hysteria, and so on, but to anxiety neurosis.

The clinical picture of anxiety neurosis comprises the following symptoms:

(1) *General irritability.* This is a common nervous symptom and as such belongs to many *status nervosi*. I mention it here because it invariably appears in anxiety neurosis and is important theoretically. Increased irritability always points to an accumulation of excitation or an inability to tolerate such an accumulation—that is, to an *absolute* or a *relative* accumulation of excitation. One manifestation of this increased irritability seems to me to deserve special mention; I refer to *auditory hyperaesthesia*, to an oversensitiveness to noise—a symptom which is undoubtedly to be explained by the innate intimate relationship between auditory impressions and fright. Auditory hyperaesthesia frequently turns out to be a cause of sleeplessness, of which more than one form belongs to anxiety neurosis.

(2) *Anxious expectation.* I cannot better describe the condition I have in mind than by this name and by adding a few examples. A woman, for instance, who suffers from anxious expectation will think of influenzal pneumonia every time her husband coughs when he has a cold, and, in her mind's eye, will see his funeral go past; if, when she is coming towards the house, she sees two people standing by her front door, she cannot avoid thinking that one of her children has fallen out of the window; when she hears the bell ring, it is someone bringing news of a death, and so on—while on all these occasions there has been no particular ground for exaggerating a mere possibility.

Anxious expectation, of course, shades off imperceptibly into normal anxiety, comprising all that is ordinarily spoken of as anxiousness—or a tendency to take a pessimistic view of things; but at every opportunity it goes beyond a plausible anxiousness of this kind, and it is frequently recognized by the patient himself as a kind of compulsion. For one form of anxious expectation —that relating to the subject's own health—we may reserve the old term *hypochondria*. The height reached by the hypochondria is not always parallel with the general anxious expectation; it requires as a precondition the existence of paraesthesias and distressing bodily sensations. Thus hypochondria is the form favoured by genuine neurasthenics when, as often happens, they fall victims to anxiety neurosis.[1]

A further expression of anxious expectation is no doubt to be found in the inclination to *moral anxiety*,[2] to scrupulousness and pedantry—an inclination which is so often present in people with more than the usual amount of moral sensitiveness and which likewise varies from the normal to an exaggerated form in *doubting mania*.

Anxious expectation is the nuclear symptom of the neurosis. It openly reveals, too, a portion of the theory of the neurosis. We may perhaps say that here a *quantum of anxiety in a freely floating state* is present, which, where there is expectation, controls the choice of ideas and is always ready to link itself with any suitable ideational content.

(3) But anxiousness—which, though mostly latent as regards consciousness, is constantly lurking in the background—has other means of finding expression besides this. It can suddenly break through into consciousness without being aroused by a train of ideas, and thus provoke an anxiety attack. An anxiety attack of this sort may consist of the feeling of anxiety, alone, without any associated idea, or accompanied by the interpretation that is nearest to hand, such as ideas of the extinction

[1] [Freud made some further remarks on the relation of hypochondria to the other neuroses in his contribution to *Studies on Hysteria* (1895*d*), Standard Ed., **2**, 258. He returned to the subject much later, particularly in Section II of his paper on narcissism (1914*c*), ibid., **14**, 83–5.]

[2] ['*Gewissensangst*', literally 'conscience anxiety'. This was to be a principal topic in some of Freud's latest writings—for instance in the latter part of *Inhibitions, Symptoms and Anxiety* (1926*d*) and in Chapters VII and VIII of *Civilization and its Discontents* (1930*a*).]

of life, or of a stroke, or of a threat of madness; or else some kind of paraesthesia (similar to the hysterical aura[1]) may be combined with the feeling of anxiety, or, finally, the feeling of anxiety may have linked to it a disturbance of one or more of the bodily functions—such as respiration, heart action, vaso-motor innervation or glandular activity. From this combination the patient picks out in particular now one, now another, factor. He complains of 'spasms of the heart', 'difficulty in breathing', 'outbreaks of sweating', 'ravenous hunger', and such like; and, in his description, the feeling of anxiety often recedes into the background or is referred to quite un-recognizably as 'being unwell', 'feeling uncomfortable', and so on.

(4) Now it is an interesting fact, and an important one from a diagnostic point of view, that the proportion in which these elements are mixed in an anxiety attack varies to a remarkable degree, and that almost every accompanying symptom alone can constitute the attack just as well as can the anxiety itself. There are consequently *rudimentary anxiety attacks* and *equivalents of anxiety attacks*, all probably having the same significance, which exhibit a great wealth of forms that has as yet been little appreciated. A closer study of these larval anxiety-states (as Hecker [1893] calls them) and their diagnostic differentiation from other attacks should soon become a necessary task for neuropathologists.

I append here a list which includes only those forms of anxiety attack which are known to me:—

(*a*) Anxiety attacks accompanied by disturbances of the *heart action*, such as palpitation, either with transitory arrhythmia or with tachycardia of longer duration which may end in serious weakness of the heart and which is not always easily differen-tiated from organic heart affection; and, again, pseudo-angina pectoris—diagnostically a delicate subject!

(*b*) Anxiety attacks accompanied by *disturbances of respiration*, several forms of nervous dyspnoea, attacks resembling asthma, and the like. I would emphasize that even these attacks are not always accompanied by recognizable anxiety.

[1] [See footnote, p. 28 above.]

(c) Attacks of *sweating*, often at night.

(d) Attacks of *tremor* and *shivering* which are only too easily confused with hysterical attacks.

(e) Attacks of *ravenous hunger*, often accompanied by vertigo.

(f) Diarrhoea coming on in attacks.

(g) Attacks of locomotor *vertigo*.

(h) Attacks of what are known as *congestions*, including practically everything that has been termed vasomotor neurasthenia.

(i) Attacks of *paraesthesias*. (But these seldom occur without anxiety or a similar feeling of discomfort.)

(5) *Waking up at night in a fright* (the *pavor nocturnus* of adults), which is usually combined with anxiety, dyspnoea, sweating and so on, is very often nothing else than a variant of the anxiety attack. This disturbance is the determinant of a second form of sleeplessness within the field of anxiety neurosis. [Cf. p. 92.] I have become convinced, moreover, that the *pavor nocturnus* of children, too, exhibits a form which belongs to anxiety neurosis. The streak of hysteria about it, the linking of the anxiety with the reproduction of an appropriate experience or a dream, causes the *pavor nocturnus* of children to appear as something special. But the *pavor* can also emerge in a pure form, without any dream or recurring hallucination.

(6) *'Vertigo'* occupies a prominent place in the group of symptoms of anxiety neurosis. In its mildest form it is best described as 'giddiness'; in its severer manifestations, as 'attacks of vertigo' (with or without anxiety), it must be classed among the gravest symptoms of the neurosis. The vertigo of anxiety neurosis is not rotatory nor does it especially affect certain planes or directions, like Ménière's vertigo. It belongs to the class of locomotor or co-ordinatory vertigo, as does the vertigo in oculomotor paralysis. It consists in a specific state of discomfort, accompanied by sensations of the ground rocking, of the legs giving way and of its being impossible to stand up any more; while the legs feel as heavy as lead and tremble or the knees bend. This vertigo never leads to a fall. On the other hand, I should like to state that an attack of vertigo of this kind may have its place taken by a profound fainting fit. Other conditions in the nature of fainting occurring in anxiety neurosis appear to depend upon cardiac collapse.

Attacks of vertigo are not seldom accompanied by the worst sort of anxiety, often combined with cardiac and respiratory disturbances. According to my observations, vertigo produced by heights, mountains and precipices is also often present in anxiety neurosis. Furthermore, I am not sure whether it is not also right to recognize alongside of this a *vertigo a stomacho laeso* [of gastric origin].

(7) On the basis of chronic anxiousness (anxious expectation) on the one hand, and a tendency to anxiety attacks accompanied by vertigo on the other, two groups of typical phobias develop, the first relating to general physiological dangers, the second relating to locomotion. To the first group belong fear of snakes, thunderstorms, darkness, vermin, and so on, as well as the typical moral over-scrupulousness and forms of doubting mania. Here the available anxiety is simply employed to reinforce aversions which are instinctively implanted in everyone. But as a rule a phobia which acts in an obsessional manner is only formed if there is added to this the recollection of an experience in which the anxiety was able to find expression— as, for instance, after the patient has experienced a thunderstorm in the open. It is a mistake to try to explain such cases as being simply a persistence of strong impressions; what makes these experiences significant and the memory of them lasting is, after all, only the anxiety which was able to emerge at the time [of the experience] and which can similarly emerge now. In other words, such impressions remain powerful only in people with 'anxious expectation'.

The other group includes *agoraphobia* with all its accessory forms, the whole of them characterized by their relation to locomotion. We frequently find that this phobia is based on an attack of vertigo that has preceded it; but I do not think that one can postulate such an attack in every case. Occasionally we see that after a first attack of vertigo without anxiety, locomotion, although henceforward constantly accompanied by a sensation of vertigo, still continues to be possible without restriction; but that, under certain conditions—such as being alone or in a narrow street—when once anxiety is added to the attack of vertigo, locomotion breaks down.

The relation of these phobias to the phobias of obsessional neurosis, whose mechanism I made clear in an earlier paper[1] in this periodical, is of the following kind. What they have in common is that in both an idea becomes obsessional as a result of being attached to an available affect. The mechanism of *transposition of affect* thus holds good for both kinds of phobia. But in the phobias of anxiety neurosis (1) this affect always has the same colour, which is that of anxiety; and (2) the affect does not originate in a repressed idea, but turns out to be *not further reducible by psychological analysis, nor amenable to psychotherapy*. The mechanism of *substitution*, therefore, does not hold good for the phobias of anxiety neurosis.

Both kinds of phobias (and also obsessions) often appear side by side; although the *atypical* phobias, which are based on obsessions, need not necessarily spring from the soil of anxiety neurosis. A very frequent and apparently complicated mechanism makes its appearance if, in what was originally a simple phobia belonging to an anxiety neurosis, the content of the phobia is replaced by another idea, so that the substitute is *subsequent* to the phobia. What are most often employed as substitutes are the '*protective measures*' that were originally used to combat the phobia. Thus, for instance, 'brooding mania' arises from the subject's endeavours to disprove that he is mad, as his hypochondriacal phobia maintains; the hesitations and doubt, and still more the repetitions, of *folie du doute* [doubting mania] arise from a justifiable doubt about the certainty of one's own train of thought, since one is conscious of its persistent disturbance by ideas of an obsessional sort, and so on. We can therefore assert that many syndromes, too, of obsessional neurosis, such as *folie du doute* and the like, are also to be reckoned, clinically if not conceptually, as belonging to anxiety neurosis.[2]

(8) The digestive activities undergo only a few disturbances in anxiety neurosis; but these are characteristic ones. Sensations such as an inclination to vomit and nausea are not rare, and the symptom of ravenous hunger may, by itself or in conjunction

[1] 'The Neuro-Psychoses of Defence' (1894a).—[The term 'obsessional neurosis (*Zwangsneurose*)' makes its first published appearance in this sentence. Freud had used it in a letter to Fliess of February 7, 1894 (Freud, 1950a, Letter 16). Löwenfeld (1904, 296 and 487) attributed the origin of both the term and the concept to Freud.—Cf. also the Editor's Appendix to 'Obsessions and Phobias', pp. 83 above.]

[2] See 'Obsessions and Phobias' (1895c) [pp. 78-9 above].

with other symptoms (such as congestions), give rise to a
rudimentary anxiety attack. As a chronic change, analogous
to anxious expectation, we find an inclination to diarrhoea,
and this has been the occasion of the strangest diagnostic
errors. Unless I am mistaken, it is this diarrhoea to which
Möbius (1894) has drawn attention recently in a short paper.
I suspect, further, that Peyer's reflex diarrhoea, which he
derives from disorders of the prostate (Peyer, 1893), is nothing
else than this diarrhoea of anxiety neurosis. The illusion of a
reflex relationship is created because the same factors come
into play in the aetiology of anxiety neurosis as are at work
in the setting up of such affections of the prostate and similar
disorders.

The behaviour of the gastro-intestinal tract in anxiety neurosis presents a sharp contrast to the influence of neurasthenia on
those functions. Mixed cases often show the familiar 'alternation between diarrhoea and constipation'. Analogous to this
diarrhoea is the need to urinate that occurs in anxiety neurosis.

(9) The *paraesthesias* which may accompany attacks of vertigo
or anxiety are interesting because they, like the sensations of the
hysterical aura, become associated in a definite sequence;
although I find that these associations, in contrast to the
hysterical ones, are atypical and changing. A further similarity
to hysteria is provided by the fact that in anxiety neurosis a
kind of *conversion*[1] takes place on to bodily sensations, which may
easily be overlooked—for instance, on to rheumatic muscles. A
whole number of what are known as rheumatic individuals—
who, moreover, can be shown to *be* rheumatic—are in reality
suffering from anxiety neurosis. Along with this increase of sensitivity to pain, I have also observed in a number of cases of
anxiety neurosis a tendency to *hallucinations*; and these could
not be interpreted as hysterical.

(10) Several of the symptoms I have mentioned, which
accompany or take the place of an anxiety attack, also appear
in a chronic form. In that case they are still less easy to recognize, since the anxious sensation which goes with them is less
clear than in an anxiety attack. This is especially true of
diarrhoea, vertigo and paraesthesias. Just as an attack of vertigo
can be replaced by a fainting fit, so chronic vertigo can be

[1] See 'The Neuro-Psychoses of Defence' (1894a) [p. 49 above].

replaced by a constant feeling of great feebleness, lassitude and so on.

II

INCIDENCE AND AETIOLOGY OF ANXIETY NEUROSIS

In some cases of anxiety neurosis no aetiology at all is to be discovered. It is worth noting that in such cases there is seldom any difficulty in establishing evidence of a grave hereditary taint.

But where there are grounds for regarding the neurosis as an *acquired* one, careful enquiry directed to that end reveals that a set of noxae and influences from *sexual life* are the operative aetiological factors.[1] These appear at first sight to be of a varied nature, but they soon disclose the common character which explains why they have a similar effect on the nervous system. Further, they are present either alone or together with other noxae of a 'stock'[2] kind, to which we may ascribe a contributory effect. This sexual aetiology of anxiety neurosis can be demonstrated with such overwhelming frequency that I venture, *for the purpose of this short paper*, to disregard those cases where the aetiology is doubtful or different.

In order that the aetiological conditions under which anxiety neurosis makes its appearance may be presented with greater accuracy, it will be advisable to consider males and females separately. In females—disregarding for the moment their innate disposition—anxiety neurosis occurs in the following cases:

(a) As *virginal anxiety* or *anxiety in adolescents*. A number of unambiguous observations have shown me that anxiety neurosis can be produced in girls who are approaching maturity by their first encounter with the problem of sex, by any more or less sudden revelation of what had till then been hidden—for instance, by witnessing the sexual act, or being told or reading

---

[1] [This passage is further discussed in connection with one of Löwenfeld's criticisms, p. 134 below.]
[2] [This word has been adopted in all these early papers as a rendering of the German-French adjective '*banal*'.]

about these things.[1] Such an anxiety neurosis is combined with hysteria in an almost typical fashion.

(b) As *anxiety in the newly-married.* Young married women who have remained anaesthetic during their first cohabitations not seldom fall ill of an anxiety neurosis, which disappears once more as soon as the anaesthesia gives place to normal sensitivity. Since most young wives remain healthy where there is initial anaesthesia of this kind, it follows that, in order that this kind of anxiety shall emerge, other determinants are required; and these I will mention later.

(c) As anxiety in women whose husbands suffer from ejaculatio praecox or from markedly impaired potency; and (d) whose husbands practise coitus interruptus or reservatus.[2] These cases [(c) and (d)] belong together, for on analysing a great number of instances it is easy to convince oneself that they depend simply on whether the woman obtains satisfaction in coitus or not. If not, the condition for the genesis of an anxiety neurosis is given. On the other hand, she is saved from the neurosis if the husband who is afflicted with ejaculatio praecox is able immediately to repeat coitus with better success. Coitus reservatus *by means of condoms* is not injurious to the woman, provided she is very quickly excitable and the husband very potent; otherwise, this kind of preventive intercourse is no less injurious than the others. Coitus interruptus is nearly always a noxa. But for the wife it is only so if the husband practises it regardlessly—that is to say, if he breaks off intercourse as soon as *he* is near emission, without troubling himself about the course of the excitation in *her.* If, on the other hand, the husband waits for his wife's satisfaction, the coitus amounts to a normal one for *her*; but *he* will fall ill of an anxiety neurosis. I have collected and analysed a large number of observations, on which these assertions are based.

(e) Anxiety neurosis also occurs as anxiety in *widows* and

---

[1] [Freud quoted part of this sentence and added a correction to it in a footnote to his second paper on the neuro-psychoses of defence (1896b), below, p. 166, footnote 1. The case of 'Katharina' in *Studies on Hysteria* was described by Freud as an example of 'virginal anxiety'. See *Standard Ed.*, **2**, 127, 134 and 260.]

[2] [Freud had mentioned his belief in the harmfulness of coitus interruptus in a letter to Fliess as early as February 4, 1888 (Freud, 1950a, Letter 3).]

intentionally *abstinent women*, not seldom in a typical combination with obsessional ideas; and

(*f*) As anxiety in the *climacteric* during the last major increase of sexual need.

Cases (*c*) (*d*) and (*e*) comprise the conditions under which anxiety neurosis in the female sex arises most frequently and most readily, independently of hereditary disposition. It is in reference to these cases of anxiety neurosis—these curable acquired cases—that I shall try to show that the sexual noxae discovered in them are really the aetiological factor of the neurosis.

Before doing so, however, I will discuss the sexual determinants of anxiety neurosis in *men*. I propose to distinguish the following groups, all of which have their analogies in women:

(*a*) Anxiety of intentionally *abstinent* men, which is frequently combined with symptoms of *defence* (obsessional ideas, hysteria). The motives which are responsible for intentional abstinence imply that a number of people with a hereditary disposition, eccentrics, etc., enter into this category.

(*b*) Anxiety in men in a state of *unconsummated excitation*[1] (e.g. during the period of engagement before marriage), or in those who (from fear of the consequences of sexual intercourse) content themselves with touching or looking at women. This group of determinants—which, incidentally, can be applied unaltered to the other sex (during engagements or relations in which sexual intercourse is avoided)—provides the purest cases of the neurosis.

(*c*) Anxiety in men who practise coitus interruptus. As has been said, coitus interruptus is injurious to the *woman* if it is practised without regard to her satisfaction; but it is injurious to the *man* if, in order to obtain satisfaction for her, he directs coitus voluntarily and postpones emission. In this way it becomes intelligible that when a married couple practise coitus interruptus, it is, as a rule, only *one* partner who falls ill. Moreover, in men coitus interruptus only rarely produces a pure anxiety neurosis; it usually produces a mixture of anxiety neurosis and neurasthenia.

(*d*) Anxiety in *senescent* men. There are men who have a

---

[1] ['*Frustrane Erregung*.' See footnote 2, p. 81 above.]

climacteric like women, and who produce an anxiety neurosis at the time of their decreasing potency and increasing libido.[1]

Finally, I must add two other cases which apply to both sexes:

(a)[2] People who, as a result of practising masturbation, have become neurasthenics,[3] fall victims to anxiety neurosis as soon as they give up their form of sexual satisfaction. Such people have made themselves particularly incapable of tolerating abstinence.

I may note here, as being important for an understanding of anxiety neurosis, that any pronounced development of that affection only occurs among men who have remained potent and women who are not anaesthetic. Among neurotics whose potency has already been severely damaged by masturbation, the anxiety neurosis resulting from abstinence is very slight and is mostly restricted to hypochondria and mild chronic vertigo. The majority of women, indeed, are to be regarded as 'potent'; a really impotent—i.e. a really anaesthetic—woman is in a similar way little susceptible to anxiety neurosis, and she tolerates the noxae I have described remarkably well.

How far, in addition to this, we are justified in postulating any constant relation between particular aetiological factors and particular symptoms in the complex of anxiety neurosis, I should not like to discuss as yet in this paper.

(β) The last of the aetiological conditions I have to bring forward appears at first sight not to be of a sexual nature at all. Anxiety neurosis also arises—and in both sexes—as a result of the factor of overwork or exhausting exertion—as, for instance, after night-watching, sick-nursing, or even after severe illness.

The main objection to my postulate of a sexual aetiology for

[1] [This seems to be Freud's first published use of the term 'libido'. Its occurrence here contradicts his apparent statement that it was used first by Moll in 1898 (cf. Freud's encyclopaedia article on 'Libido' (1923a), Standard Ed., 18, 255); and, indeed, at the beginning of Chapter VI of Civilization and its Discontents (1930a), ibid., 21, 117, he mentions having introduced the term himself, presumably in the present passage. He had used it a few months earlier than this, on August 18, 1894 (Freud, 1950a, Draft F) or perhaps earlier still (Draft E).]
[2] [In the editions previous to 1925 this and the next class of cases were marked 'ε' and 'ζ' instead of 'α' and 'β'.]
[3] [See below, p. 109, footnote 1.]

anxiety neurosis will probably be to the following effect. Abnormal conditions in sexual life of the kind I have described are found so extremely frequently that they are bound to be forthcoming wherever one looks for them. Their presence in the cases of anxiety neurosis which I have enumerated does not, therefore, prove that we have unearthed in them the aetiology of the neurosis. Moreover, the number of people who practise coitus interruptus and the like is incomparably larger than the number who are afflicted with anxiety neurosis, and the great majority of the former tolerate this noxa very well.

To this I must reply in the first place that, considering the admittedly enormous frequency of the neuroses and especially of anxiety neurosis, it would certainly not be right to expect to find an aetiological factor for them that is of *rare* occurrence; in the second place, that a postulate of pathology is in fact satisfied, if in an aetiological investigation it can be shown that the *presence* of an aetiological factor is more frequent than its effects, since, in order for these latter to occur, other conditions may have to exist in addition (such as disposition, summation of specific aetiological elements, or reinforcement by other, stock noxae);[1] and further, that a detailed dissection of suitable cases of anxiety neurosis proves beyond question the importance of the sexual factor. I will confine myself here, however, to the single aetiological factor of coitus interruptus and to bringing out certain observations which confirm it.

(1) So long as an anxiety neurosis in young married women is not yet established, but only appears in bouts and disappears again spontaneously, it is possible to demonstrate that each such bout of the neurosis is traceable to a coitus which was deficient in satisfaction. Two days after this experience—or, in the case of people with little resistance, the day after—the attack of anxiety or vertigo regularly appears, bringing in its train other symptoms of the neurosis. All this vanishes once more, provided that marital intercourse is comparatively rare. A chance absence of the husband from home, or a holiday in the mountains which necessitates a separation of the couple, has a good effect. The gynaecological treatment which is usually resorted to in the first instance is beneficial because, while it lasts, marital

[1] [This argument is more clearly stated in a later paper, 1896c, p. 209 below.]

intercourse is stopped. Curiously enough the success of local treatment is only transitory: the neurosis sets in again in the mountains, as soon as the husband begins his holiday too; and so on. If, as a physician who understands this aetiology, one arranges, in a case in which the neurosis has not yet been established, for coitus interruptus to be replaced by normal intercourse, one obtains a *therapeutic* proof of the assertion I have made. The anxiety is removed, and—unless there is fresh cause for it of the same sort—it does not return.

(2) In the anamneses of many cases of anxiety neurosis we find, both in men and women, a striking oscillation in the intensity of its manifestations, and, indeed, in the coming and going of the whole condition. One year, they will tell you, was almost entirely good, but the next one was dreadful; on one occasion the improvement seemed to be due to a particular treatment, which, however, turned out to be quite useless at the next attack; and so on. If we enquire into the number and sequence of the children and compare this record of the marriage with the peculiar history of the neurosis, we arrive at the simple solution that the periods of improvement or good health coincided with the wife's pregnancies, during which, of course, the need for preventive intercourse was no longer present. The husband benefited by the treatment after which he found his wife pregnant—whether he received it from Pastor Kneipp[1] or at a hydropathic establishment.

(3) The anamnesis of patients often discloses that the symptoms of anxiety neurosis have at some definite time succeeded the symptoms of some other neurosis—neurasthenia, perhaps— and have taken their place. In these instances it can quite regularly be shown that, shortly before this change of the picture, a corresponding change has occurred in the form of the sexual noxa.

Observations of this sort, which can be multiplied at will, positively thrust a sexual aetiology on the doctor for a certain category of cases. And other cases, which would otherwise remain unintelligible, can at least be understood and classified without inconsistency by employing that aetiology as a key. I

---

[1] [The episode to which this refers is described in detail in a later paper 'Sexuality in the Aetiology of the Neuroses' (1898*a*), p. 272 f. below.]

have in mind those very numerous cases in which, it is true, everything is present that has been found in the previous category—on the one hand the manifestations of anxiety neurosis, and on the other the specific factor of coitus interruptus—but in which something else as well intrudes itself: namely, a long interval between the presumed aetiology and its effects, and also perhaps aetiological factors that are not of a sexual nature. Take, for instance, a man who, on receiving news of his father's death, had a heart attack and from that moment fell a victim to an anxiety neurosis. The case is not comprehensible, for, till then, the man was not neurotic. The death of his father, who was well advanced in years, did not take place under in any way special circumstances, and it will be admitted that the normal and expected decease of an aged father is not one of those experiences which usually cause a healthy adult to fall ill. Perhaps the aetiological analysis will become clearer if I add that this man had been practising coitus interruptus for eleven years, with due consideration for his wife's satisfaction. The clinical symptoms are, at least, exactly the same as those which appear in other people after only a short sexual noxa of the same kind, and without the interpolation of any other trauma.[1] A similar assessment must be made of the case of a woman whose anxiety neurosis broke out after the loss of her child, or of the student whose preparatory studies for his final examination were interfered with by an anxiety neurosis. I think that in these instances, too, the effect is not explained by the ostensible aetiology. One is not necessarily 'overworked' by study,[2] and a healthy mother as a rule reacts only with normal grief to the loss of a child. Above all, however, I should have expected the student, as a result of his overwork, to acquire cephalasthenia,[3] and the mother, as a result of her bereavement, hysteria. That both should have been overtaken by anxiety neurosis leads me to attach importance to the fact that the mother had been

[1] [This case and that of the student below are referred to again in the second paper on anxiety neurosis (1895f), p. 127 f. below. Freud had described the former shortly in a letter to Fliess of October 6, 1893 (Freud, 1950a, Letter 14).]

[2] [Cf. some discussion of 'overwork' in the later paper on 'Sexuality in the Aetiology of the Neuroses' (1898a), p. 272 below.]

[3] [In referring to this same case below (p. 128), Freud uses the term 'cerebral neurasthenia'.]

living for eight years in conditions of marital coitus interruptus, and that the student had for three years had an ardent love-affair with a 'respectable' girl whom he had to avoid making pregnant.

These considerations lead us to the conclusion that the specific sexual noxa of coitus interruptus, even when it is not able on its own account to provoke an anxiety neurosis in the subject, does at least *dispose* him to acquire it. The anxiety neurosis breaks out as soon as there is added to the latent effect of the specific factor the effect of another, stock noxa. The latter can act in the sense of the specific factor quantitatively but cannot replace it qualitatively. The specific factor always remains decisive for the *form* taken by the neurosis. I hope to be able to prove this assertion concerning the aetiology of the neuroses more comprehensively too.

In addition, these latter remarks contain an assumption which is not in itself improbable, to the effect that a sexual noxa like coitus interruptus comes into force through summation. A shorter or longer time is needed—depending on the individual's disposition and any other inherited weaknesses of his nervous system—before the effect of this summation becomes visible. Those individuals who apparently tolerate coitus interruptus without harm, in fact become disposed by it to the disorders of anxiety neurosis, and these may break out at some time or other, either spontaneously or after a stock trauma which would not ordinarily suffice for this; just as, by the path of summation, a chronic alcoholic will in the end develop a cirrhosis or some other illness, or will, under the influence of a fever, fall a victim to delirium.[1]

III

First Steps towards a Theory of Anxiety Neurosis

The following theoretical discussion can only claim to have the value of a first, groping attempt; criticism of it ought not to affect an acceptance of the *facts* which have been brought

[1] [Cf. below, p. 130. The 'summation' of traumas in cases of hysteria had been discussed by Freud in *Studies on Hysteria* (1895*d*), *Standard Ed.*, **2**, 173–4. The importance of summation in the aetiology of migraine was strongly emphasized by him in an unpublished paper of about this date. See Freud, 1950*a* Draft I. Cf. p. 133 below.]

forward above. Moreover, an assessment of this 'theory of anxiety neurosis' is made the more difficult from being only a fragment of a more comprehensive account of the neuroses.

What we have so far said about anxiety neurosis already provides a few starting points for gaining an insight into the mechanism of this neurosis. In the first place there was our suspicion that we had to do with an accumulation of excitation [p. 92]; and then there was the extremely important fact that the anxiety which underlies the clinical symptoms of the neurosis can be traced to *no psychical origin*. Such an origin would exist, for instance, if it was found that the anxiety neurosis was based on a single or repeated justifiable fright, and that that fright had since provided the source for the subject's readiness for anxiety. But this is not so. Hysteria or a traumatic neurosis can be acquired from a single fright, but never anxiety neurosis. Since coitus interruptus takes such a prominent place among the causes of anxiety neurosis, I thought at first that the source of the continuous anxiety might lie in the fear, recurring every time the sexual act was performed, that the technique might go wrong and conception consequently take place. But I have found that this state of feeling, either in the man or the woman, during coitus interruptus has no influence on the generation of anxiety neurosis, that women who are basically indifferent about the consequence of a possible conception are just as liable to the neurosis as those who shudder at the possibility, and that everything depends simply on which partner has forfeited satisfaction in this sexual technique.

A further point of departure is furnished by the observation, not so far mentioned, that in whole sets of cases anxiety neurosis is accompanied by a most noticeable decrease of sexual libido or *psychical desire*,[1] so that on being told that their complaint results from 'insufficient satisfaction', patients regularly reply that that is impossible, for precisely now all sexual need has become extinguished in them. From all these indications—that we have to do with an accumulation of excitation; that the anxiety which probably corresponds to this accumulated excitation is of somatic origin, so that what is being accumulated is a *somatic* excitation; and, further, that this somatic excitation is of a sexual nature and that a decrease of *psychical* participation

[1] [See Editor's Note, p. 88 above.]

in the sexual processes goes along with it—all these indications, I say, incline us to expect that *the mechanism of anxiety
neurosis is to be looked for in a deflection of somatic sexual excitation
from the psychical sphere, and in a consequent abnormal employment of
that excitation.*

This concept of the mechanism of anxiety neurosis can be
made clearer if one accepts the following view of the sexual process, which applies, in the first instance, to men. In the sexually
mature male organism somatic sexual excitation is produced—
probably continuously—and periodically becomes a stimulus to
the psyche. In order to make our ideas on this point firmer, I
will add by way of interpolation that this somatic excitation is
manifested as a pressure on the walls of the seminal vesicles,
which are lined with nerve endings; thus this visceral excitation
will develop continuously, but it will have to reach a certain
height before it is able to overcome the resistance of the intervening path of conduction to the cerebral cortex and express
itself as a psychical stimulus.[1] When this has happened, however, the group of sexual ideas which is present in the psyche
becomes supplied with energy[2] and there comes into being the
psychical state of libidinal tension which brings with it an urge
to remove that tension. A psychical unloading of this kind is
only possible by means of what I shall call *specific* or *adequate*
action.[3] This adequate action consists, for the male sexual instinct, in a complicated spinal reflex act which brings about the
unloading of the nerve-endings, and in all the psychical preparations which have to be made in order to set off that reflex.
Anything other than the adequate action would be fruitless,
for once the somatic sexual excitation has reached threshold
value it is turned continuously into psychical excitation, and
something must positively take place which will free the nerve-
endings from the load of pressure on them—which will, accordingly, remove the whole of the existing somatic excitation and

[1] [This theory of the process of sexual excitation was stated again by
Freud in Section 2 of the third of his *Three Essays* (1905*d*), *Standard Ed.*,
7, 213; but he there also stated certain objections to it.]

[2] [See footnote 2, p. 48 above.]

[3] [This whole account will be found repeated in similar terms in
Draft E, 'How Anxiety Originates', in the Fliess correspondence
(Freud, 1950*a*). It is further illustrated by a diagram in Draft G (ibid.).
Cf. Editor's Note, p. 88 above.]

allow the subcortical path of conduction to re-establish its resistance.

I shall refrain from describing more complicated instances of the sexual process in a similar way. I will only state that in essentials this formula is applicable to women as well, in spite of the confusion introduced into the problem by all the artificial retarding and stunting of the female sexual instinct. In women too we must postulate a somatic sexual excitation and a state in which this excitation becomes a psychical stimulus—libido— and provokes the urge to the specific action to which voluptuous feeling is attached. Where women are concerned, however, we are not in a position to say what the process analogous to the relaxation of tension of the seminal vesicles may be.

We can include within the framework of this description of the sexual process not only the aetiology of anxiety neurosis but that of genuine neurasthenia. Neurasthenia develops whenever the adequate unloading (the adequate action) is replaced by a less adequate one—thus, when normal coition, carried out in the most favourable conditions, is replaced by masturbation or spontaneous emission.[1] Anxiety neurosis, on the other hand, is the product of all those factors which prevent the somatic sexual excitation from being worked over psychically.[2] The manifestations of anxiety neurosis appear when the somatic excitation which has been deflected from the psyche is expended subcortically in totally inadequate reactions.

I will now attempt to discover whether the aetiological conditions for anxiety neurosis which I set out above [p. 99 ff.] exhibit the common character that I have just attributed to them. The first aetiological factor I postulated for men was intentional abstinence [p. 101]. Abstinence consists in the withholding of the specific action which ordinarily follows upon libido. Such withholding may have two consequences. In the first place, the somatic excitation accumulates; it is then deflected into other paths, which hold out greater promise of

[1] [The role of masturbation in the aetiology of neurasthenia is shortly mentioned in the paper on 'Heredity and the Aetiology of the Neuroses' (1896a), p. 150 below; but the subject is somewhat more fully discussed in a later work, 'Sexuality in the Aetiology of the Neuroses' (1898a), p. 275 below.]

[2] [Freud was still able to repeat these words with approval in Chapter VIII of Inhibitions, Symptoms and Anxiety (1926d), Standard Ed., 20, 141.]

110   THE ANXIETY NEUROSIS (I)

discharge than does the path through the psyche. Thus the
libido will in the end sink, and the excitation will manifest
itself subcortically as anxiety. In the second place, if the libido
is *not* diminished, or if the somatic excitation is expended, by
a short cut, in emissions, or if, in consequence of being forced
back, the excitation really ceases, then all kinds of things other
than an anxiety neurosis will ensue. Abstinence, then, leads to
anxiety neurosis in the manner described above. But it is also
the operative agent in my second aetiological group, that of
unconsummated excitation [p. 101]. My third group, that of
coitus reservatus with consideration for the woman [ibid.],
operates by disturbing the man's psychical preparedness for the
sexual process, in that it introduces alongside of the task of
mastering the sexual affect another psychical task, one of a
deflecting sort. In consequence of this psychical deflection, once
more, libido gradually disappears, and the further course of
things is then the same as in the case of abstinence. Anxiety in
senescence (the male climacteric) [pp. 101–2] requires another
explanation. Here there is no diminution of libido; but, as in
the female climacteric, so great an increase occurs in the production of somatic excitation that the psyche proves relatively
insufficient to master it.

The aetiological conditions applying to women can be
brought into the framework of my scheme with no greater
difficulties than in the case of men. Virginal anxiety [p. 99]
is a particularly clear example. For here the groups of ideas to
which the somatic sexual excitation should become attached are
not yet enough developed. In the newly-married woman who is
anaesthetic [p. 100], anxiety only appears if the first cohabitations arouse a sufficient amount of somatic excitation. When the
local indications of such excitement (spontaneous sensations of
stimulation, desire to micturate and so on) are lacking, anxiety
is also absent. The case of ejaculatio praecox and of coitus
interruptus [ibid.] can be explained on the same lines as in
men, namely that the libidinal desire for the psychically un-
satisfying act gradually disappears, while the excitation which
has been aroused during the act is expended subcortically. The
alienation between the somatic and the psychical sphere[1] is

―――――――
[1] [The phrase is found towards the end of Draft E and in the discussion of Case 1 in Draft F of the Fliess papers (1950*a*).]

established more readily and is more difficult to remove in women than in men. The cases of widowhood and of voluntary abstinence, and also that of the climacteric [p. 100 f.], are dealt with in the same way in both sexes; but where abstinence is concerned there is in the case of women no doubt the further matter of intentional repression of the sexual circle of ideas, to which an abstinent woman, in her struggle against temptation, must often make up her mind. The horror which, at the time of the menopause, an ageing woman feels at her unduly increased libido may act in a similar sense.

The two last aetiological conditions on our list seem to fall into place without difficulty. The tendency to anxiety in masturbators who have become neurasthenic [p. 102] is explained by the fact that it is very easy for them to pass into a state of 'abstinence' after they have been accustomed for so long to discharging even the smallest quantity of somatic excitation, faulty though that discharge is. Finally, the last case,—the generation of anxiety neurosis through severe illness, overwork, exhausting sick-nursing, etc. [ibid.],—finds an easy interpretation when brought into relation with the effects of coitus interruptus. Here the psyche, on account of its deflection, would seem to be no longer capable of mastering the somatic excitation, a task on which, as we know, it is continuously engaged. We are aware to what a low level libido can sink under these conditions; and we have here a good example of a neurosis which, although it exhibits *no sexual aetiology, nevertheless exhibits a sexual mechanism.*

The view here developed depicts the symptoms of anxiety neurosis as being in a sense *surrogates* of the omitted specific action following on sexual excitation. In further support of this view, I may point out that in normal copulation too the excitation expends itself, among other things, in accelerated breathing, palpitation, sweating, congestion, and so on. In the corresponding anxiety attacks of our neurosis we have before us the dyspnoea, palpitations, etc. of copulation in an isolated and exaggerated form.[1]

[1] [This theory, already put forward in Draft E of the Fliess papers (Freud, 1950a), was brought up again by Freud in Chapter II of the 'Dora' case history (1905e), *Standard Ed.*, **7**, 80. Later on, in Chapter VIII of *Inhibitions, Symptoms and Anxiety* (1926d), ibid., **20**, 132–3, he related these same symptoms of anxiety to the accompaniments of birth.]

A further question may be asked. Why, under such conditions of psychical insufficiency in mastering sexual excitation, does the nervous system find itself in the peculiar affective state of *anxiety?* An answer may be suggested as follows. The psyche finds itself in the *affect* of anxiety if it feels unable to deal by appropriate reaction with a task (a danger) *approaching from outside*; it finds itself in the *neurosis* of anxiety if it notices that it is unable to even out the (sexual) excitation originating *from within*—that is to say, *it behaves as though it were projecting that excitation outwards*. The affect and its corresponding neurosis are firmly related to each other. The first is a reaction to an exogenous excitation, the second a reaction to the analogous endogenous one. The affect is a state which passes rapidly, the neurosis is a chronic one; because, while exogenous excitation operates with a single impact, the endogenous excitation operates as a constant force.[1] *In the neurosis, the nervous system is reacting against a source of excitation which is internal, whereas in the corresponding affect it is reacting against an analogous source of excitation which is external.*

IV

RELATION TO OTHER NEUROSES

There are still a few words to be said about the relations of anxiety neurosis to the other neuroses as regards their onset and their internal connections.

The purest cases of anxiety neurosis are usually the most marked. They are found in sexually potent youthful individuals, with an undivided aetiology, and an illness that is not of too long standing.

More often, however, symptoms of anxiety occur at the same time as, and in combination with, symptoms of neurasthenia, hysteria, obsessions or melancholia. If we were to allow ourselves to be restrained by a clinical intermixture like this from acknowledging anxiety neurosis as an independent entity, we

---

[1] [Freud stated this again twenty years later in almost identical words, except that instead of 'exogenous excitation' and 'endogenous excitation' he spoke of 'stimulus' and 'instinct'. See the metapsychological paper on 'Instincts and their Vicissitudes' (1915c), *Standard Ed.*, **14**, 118.]

ought, logically, also to abandon once more the separation which has been so laboriously achieved between hysteria and neurasthenia.

For the purposes of analysing 'mixed neuroses' I can state this important truth: *Wherever a mixed neurosis is present, it will be possible to discover an intermixture of several specific aetiologies.*

A multiplicity of aetiological factors such as this, which determine a mixed neurosis, may occur purely fortuitously. For instance, a fresh noxa may add its effects to those of an already existing one. Thus, a woman who has always been hysterical may begin at a certain point in her marriage to experience coitus reservatus; she will then acquire an anxiety neurosis in addition to her hysteria. Or again, a man who has hitherto masturbated and has become neurasthenic, may get engaged and become sexually excited by his fiancée; his neurasthenia will now be joined by a new anxiety neurosis.

In other cases the multiplicity of aetiological factors is by no means fortuitous: one of the factors has brought the other into operation. For example, a woman with whom her husband practises coitus reservatus without regard to her satisfaction may find herself compelled to masturbate in order to put an end to the distressing excitation that follows such an act; as a result, she will produce, not an anxiety neurosis pure and simple, but an anxiety neurosis accompanied by symptoms of neurasthenia. Another woman suffering from the same noxa may have to fight against lascivious images against which she tries to defend herself; and in this way she will, through the coitus interruptus, acquire obsessions as well as an anxiety neurosis. Finally, as a result of coitus interruptus, a third woman may lose her affection for her husband and feel an attraction for another man, which she carefully keeps secret; in consequence, she will exhibit a mixture of anxiety neurosis and hysteria.

In a third category of mixed neuroses the interconnection between the symptoms is still more intimate, in that the same aetiological determinant regularly and simultaneously provokes both neuroses. Thus, for instance, the sudden sexual enlightenment, which we have found present in virginal anxiety, always gives rise to hysteria as well [as anxiety neurosis]; by far the majority of cases of intentional abstinence become linked from the beginning with true obsessional ideas; coitus interruptus in men never seems to me to be able to provoke a pure anxiety neurosis, but always a mixture of it with neurasthenia.

From these considerations it appears that we must further distinguish the aetiological conditions for the *onset* of the neuroses from their specific aetiological factors. The former— for example, coitus interruptus, masturbation or abstinence— are still ambiguous, and each of them can produce different neuroses. Only the aetiological factors which can be picked out in them, such as *inadequate disburdening, psychical insufficiency or defence accompanied by substitution*, have an unambiguous and specific relation to the aetiology of the individual major neuroses.[1]

As regards its intimate nature, anxiety neurosis presents the most interesting agreements with, and differences from, the other major neuroses, in particular neurasthenia and hysteria. It shares with neurasthenia one main characteristic—namely that the source of excitation, the precipitating cause of the disturbance, lies in the somatic field instead of the psychical one, as is the case in hysteria and obsessional neurosis. In other respects we rather find a kind of antithesis between the symptoms of anxiety neurosis and of neurasthenia, which might be brought out by such labels as 'accumulation of excitation' and 'impoverishment of excitation'. This antithesis does not prevent the two neuroses from being intermixed with each other; but it nevertheless shows itself in the fact that the most extreme forms of each are in both cases also the purest.

The symptomatology of hysteria and anxiety neurosis show many points in common, which have not yet been sufficiently considered. The appearance of symptoms either in a chronic form or in attacks, the paraesthesias, grouped like aurae, the hyperaesthesias and pressure-points which are found in certain surrogates of an anxiety attack (in dyspnoea and heart-attacks), the intensification, through conversion, of pains which perhaps have an organic justification—these and other features which the two illnesses have in common even allow of a suspicion that not a little of what is attributed to hysteria might with more

[1] [The question of aetiology is discussed in great detail in the following paper (1895*f*), p. 135 ff. below.]

justice be put to the account of anxiety neurosis. If one goes into the mechanism of the two neuroses, so far as it has been possible to discover it hitherto, aspects come to light which suggest that anxiety neurosis is actually the somatic counterpart to hysteria. In the latter just as in the former there is an accumulation of excitation (which is perhaps the basis for the similarity between their symptoms we have mentioned). In the latter just as in the former we find a *psychical insufficiency, as a consequence of which abnormal somatic processes arise.* In the latter just as in the former, too, instead of a psychical working-over of the excitation, a deflection of it occurs into the somatic field; the difference is merely that in anxiety neurosis the excitation, in whose displacement the neurosis expresses itself, is purely somatic (somatic sexual excitation), whereas in hysteria it is psychical (provoked by conflict). Thus it is not to be wondered at that hysteria and anxiety neurosis regularly combine with each other, as is seen in 'virginal anxiety' or in 'sexual hysteria', and that hysteria simply borrows a number of its symptoms from anxiety neurosis, and so on. These intimate relations which anxiety neurosis has with hysteria provide a fresh argument, moreover, for insisting on the detachment of anxiety neurosis from neurasthenia; for if this detachment is not granted, we shall also be unable any longer to maintain the distinction which has been acquired with so much labour and which is so indispensable for the theory of the neuroses, between neurasthenia and hysteria.

VIENNA, *December* 1894.

APPENDIX

THE TERM '*ANGST*' AND ITS ENGLISH TRANSLATION

There are at least three passages in which Freud discusses the various shades of meaning expressed by the German word '*Angst*' and the cognate '*Furcht*' and '*Schreck*'.[1] Though he stresses the anticipatory element and absence of an object in '*Angst*', the distinctions he draws are not entirely convincing, and his actual usage is far from invariably obeying them. And this is scarcely surprising, since '*Angst*' is a word in common use in ordinary German speech and by no means exclusively a technical psychiatric term. It may on occasion be translated by any one of half a dozen similarly common English words—'fear', 'fright', 'alarm' and so on—and it is therefore quite unpractical to fix on some single English term as its sole translation. Nevertheless '*Angst*' does often appear as a psychiatric term (particularly in such combinations as '*Angstneurose*' or '*Angstanfall*') and for such occasions an English technical equivalent seems to be called for. The word universally, and perhaps unfortunately, adopted for the purpose has been 'anxiety'—unfortunately, since 'anxiety' too has a current everyday meaning, and one which has only a rather remote connection with any of the uses of the German '*Angst*'. There is, however, a well-established psychiatric, or at least medical, use of the English 'anxiety', going back (so the *Oxford Dictionary* tells us) to the middle of the seventeenth century. Indeed, the psychiatric use of the two words brings to light their parallel origins. '*Angst*' is akin to '*eng*', the German word for 'narrow', 'restricted'; 'anxiety' is derived from the Latin '*angere*', 'to throttle' or 'squeeze'; in both cases the reference is to the choking feelings which characterize severe forms of the psychological state in question. A still more acute condition is described in English by the word 'anguish', which has

[1] See *Beyond the Pleasure Principle* (1920g), *Standard Ed.*, **18**, 12, *Inhibitions, Symptoms and Anxiety* (1926d), ibid. **20**, 164–5 and a paragraph near the beginning of Lecture XXV of the *Introductory Lectures* (1916–17).

the same derivation; and it is to be remarked that Freud in his French papers uses the kindred word '*angoisse*' (as well as the synonymous '*anxiété*') to render the German '*Angst*' (See above, p. 75.)

The English translator is thus driven to compromise: he must use 'anxiety' in technical or semi-technical connections, and must elsewhere choose whatever everyday English word seems most appropriate. Incidentally, the solution adopted in many of the earlier Freud translations of rendering '*Angst*' by 'morbid anxiety' seems especially ill-judged. One of the main theoretical problems discussed by Freud is precisely whether, and if so why, '*Angst*' is sometimes pathological and sometimes normal. (See, for instance, Addendum B to *Inhibitions, Symptoms and Anxiety*, *Standard Ed.*, **20**, 164 ff.)

A REPLY TO CRITICISMS OF MY PAPER ON ANXIETY NEUROSIS

(1895)

EDITOR'S NOTE

ZUR KRITIK DER 'ANGSTNEUROSE'

(a) German Editions:
1895 *Wien. klin. Rdsch.*, **9** (27), 417–19, (28), 435–7, and (29), 451–2. (July 7, 14 and 21.)
1906 *S.K.S.N.*, **1**, 94–111. (1911, 2nd ed.; 1920, 3rd ed.; 1922, 4th ed.)
1925 *G.S.*, **1**, 343–62.
1952 *G.W.*, **1**, 357–76.

(b) English Translation:
'A Reply to Criticisms on the Anxiety-Neurosis'
1924 *C.P.*, **1**, 107–27. (Tr. J. Rickman.)

Included (No. XXXIII) in Freud's own collection of abstracts of his early works (1897*b*). The present translation, with a changed title, is based on that of 1924.

Freud's first paper on the anxiety neurosis having appeared in January, 1895, a criticism of it by Löwenfeld was published in the March issue of the *Neurologisches Zentralblatt*. The present paper is Freud's rejoinder. Leopold Löwenfeld (1847–1923) was a well-known psychiatrist practising in Munich. He was an acquaintance of Freud's and continued to be on friendly terms with him. He included chapters by Freud in two of his own books, he attended the first two Psycho-Analytical Congresses, in 1908 and 1910, and even read a paper (on hypnotism) at the latter. In spite of this, however, he never fully accepted Freud's ideas. A reference to the fact that the present controversy did not affect their good relations occurs in Lecture XVI of the *Introductory Lectures* (1916–17).

The main importance of the present paper is the elaborate discussion in it of what Freud here calls 'the aetiological equation'—the interrelations between the different *sorts* of causes concerned in bringing about a neurosis (or, indeed, any other illness). The question had already been sketched out in a communication to Fliess on February 8, 1893 (Freud, 1950a, Draft B),[1] and was dealt with again later in the French paper on 'Heredity and the Aetiology of the Neuroses' (1896a). The 'aetiological equation', all the terms of which must be satisfied before a neurosis can become manifest, is alluded to again ten years later in the paper on sexuality in the neuroses (1906a), *Standard Ed.*, **7**, 279 and re-appears in the Nuremberg Congress address (1910d), *Standard Ed.*, **11**, 149. But thereafter it gradually boils down into the interlocking between inheritance and experience—the two main sets of determinants of neurosis—and ends in the introduction of the concept of 'complemental series' in Lectures XXII and XXIII of the *Introductory Lectures* (1916–17). There is a passage in the *Three Essays* in which the transition is clearly shown. In some sentences added to that work in 1915, Freud twice referred to an 'aetiological series', 'in which the diminishing intensity of one factor is balanced by the increasing intensity of the other'. Then in 1920, *after* writing the *Introductory Lectures*, he changed the phrase in the *Three Essays* to 'complemental series'; at least he changed *one* of its occurrences, but he overlooked the second. So that the two versions of the term are preserved within a few lines of each other (*Standard Ed.*, **7**, 239–40), and the line of descent from the aetiological equation to the complemental series is revealed.

[1] The concept goes back still further; for, except in name, it appears in some of the very earliest of Freud's psychological writings that have survived, in one of his drafts ('III') for the 'Preliminary Communication' (1941b [1892]) and in the even earlier letter to Breuer of June 29, 1892 (1941a).

A REPLY TO CRITICISMS OF MY
PAPER ON ANXIETY NEUROSIS

In the second number of Mendel's *Neurologisches Zentralblatt* for 1895, I published a short paper in which I ventured an attempt to detach a number of nervous states from neurasthenia and to establish them as an independent entity under the name of 'anxiety neurosis'.[1] I was led to do so by the presence of a constant conjunction of certain clinical features with certain aetiological ones—a thing which, in general, should permit us to make a separation of this kind. I found—and in this Hecker[2] (1893) had anticipated me—that the neurotic symptoms in question could all be classed together as constituting expressions of anxiety; and, from my study of the aetiology of the neuroses, I was able to add that these portions of the complex of the 'anxiety neurosis' exhibit special aetiological preconditions which are almost the opposite of the aetiology of neurasthenia. My observations had shown me that in the aetiology of the neuroses (at all events of *acquired* cases and *acquirable* forms) sexual factors play a predominant part and one which has been given far too little weight; so that a statement such as that 'the aetiology of the neuroses lies in sexuality', with all its unavoidable incorrectness *per excessum et defectum* [in respect of exaggeration and omission], nevertheless comes nearer to the truth than do the other doctrines, which hold the field at the present time. A further assertion which my observations forced me to make was to the effect that the various sexual noxae are not to be found in the aetiology of every neurosis indifferently, but that unmistakable special relationships hold between particular noxae and particular neuroses. Thus I could assume that I had discovered the *specific* causes of the various neuroses. I then sought to formulate shortly

[1] 'On the Grounds for Detaching a Particular Syndrome from Neurasthenia under the Description "Anxiety Neurosis" ' (1895*b*) [p. 90 above].

[2] [Cf. p. 91 above. Freud had also mentioned Hecker's paper in *Studies on Hysteria* (1895*d*), *Standard Ed.*, **2**, 258.]

the special character of the sexual noxae which constitute the aetiology of anxiety neurosis, and, on the basis of my view of the sexual process (p. 108), I arrived at the proposition: anxiety neurosis is created by everything which keeps somatic sexual tension away from the psychical sphere, which interferes with its being worked over psychically. If we go back to the concrete circumstances in which this factor becomes operative, we are led to assert that [sexual] abstinence, whether voluntary or involuntary, sexual intercourse with incomplete satisfaction, coitus interruptus, deflection of psychical interest from sexuality, and similar things, are the specific aetiological factors of the states to which I have given the name of anxiety neurosis.

When I published the paper I have mentioned, I was under no illusion as to its power to carry conviction. In the first place, I was aware that the account I had given was only a brief and incomplete one and even in places hard to understand—just enough, perhaps, to arouse the reader's expectations. Then, too, I had scarcely brought forward any examples and given no figures. Nor had I touched on the technique of collecting anamneses or done anything to prevent misunderstandings. I had not given consideration to any but the most obvious objections; and, as regards the theory itself, I had laid stress only on its main proposition and not on its qualifications. Accordingly, each reader was in fact at liberty to form his own opinion as to the binding force of the whole hypothesis. I could, moreover, reckon upon another difficulty in the way of its acceptance. I know very well that in putting forward my 'sexual aetiology' of the neuroses, I have brought up nothing new, and that undercurrents in medical literature taking these facts into account have never been absent. I know, too, that official academic medicine has in fact also been aware of them. But it has acted as if it knew nothing about the matter. It has made no use of its knowledge and has drawn no inferences from it. Such behaviour must have a deep-seated cause, originating perhaps in a kind of reluctance to look squarely at sexual matters, or in a reaction against older attempts at an explanation, which are regarded as obsolete. At all events, one had to be prepared to meet with resistance in venturing upon an attempt to make something credible to other people which they could without any trouble have discovered for themselves.

In such circumstances it would perhaps be more expedient not to answer critical objections until I had myself expressed my views on this complicated subject in greater detail and had made them more intelligible. Nevertheless, I cannot resist the motives which prompt me to make an immediate answer to a criticism of my theory of anxiety neurosis which has appeared in recent days. I do so because its author, L. Löwenfeld of Munich, the author of *Pathologie und Therapie der Neurasthenie*, is a man whose judgement undoubtedly carries great weight with the medical public; because of a mistaken view which Löwenfeld's account imputes to me; and finally because I wish to combat at the very start the impression that my theory can be refuted quite so easily by the first objections that come to hand.

With an unerring eye Löwenfeld (1895) detects the essential feature of my paper—namely, my assertion that anxiety-symptoms have a specific and uniform aetiology of a sexual nature. If this cannot be established as a fact, then the main reason for detaching an independent anxiety neurosis from neurasthenia disappears as well. There remains, it is true, one difficulty to which I called attention [p. 114 f.]: the fact that anxiety-symptoms also have such very unmistakable connections with hysteria, so that a decision on Löwenfeld's lines would prejudice the separation between hysteria and neurasthenia. This difficulty, however, is met by a recourse to heredity as the common cause of all these neuroses (a view which I will go into later).

What arguments, then, does Löwenfeld use to support his objection to my theory?

(1) I emphasized as a point essential to an understanding of anxiety neurosis that the anxiety appearing in it does not admit of a psychical derivation—that is to say that the preparedness for anxiety, which constitutes the nucleus of the neurosis, cannot be acquired by a single or repeated affect of psychically justified fright. Fright, I maintained, might result in hysteria or a traumatic neurosis, but not in an anxiety neurosis. This denial, it is easy to see, is nothing else than the counterpart to my contention, on the positive side, that the anxiety appearing

in my neurosis corresponds to a somatic sexual tension which has been deflected from the psychical field—a tension which would otherwise have made itself felt as libido.

Against this, Löwenfeld insists on the fact that in a number of cases 'states of anxiety appear immediately or shortly after a psychical shock (fright alone, or accidents which were accompanied by fright), and in such situations there are sometimes circumstances which make the simultaneous operation of sexual noxae of the kind mentioned extremely improbable.' He gives, shortly, as a particularly pregnant example, one clinical observation (to serve instead of many). This example concerns a woman of thirty, with a hereditary taint, who had been married for four years and who had had a first, difficult, confinement a year before. A few weeks after this event her husband had an attack of illness which frightened her, and in her agitation she ran about the cold room in her chemise. From that time on she was ill. First she had states of anxiety and palpitations in the evening, then came attacks of convulsive trembling, and after that phobias, and so on. It was the picture of a fully-developed anxiety neurosis. 'Here,' concludes Löwenfeld, 'the anxiety states are obviously of psychical origin, brought about by the single fright.'

I do not doubt that my respected critic can produce many similar cases. I myself can supply a long list of analogous examples. Anyone who has not seen such cases—and they are extremely common—of an outbreak of anxiety neurosis after a psychical shock, ought not to regard himself as qualified to take part in discussions about anxiety neurosis. I will only remark in this connection that neither fright nor anxious expectation need always be found in the aetiology of such cases; any other emotion will do as well. If I hastily recall a few cases from my memory, I think of a man of forty-five who had his first attack of anxiety (with cardiac collapse) at the news of the death of his father, who was an old man; from that time on he developed a complete and typical anxiety neurosis with agoraphobia. Again, I think of a young man who was overtaken by the same neurosis on account of his agitation about the disagreements between his young wife and his mother and who had a fresh onset of agoraphobia after every domestic quarrel. Then, there was a student, something of an idler, who produced his first anxiety attacks during a period in which, under the spur of his father's displeasure, he was working hard for an examination. I recall, too, a woman, herself childless, who fell ill as a result of anxiety about the health of a small niece. And other similar instances. About the facts themselves, which Löwenfeld uses against me, there is not the slightest doubt.

But there *is* doubt about their interpretation. Are we to accept the *post hoc ergo propter hoc* conclusion straight away and spare ourselves any critical consideration of the raw material? There are examples enough in which the final, releasing cause has not, in the face of critical analysis, maintained its position as the *causa efficiens*. One has only to think, for instance, of the relationship between trauma and gout. The role of a trauma in provoking an attack of gout in the injured limb is probably no different from the role it plays in the aetiology of tabes and general paralysis of the insane; only in the case of gout it is clear to the meanest capacity that it is absurd to suppose that the trauma has 'caused' the gout instead of having merely provoked it. It is bound to make us thoughtful when we come across aetiological factors of this sort—'stock' factors, as I should like to call them[1]—in the aetiology of the most varied forms of illness. Emotion, fright, is also a stock factor of this kind. Fright can provoke chorea, apoplexy, paralysis agitans and many other things just as well as it can provoke anxiety neurosis. I must not go on to argue, of course, that, because of their ubiquity, the stock causes do not satisfy our requirements and that there must be specific causes as well; to do so would be to beg the question in favour of the proposition I want to prove. But I am justified in drawing the following conclusion: if the same specific cause can be shown to exist in the aetiology of all, or the great majority, of cases of anxiety neurosis, our view of the matter need not be shaken by the fact that the illness does not break out until one or other stock factor, such as emotion, has come into operation.

So it was with my cases of anxiety neurosis. Let us take the man who [p. 105], after receiving the news of his father's death, fell ill so inexplicably. (I add 'inexplicably' because the death was not unexpected and did not occur in unusual or shattering circumstances.) This man had carried out coitus interruptus for

[1] [See footnote 2 ,p. 99 above.]

eleven years with his wife, whom he tried for the most part to satisfy. Again, the young man who was not equal to the quarrels between his wife and his mother, had practised withdrawal with his young wife from the first, in order to spare himself the burden of children. Then we have the student who acquired an anxiety neurosis from overwork, instead of the cerebral neuras-thenia that was to be expected: he had maintained a relation-ship for three years with a girl whom it was not permissible for him to make pregnant. Again, there was the woman who, childless herself, was overtaken by an anxiety neurosis about a niece's illness: she was married to an impotent man and had never been sexually satisfied. And so on. Not all these cases are equally clear or equally good evidence for my thesis; but when I add them to the very considerable number of cases in which the aetiology shows nothing but the specific factor, they fit without contradiction into the theory I have put forward and they allow of an extension of our aetiological understanding beyond the boundaries hitherto in force.

If anyone wants to prove to me that in these remarks I have unduly neglected the significance of the stock aetiological factors, he must confront me with observations in which my specific factor is missing—that is, with cases in which anxiety neurosis has arisen after a psychical shock although the subject has (on the whole) led *a normal vita sexualis*. Let us see now whether Löwenfeld's case fulfils this condition. My respected opponent has evidently not been clear about this necessity in his own mind, otherwise he would not have left us so completely in the dark about his patient's *vita sexualis*. I will leave on one side the fact that this case of a lady of thirty is obviously com-plicated by a hysteria as to the psychical origin of which I have not the least doubt; and I naturally admit without raising any objection the presence of an anxiety neurosis alongside of this hysteria. But before I turn a case to account for or against the theory of the sexual aetiology of the neuroses, I must first have studied the patient's sexual behaviour more closely than Löwen-feld has done here. I should not be content to conclude that, because the time at which the lady received her psychical shock was shortly after a confinement, coitus interruptus could not have played a part during the previous year, and that therefore sexual noxae are ruled out. I know cases of women who were made pregnant every year, and who yet had anxiety neurosis, because—incredible as it may seem—all sexual relations were stopped after the first fertilizing coition, so that in spite of having many children they suffered from sexual privation through all these years. No doctor is ignorant of the fact that women conceive from men whose potency is very slight and who are not able to give them satisfaction. Finally (and this is a consideration which should be taken into account precisely by the upholders of a hereditary aetiology), there are plenty of women who are afflicted with congenital anxiety neurosis—that is to say, who inherit, or who develop without any demonstrable disturbance from outside, a *vita sexualis* which is the same as the one usually acquired through coitus interruptus and similar noxae. In a number of these women we are able to discover a hysterical illness in their youth, since which their *vita sexualis* has been disturbed and a deflection of sexual tension from the psychical sphere has been established. Women with this kind of sexuality are incapable of obtaining real satisfaction even from normal coitus, and they develop anxiety neurosis either spontaneously or after further operative factors have supervened. Which of all these elements were present in Löwenfeld's case? I do not know. But I repeat: this case is evidence against me only if the lady who responded to a single fright with an anxiety neurosis had before then enjoyed a normal *vita sexualis*.

It is impossible to pursue an aetiological investigation based on anamneses if we accept those anamneses as the patients present them, or are content with what they are willing to volunteer. If syphilidologists still depended on the statements of their patients for tracing back an initial infection of the genitals to sexual intercourse, they would be able to attribute an imposing number of chancres in allegedly virginal persons to catching a chill; and gynaecologists would have little difficulty in confirming the miracle of parthenogenesis among their unmarried lady clients. I hope that one day the idea will prevail that neuropathologists, too, in collecting the anamneses of major neuroses, may proceed upon aetiological prejudices of a similar kind.

(2) Löwenfeld says further that he has repeatedly seen

anxiety states appear and disappear where a change in the subject's sexual life had certainly not taken place but where other factors were in play.

I, too, have made exactly the same observation, without, however, being misled by it. I myself have caused anxiety attacks to disappear by means of psychical treatment, improvement of the patient's general health, and so on; but I have naturally not concluded from this that what had caused the anxiety attack was a lack of treatment. Not that I should like to foist a conclusion of this sort upon Löwenfeld. My joking remark is only intended to show that the state of affairs may easily be complicated enough to render Löwenfeld's objection quite invalid. I have not found it difficult to reconcile the fact brought forward here with my assertion that anxiety neurosis has a specific aetiology. It will readily be granted that there are aetiological factors which, in order to exercise their effect, must operate with a certain intensity (or quantity)[1] and over a certain period of time—which, that is to say, become *summated*.[2] The effects of alcohol are a standard example of causation like this through summation. It follows that there must be a period of time in which the specific aetiology is at work but in which its effect is not yet manifest. During this time the subject is not ill as yet, but he is predisposed to a particular illness—in our case, to anxiety neurosis—and now the addition of a stock noxa will be able to set the neurosis off, just as would a further intensification of the operation of the specific noxa. The situation may also be expressed as follows: it is not enough for the specific noxa to be present; it must also reach a definite amount; and, in the process of reaching that limit, a quantity of specific noxa can be replaced by a quota of stock noxa. If the latter is removed once more, we find ourselves below a certain threshold and the clinical symptoms depart once more. The whole therapy of the neuroses rests upon the fact that the total load upon the nervous system, to which it has succumbed, can be brought below this threshold by influencing the aetiological mixture in a great variety of ways. From these circumstances we can draw no

---

[1] [Cf. an Editor's footnote to the late paper on 'Female Sexuality' (1931b), *Standard Ed.*, **21**, 242–3, and a passage in Chapter VII (E) of *The Interpretation of Dreams* (1900a), ibid., **5**, 602; cf. also p. 67 above.]
   [Cf. footnote, p. 106 above.]

conclusion as to the existence or non-existence of a specific aetiology. These considerations are surely indisputable and assured. But anyone who does not think them sufficient may be influenced by the following argument. According to the views of Löwenfeld and very many others, the aetiology of anxiety states is to be found in heredity. Now heredity is certainly immune to alteration; thus if anxiety neurosis is curable by treatment, we should have to conclude according to Löwenfeld's argument that its aetiology *cannot* reside in heredity.

For the rest, I might have been spared having to defend myself against these two objections of Löwenfeld's, if my respected opponent had paid greater attention to my paper itself. In it, both these objections are anticipated and answered (p. 104 ff. I have only been able to repeat here what I said there; and I have even purposely analysed the same cases over again. Moreover the aetiological formulas on which I have just laid weight are contained in the text of my paper [p. 106]. I will repeat them once more. I maintain that *there exists a specific aetiological factor for anxiety neurosis which can be replaced in its operation by stock noxae in a* QUANTITATIVE *sense, but not in a* QUALITATIVE *one;* I furthermore maintain that *this specific factor determines above all the* FORM *of the neurosis; whether a neurotic illness occurs at all depends on the total load upon the nervous system (in proportion to its capacity to carry the load).* As a rule the neuroses are *overdetermined;*[1] that is to say, several factors operate together in their aetiology.

(3) I need not concern myself so much about refuting Löwenfeld's next comments, since on the one hand they damage my theory very little and on the other they raise difficulties whose existence I acknowledge. Löwenfeld writes: 'The Freudian theory is totally insufficient to explain the appearance or non-appearance of anxiety attacks in individual instances. If anxiety-states—i.e. the clinical symptoms of anxiety neurosis—occurred solely through a subcortical storing-up of somatic sexual excitation and an abnormal employment of it, then every person who is afflicted with anxiety-states ought, so long as no changes take place in his sexual life, to have an anxiety attack from time

[1] [Freud had made this point in Section IV of *Studies on Hysteria* (1895*d*), *Standard Ed.*, **2**, 263.]

to time, just as an epileptic has his attack of *grand* and *petit mal*. But this, as everyday experience shows, is by no means so. The anxiety attacks happen in the great majority of instances only on definite occasions; if the patient avoids these occasions or is able to paralyse their influence by taking some precaution, he remains exempt from anxiety attacks, whether he is consistently given over to coitus interruptus or to abstinence, or whether he enjoys a normal sexual life.'

There is a great deal to be said about this. In the first place, Löwenfeld forces upon my theory an inference which it is not bound to accept. To suppose that in the storing-up of somatic sexual excitation the same thing must be happening as in the accumulation of the stimulus which leads to an epileptic convulsion, is to make a far too detailed hypothesis, and I have given no occasion for it; nor is it the only one that presents itself. I need only assume that the nervous system has the power to master a certain amount of somatic sexual excitation even when the latter is deflected from its aim, and that disturbances only occur when that quantum of excitation receives a sudden increment, and Löwenfeld's claim would be disposed of. I have not ventured to extend my theory in that direction, chiefly because I did not expect to find any solid points of support along that path. I should merely like to indicate that we ought not to think of the *production* of sexual tension independently of its *distribution*; that in normal sexual life this production, when it is stimulated by a sexual object, takes on a substantially different form from what it does in a state of psychical quiescence;[1] and so on.

It must be admitted that the condition of affairs here is in all probability different from what prevails in the tendency to epileptic convulsions, and that it cannot yet be consistently derived from the theory of the accumulation of somatic sexual excitation.

Against Löwenfeld's further assertion—that anxiety-states only appear under certain conditions and fail to appear when

[1] [This is perhaps a first hint at the theory that psychical energy occurs in two forms, quiescent and mobile, which was to be expounded a few months after this in Section 1 of Part III of the 'Project' (1950a), though only published in *The Interpretation of Dreams* (1900a), *Standard Ed.*, 5, 599 ff. Cf. footnote, p. 65 above.]

those conditions are avoided, regardless of what the subject's *vita sexualis* may be—it must be pointed out that he clearly has in mind here only the anxiety of *phobias*, as, indeed, is shown by the examples attached to the passage I have quoted. He says nothing at all about the spontaneous anxiety attacks which take the form of vertigo, palpitation, dyspnoea, trembling, sweating, and so on. My theory, on the contrary, seems by no means unequal to explaining the emergence or non-emergence of these attacks of anxiety. For in a whole number of such cases of anxiety neurosis there does in fact appear to be a periodicity in the emergence of the states of anxiety, similar to what has been observed in epilepsy, except that in the latter the mechanism of the periodicity is more transparent. On closer examination we discover the presence, with great regularity, of an excitatory sexual process (that is, a process which is able to generate somatic sexual tension), and which, after the lapse of a definite and often constant interval of time, is followed by the anxiety attack. This [excitatory] role is played, in abstinent women, by menstrual excitation; it is played, too, by nocturnal pollutions, which also recur periodically. Above all, it is played by sexual intercourse itself (harmful from its being incomplete), which carries over its own periodicity to the effects it brings about, viz. to the anxiety attacks. If anxiety attacks occur which break through the usual periodicity, it is generally possible to trace them back to an incidental cause of rare and irregular occurrence —to a single sexual experience, something read or seen, and the like. The interval I have mentioned varies from a few hours to two days; it is the same as that which elapses in other people between the occurrence of the same causes and the onset of the well-known sexual migraine, which has well-established connections with the syndrome of anxiety neurosis.[1]

Besides this, there are plenty of cases in which a single anxiety-state is provoked by the extra addition of a stock factor, by an excitement of some kind or other. The same holds good, therefore, for the aetiology of the individual anxiety attack as for the causation of the whole neurosis. It is not very strange that the anxiety of the phobias should obey different conditions;

---

[1] [A paper on migraine, dealing with these connections, had been sent by Freud to Fliess, probably at about this time. See Freud, 1950a, Draft I. This was never published by Freud. Cf. footnote, p. 106 above.]

they have a more complicated structure than purely somatic anxiety attacks. In phobias the anxiety is linked to a definite ideational or perceptual content, and the arousal of this psychical content is the chief condition for the emergence of the anxiety. When this happens, anxiety is 'generated', just as for instance sexual tension is generated by the arousal of libidinal ideas. The connection of this process, however, with the theory of anxiety neurosis has not yet been elucidated.

I see no reason why I should try to hide the gaps and weaknesses in my theory. The main thing about the problem of the phobias seems to me to be that *when the vita sexualis is normal*— when the specific condition, a disturbance of sexual life in the sense of a deflection of the somatic from the psychical, is not fulfilled—*phobias do not appear at all*. However much else may be obscure about the mechanism of phobias, my theory can only be refuted when I have been shown phobias where sexual life is normal or even where there is a disturbance of it of a non-specific sort.

(4) I now pass on to a remark by my esteemed critic which I cannot leave uncontradicted. In my paper on anxiety neurosis I had written (p. 99):

'In some cases of anxiety neurosis no aetiology at all is to be discovered. It is worth noting that in such cases there is seldom any difficulty in establishing evidence of a grave hereditary taint.

'But where there are grounds for regarding the neurosis as an *acquired* one, careful enquiry directed to that end reveals that a set of noxae and influences from *sexual life* . . . [are the operative aetiological factors].' Löwenfeld quotes this passage and adds the following gloss: 'From this it appears that Freud always regards a neurosis as "acquired" whenever incidental causes are to be found for it.'

If this meaning follows naturally from my text, then the latter gives a very distorted expression to my thoughts. Let me point out that in the preceding pages I have shown myself far stricter than Löwenfeld in my evaluation of incidental causes. If I were myself to elucidate the meaning of the passage I wrote I should add, after the subordinate clause 'But where there are grounds for regarding the neurosis as an *acquired* one . . .', the words '*because evidence (referred to in the previous sentence) of a hereditary taint is not forthcoming . . .*' What this means is that I hold the case to be an acquired one, since no heredity is to be discovered in it. In doing so I am behaving like everyone else, perhaps with the slight difference that others may declare the case to be determined by heredity even when there is no heredity, so that they overlook the whole category of acquired neuroses. But this difference runs in my favour. I admit, however, that I am myself to blame for this misunderstanding, on account of the way in which I expressed myself in the first sentence: 'no aetiology at all is to be discovered'. I shall certainly be taken to task from other directions as well and be told that I have created useless trouble for myself by searching for the specific causes of neuroses. Some will say that the true aetiology of anxiety neurosis, as of neuroses in general, is known: it is heredity. And two real causes cannot exist side by side. I have not, they will say, denied the aetiological role of heredity; but if so, all other aetiologies are merely incidental causes and equal to one another in value or want of value.

I do not share this view of the role of heredity; and since in my short paper on anxiety neurosis it is precisely to this theme that I have paid least attention, I will now try to make good some of what I have omitted in it and to remove the impression that in writing my paper I had not attended to all the relevant problems.

I think we can arrive at a picture of the probably very complicated aetiological situation which prevails in the pathology of the neuroses if we postulate the following concepts:

(*a*) *Precondition*, (*b*) *Specific Cause*, (*c*) *Concurrent Causes*, and, as a term which is not equivalent to the foregoing ones, (*d*) *Precipitating or Releasing Cause.*

In order to meet every possibility, let us assume that the aetiological factors we are concerned with are capable of a quantitative change—that is of increase or decrease.

If we accept the idea of an aetiological equation of several terms which must be satisfied if the effect is to take place,[1] then we may characterize as the *precipitating* or releasing cause the one which makes its appearance last in the equation, so that it

[1] [See Editor's Note, p. 121 f. above.]

immediately precedes the emergence of the effect. It is this chronological factor alone which constitutes the essential nature of a precipitating cause. Any of the other causes, too, can in a particular case play the role of precipitating cause; and [the factor playing] this role can change within the same aetiological combination.

The factors which may be described as *preconditions* are those in whose absence the effect would never come about, but which are incapable of producing the effect by themselves alone, no matter in what amount they may be present. For the specific cause is still lacking.

The *specific cause* is the one which is never missing in any case in which the effect takes place, and which moreover suffices, if present in the required quantity or intensity, to achieve the effect, provided only that the preconditions are also fulfilled.

As *concurrent causes* we may regard such factors as are not necessarily present every time, nor able, whatever their amount, to produce the effect by themselves alone, but which operate alongside of the preconditions and the specific cause in satisfying the aetiological equation.

The distinctive character of the concurrent, or auxiliary, causes seems clear; but how do we distinguish between a precondition and a specific cause, since both are indispensable and yet neither suffices alone to act as a cause?

The following considerations seem to allow us to arrive at a decision. Among the '*necessary causes*' we find several which reappear in the aetiological equations concerned in many other effects and thus exhibit no special relationship to any one particular effect. One of these causes, however, stands out in contrast to the rest from the fact that it is found in no other aetiological equation, or in very few; and this one has a right to be called the *specific* cause of the effect concerned. Furthermore, preconditions and specific causes are especially distinct from each other in those cases in which the preconditions have the characteristic of being long-standing states that are little susceptible to alteration, while the specific cause is a factor which has recently come into play.

I will try to give an example of this complete aetiological schematic picture:

Effect: Phthisis pulmonum.

Precondition: Disposition, for the most part laid down through heredity, by the organic constitution.

Specific Cause: Bacillus Kochii.

Auxiliary Causes: Anything that diminishes the powers—emotions as well as suppurations or colds.

The schematic picture for the aetiology of anxiety neurosis seems to me to be on the same lines:

Precondition: Heredity.

Specific Cause: A sexual factor, in the sense of a deflection of sexual tension away from the psychical field.

Auxiliary Causes: Any stock noxae—emotion, fright, and also physical exhaustion through illness or over-exertion.

If I consider this aetiological formula for anxiety neurosis in detail, I am able to add the following remarks. Whether a special personal constitution (which need not be produced by heredity) is absolutely necessary for the production of an anxiety neurosis, or whether any normal person can be made to have an anxiety neurosis by some given quantitative increase of the specific factor—this I am not able to decide with certainty; but I incline strongly to the latter view.—Hereditary disposition is the most important precondition for anxiety neurosis; but it is not an *indispensable* one, since it is absent in a class of borderline cases.—The presence of the specific sexual factor can, in the majority of cases, be demonstrated with certainty. In one series of cases (congenital ones) this factor is not separated from the precondition of heredity, but is fulfilled with the help of it. That is to say, in some patients this peculiarity of the *vita sexualis*—psychical inadequacy in mastering somatic sexual tension—is innate in the form of a stigma[1] whereas ordinarily it is *viâ* that peculiarity that they acquire the neurosis. In another class of borderline cases the specific cause is contained in a contributory one. This is when the psychical inadequacy which I have just mentioned is brought about by exhaustion and such causes. All these cases fall into classes which melt into one another and do not form separate categories. In all of them, moreover, we find that the sexual tension undergoes the same vicissitudes; and for most of them the distinction between

[1] [See footnote 2, p. 192 f. below.]

precondition, specific and auxiliary cause holds good, in conformity with the solution of the aetiological equation which I have given above.

When I consult my experience on this point, I cannot find that there is any antithetic relation as regards anxiety neurosis between hereditary disposition and the specific sexual factor. On the contrary, the two aetiological factors support and supplement each other. The sexual factor is usually only operative in those who have an innate hereditary taint as well; heredity alone is usually not able to produce an anxiety neurosis, but waits for the occurrence of a sufficient amount of the specific sexual noxa. The discovery of the hereditary element does not, therefore, exempt us from searching for a specific factor. On its discovery, incidentally, all our therapeutic interest as well depends. For what can we do therapeutically about heredity as an aetiological element? It has always been there in the patient and will continue to be there until the end of his life. Taken by itself, it cannot help us to understand either the episodic onset of a neurosis or the cessation of a neurosis as a result of treatment. It is nothing but a *precondition* of the neurosis —an inexpressibly important precondition, it is true, but nevertheless one which has been over-estimated, to the detriment of therapy and theoretical comprehension. To be convinced by the contrasting state of affairs, one has only to think of the cases of nervous diseases that run in families (such as chorea chronica, Thomsen's disease, and so on), in which heredity unites in itself all the aetiological preconditions.

In conclusion, I should like to repeat the few statements in which I am accustomed, as a first approximation to the truth, to express the mutual relationships between the various aetiological factors:

(1) Whether a neurotic illness *occurs at all* depends upon a quantitative factor—upon the total load on the nervous system as compared with the latter's capacity for resistance. Everything which can keep this quantitative factor below a certain threshold-value, or can bring it back to that level, has a therapeutic effect, since by so doing it keeps the aetiological equation unsatisfied.

What is to be understood by the 'total load' and by the 'capacity for resistance' of the nervous system, could no doubt be more clearly explained on the basis of certain hypotheses regarding the function of the nerves.[1]

(2) What *dimensions* the neurosis attains depends in the first instance on the amount of the hereditary taint. Heredity acts like a multiplier introduced into an electric circuit, which increases the deviation of the needle many times over.[2]

(3) But what *form* the neurosis assumes—what direction the deviation takes—is solely determined by the specific aetiological factor arising from sexual life.

Although I am aware of the many still unsolved difficulties of the subject, I hope that, on the whole, my hypothesis of an anxiety neurosis will prove more fruitful for an understanding of the neuroses than Löwenfeld's attempt to account for the same facts by postulating '*a combination of neurasthenic and hysterical symptoms in the form of an attack.*'

VIENNA, *beginning of May* 1895.

[1] [This is no doubt an allusion to the 'principle of constancy'. See above, p. 65.]

[2] [This analogy is found already in Draft A in the Fliess papers (1950*a*), which possibly dates from the end of 1892. It occurs again in the French paper on 'Heredity and the Aetiology of the Neuroses' (1896*a*), p. 147 below, as well as in Freud's abstract of the present paper, p. 252 below.]

HEREDITY AND THE AETIOLOGY OF THE NEUROSES

(1896)

L'HÉRÉDITÉ ET L'ÉTIOLOGIE DES NÉVROSES

(*a*) FRENCH EDITIONS:

1896   *Rev. neurol.*, **4** (6), 161–9. (March 30.)
1906   *S.K.S.N.*, **1**, 135–48. (1911, 2nd ed.; 1920, 3rd ed.;
        1922, 4th ed.)
1925   *G.S.*, **1**, 388–403.
1952   *G.W.*, **1**, 407–422.

(*b*) ENGLISH TRANSLATION:
        'Heredity and the Aetiology of the Neuroses'
1924   *C.P.*, **1**, 138–154. (Tr. M. Meyer.)

Included (No. XXXVII) in Freud's own collection of abstracts of his early works (1897*b*). The original is in French. The present translation is a new one by James Strachey.

This paper and the next one, the second on the neuro-psychoses of defence (1896*b*), were sent off to their respective publishers on the same day, February 5, 1896, as Freud reported to Fliess in a letter the day after (Freud, 1950*a*, Letter 40). The French paper was published at the end of March, some six weeks before the other, and it consequently has priority over it for the first published appearance of the word 'psycho-analysis' (p. 151). The paper is a summary of Freud's contemporary views on the aetiology of all four of what he then regarded as the main types of neurosis: the two 'psychoneuroses', hysteria and obsessional neurosis, and the two 'actual neuroses' (as they were later to be called, see footnote 1, p. 279 below), neurasthenia and anxiety neurosis. The earlier part of the paper is to a great extent a repetition of the discussion on aetiology in the second paper on anxiety neurosis (1895*f*), while the later part covers very shortly the same ground as its contemporary, the second paper on the neuro-psychoses of defence (1896*b*). The reader may therefore be referred to these and to the editorial comments on them for further information.

HEREDITY AND THE AETIOLOGY
OF THE NEUROSES

I AM addressing in particular the disciples of J.-M. Charcot, in order to put forward some objections to the aetiological theory of the neuroses which was handed on to us by our teacher.

The role attributed in that theory to nervous heredity is well known: it is the sole true and indispensable cause of neurotic affections, and the other aetiological influences can aspire only to the name of *agents provocateurs*. Such was the opinion laid down by the great man himself and by his pupils, MM. Guinon, Gilles de la Tourette, Janet and others, in regard to the major neurosis, hysteria; and I believe the same view is held in France and in most other places in regard to the other neuroses, though, where these states analogous to hysteria are concerned, it has not been promulgated in so solemn and decided a manner.

I have long entertained doubts on this subject, but I have had to wait to find corroborative facts in my daily experience as a doctor. My objections are now of a double order: factual arguments and arguments derived from speculation. I will begin with the former, arranging them according to the importance I ascribe to them.

I

(*a*) Affections which are fairly often remote from the domain of neuropathology, and which do not necessarily depend on a disease of the nervous system, have sometimes been regarded as nervous and as showing the presence of a hereditary neuropathic tendency. This has been so with true facial neuralgias and with many headaches which were thought to be nervous but which arose rather from post-infectious pathological changes and suppuration in the pharyngo-nasal cavities. I feel convinced that the patients would benefit if we were more often to hand over the treatment of these affections to the rhinological surgeons.

(*b*) All the nervous affections found in a patient's family, without consideration of their frequence or severity, have been accepted as a basis for charging him with a hereditary nervous taint. Does not this way of looking at things imply drawing a sharp line between families which are clear of all nervous predisposition and families which are subject to them to an unlimited extent? And do not the facts argue in favour of the contrary view that there are transitions and degrees in nervous disposition and that no family escapes it altogether?

(c) Our opinion of the aetiological role of heredity in nervous illnesses ought decidedly to be based on an impartial statistical examination and not on a *petitio principii*. Until such an examination has been made we ought to believe that the existence of acquired nervous disorders is just as possible as that of hereditary ones. But if there can be nervous disorders that are acquired by people without a predisposition, it can no longer be denied that the nervous affections met with in our patient's relatives may partly have arisen in that way. It will then no longer be possible to quote them as conclusive evidence of the hereditary disposition imputed to the patient by reason of his family history, for a retrospective diagnosis of the illnesses of ancestors or absent members of a family can only very rarely be successfully made.

(d) Those who are adherents of M. Fournier and M. Erb in the matter of the part played by syphilis in the aetiology of tabes dorsalis and progressive paralysis have learned that powerful aetiological influences must be recognized whose collaboration is indispensable for the pathogenesis of certain illnesses which could not be produced by heredity alone. Nevertheless M. Charcot remained to the very last (as I know from a private letter I had from him) strictly opposed to Fournier's theory, which is, however, gaining ground every day.

(e) There is no doubt that certain nervous disorders can develop in people who are perfectly healthy and whose family is above reproach. This is a matter of daily observation in cases of Beard's neurasthenia; if neurasthenia were restricted to people who were predisposed, it would never have attained the importance and extent with which we are familiar.

(f) In nervous pathology there is *similar heredity* and what is known as *dissimilar heredity*. No objection can be made to the former; it is in fact a very remarkable thing that in the disorders which depend on similar heredity (Thomsen's disease, Fried-reich's disease, the myopathies, Huntington's chorea, etc.) we never come across a trace of any other accessory aetiological influence. But dissimilar heredity, which is much more important than the other, leaves gaps which would have to be filled before a satisfactory solution of aetiological problems could be reached. Dissimilar heredity consists in the fact that the members of the same family are found to be affected by the most various nervous disorders, functional and organic, without its being possible to discover any law determining the replacement of one illness by another or the order of their succession through the generations. Alongside of the sick members of these families there are others who remain healthy; and the theory of dissimilar heredity does not tell us why one person tolerates the same hereditary load without succumbing to it or why another person, who is sick, should choose this particular nervous affection from among all the illnesses which make up the great family of nervous diseases instead of choosing another one—hysteria instead of epilepsy or insanity, and so on. Since there is no such thing as chance in neurotic pathogenesis any more than anywhere else, it must be allowed that it is not heredity that presides over the choice of the particular nervous disorder which is to develop in the predisposed member of a family, but that there are grounds for suspecting the existence of other aetiological influences, of a less incomprehensible[1] nature, which would then deserve to be called the *specific aetiology* of such and such a nervous affection. Without the existence of this special aetiological factor, heredity could have done nothing; it would have lent itself to the production of another nervous disorder if the specific aetiology in question had been replaced by some other influence.

II

There has been too little research into these specific and determining causes of nervous disorders, for the attention of

[1] [The original publication of 1896 gives '*compréhensible*'. All the subsequent reprints from 1906 up to and including 1925 give '*incompréhensible*'; but the latest reprint (*G.W.*, 1952) returns to the original '*compréhensible*'. Arguments can be found in favour of either alternative. Cf. Editor's Note to 'Obsessions and Phobias', pp. 72–3 above.]

physicians has remained dazzled by the grandiose prospect of the aetiological precondition of heredity. Those causes nevertheless deserve to be made the object of industrious study. Although their pathogenic power is in general only accessory to that of heredity, great practical interest attaches to the knowledge of this specific aetiology; it will allow our therapeutic efforts to find a path of access, whereas hereditary disposition, which is something fixed in advance for the patient from his birth, brings our efforts to a halt with its unapproachable power.[1]

I have been engaged for years in researches into the aetiology of the major neuroses (functional nervous states analogous to hysteria) and it is the result of those studies that I propose to describe to you in the following pages. To avoid any possible misunderstanding I shall begin by making two remarks on the nosography of the neuroses and on the aetiology of the neuroses in general.

I was obliged to begin my work with a nosographic innovation. I found reason to set alongside of hysteria the obsessional neurosis (*Zwangsneurose*) as a self-sufficient and independent disorder, although the majority of the authorities place obsessions among the syndromes constituting mental degeneracy or confuse them with neurasthenia. I for my part, by examining the psychical mechanism of obsessions, had learnt that they are connected with hysteria more closely than one might suppose.

Hysteria and obsessional neurosis form the first group of the major neuroses studied by me. The second contains Beard's neurasthenia, which I have divided up into two functional states separated by their aetiology as well as by their symptomatic appearance—*neurasthenia* proper and the *anxiety neurosis* (*Angstneurose*), a name which, I may say in passing, I am not pleased with myself. I gave my detailed reasons for making this separation, which I consider necessary, in a paper published in 1895 [Freud, 1895*b*].

As regards the aetiology of the neuroses, I think it should be recognized in theory that aetiological influences, differing among themselves in their importance and in the manner in which they are related to the effect they produce, can be

[1] [In the 1952 edition only, this has been changed to 'opposes an unapproachable obstacle to our efforts'.]

grouped in three classes:[1] (1) *Preconditions,* which are indispensable for producing the disorder concerned but which are of a general nature and are equally met with in the aetiology of many other disorders; (2) *Concurrent Causes,* which share the character of preconditions in that they function in the causation of other disorders as well as in that of the disorder under consideration, but which are not indispensable for the production of the latter; and (3) *Specific Causes,* which are as indispensable as the preconditions, but are of a limited nature and appear only in the aetiology of the disorder for which they are specific.

In the pathogenesis of the major neuroses, then, heredity fulfils the role of a *precondition,* powerful in every case and even indispensable in most cases. It could not do without the collaboration of the specific causes; but the importance of hereditary disposition is proved by the fact that the same specific causes acting on a healthy individual produce no manifest pathological effect, whereas in a predisposed person their action causes the neurosis to come to light, whose development will be proportionate in intensity and extent to the degree of the hereditary precondition.

Thus the action of heredity is comparable to that of a multiplier in an electric circuit, which exaggerates the visible deviation of the needle, but which cannot determine its direction.

There is yet another thing to be noted in the relations between the hereditary precondition and the specific causes of neuroses. Experience shows—what one might have guessed in advance—that in these questions of aetiology one should not neglect the relative quantities, so to speak, of the aetiological influences. But one could not have guessed the following fact, which seems to arise from my observations: namely that heredity and the specific causes can replace each other as regards quantity, that the same pathological effect will be produced by the coincidence of a very serious specific aetiology with a moderate disposition or of a severely loaded nervous heredity with a slight specific influence. And we shall simply be meeting not unexpected extreme instances in this series if we come upon cases of neurosis in which we shall look in vain for any appreciable

[1] [Much of what follows for the next few pages is a close repetition of the latter part of the second paper on anxiety neurosis (1895*f*).]

degree of hereditary disposition, provided that what is lacking is made up for by a powerful specific influence.

As *concurrent* (or auxiliary) *causes* of neuroses may be enumerated all the stock agents met with elsewhere: emotional disturbance, physical exhaustion, acute illnesses, intoxications, traumatic accidents, intellectual overwork, etc. I maintain that none of these, not even the last, enters into the aetiology of the neuroses regularly or necessarily, and I am aware that to declare this opinion is to put oneself in direct opposition to a theory which is looked upon as universally accepted and irreproachable. Since Beard declared that neurasthenia was the fruit of our modern civilization, he has only met with believers; but I find it impossible to accept this view. A laborious study of the neuroses has taught me that the specific aetiology of the neuroses has escaped Beard's notice.[1]

I have no desire to depreciate the aetiological importance of these stock agents. Since they are very various, occur very frequently and are most often named by patients themselves, they become more prominent than the specific causes of the neuroses —an aetiology which is either hidden or unknown. Fairly frequently they fulfil the function of *agents provocateurs* which render manifest a neurosis that has previously been latent; and a practical interest attaches to them, for a consideration of these stock causes may offer lines of approach to a therapy which does not aim at a radical cure and is content with repressing the illness to its former state of latency.

But it is not possible to establish any constant and close relation between one of these stock causes and one or other form of nervous affection. Emotional disturbance, for instance, is found equally in the aetiology of hysteria, obsessions and neurasthenia, as well as in that of epilepsy, Parkinson's disease, diabetes and many others.

Stock concurrent causes can also replace the specific aetiology in respect of quantity, but can never take its place entirely. There are numerous cases in which all the aetiological influences are represented by the hereditary precondition and the specific cause, stock causes being absent. In the other cases the

---

[1] [Freud discussed this question more fully ten years later in his paper on ' "Civilized" Sexual Ethics and Modern Nervous Illness' (1908*d*), and, of course, in many later writings.]

indispensable aetiological factors are not in themselves sufficient in quantity to bring about an outbreak of neurosis; a state of apparent health may be maintained for a long time, though it is in reality a state of predisposition to neurosis. It is then enough for a stock cause to come into action as well, and the neurosis becomes manifest. But it must be clearly pointed out that under these conditions the nature of the stock cause which supervenes is a matter of complete indifference—whether it is an emotion, a trauma, an infectious illness or anything else. The pathological effect will not be modified according to this variation; the nature of the neurosis will always be dominated by the pre-existing specific cause.

What, then, are the specific causes of neuroses? Is there a single one or are there several? And is it possible to establish a constant aetiological relation between a particular cause and a particular neurotic effect, in such a way that each of the major neuroses can be attributed to a special aetiology?

On the basis of a laborious examination of the facts, I shall maintain that this last supposition is quite in agreement with reality, that each of the major neuroses which I have enumerated has as its immediate cause one particular disturbance of the economics of the nervous system, and that these functional pathological modifications *have as their common source the subject's sexual life, whether they lie in a disorder of his contemporary sexual life or in important events in his past life.*

This, to tell the truth, is no new, unheard-of proposition. Sexual disorders have always been admitted among the causes of nervous illness, but they have been subordinated to heredity and co-ordinated with the other *agents provocateurs*; their aetiological influence has been restricted to a limited number of observed cases. Physicians had even fallen into the habit of not investigating them unless the patient brought them up himself. What gives its distinctive character to my line of approach is that I elevate these sexual influences to the rank of specific causes, that I recognize their action in every case of neurosis, and finally that I trace a regular parallelism, a proof of a special aetiological relation between the nature of the sexual influence and the pathological species of the neurosis.

I am quite sure that this theory will call up a storm of

contradictions from contemporary physicians. But this is not the place in which to present the documents and the experiences which have forced me to my conviction, nor to explain the true meaning of the rather vague expression 'disorders of the economics of the nervous system'. This will be done, most fully, I hope, in a work on the subject which I have in preparation.[1] In the present paper I limit myself to reporting my findings.

Neurasthenia proper, if we detach anxiety neurosis from it, has a very monotonous clinical appearance: fatigue, intracranial pressure, flatulent dyspepsia, constipation, spinal paraesthesias, sexual weakness, etc. The only specific aetiology it allows of is (immoderate) masturbation or spontaneous emissions.

It is the prolonged and intense action of this pernicious sexual satisfaction which is enough on its own account to provoke a neurasthenic neurosis or which imposes on the subject the special neurasthenic stamp that is manifested later under the influence of an incidental accessory cause. I have also come across people presenting the indications of a neurasthenic constitution in whom I have not succeeded in bringing to light the aetiology I have mentioned; but I have at least shown that the sexual function has never developed to its normal level in these patients; they seemed to have been endowed by heredity with a sexual constitution analogous to what is brought about in a neurasthenic as a result of masturbation.[2]

The anxiety neurosis exhibits a much richer clinical picture: irritability, states of anxious expectation, phobias, anxiety attacks, complete or rudimentary, attacks of fear and of vertigo, tremors, sweating, congestion, dyspnoea, tachycardia, etc., chronic diarrhoea, chronic locomotor vertigo, hyperaesthesia, insomnia, etc.[3] It is easily revealed as being the specific effect of various disorders of sexual life which possess a characteristic common to all of them. Enforced abstinence, unconsummated[4]

---

[1] [See footnote 2, p. 162 f. below.]
[2] [See a fuller discussion of masturbation in 'Sexuality in the Aetiology of the Neuroses' (1898a), p. 275 below.]
[3] For the symptomatology as well as for the aetiology of anxiety neurosis, see my paper referred to above [Freud, 1895b].
[4] ['Fruste' in the original. See footnote 2, p. 81.]

genital excitation (excitation which is not relieved by a sexual act), coition which is imperfect or interrupted (which does not end in gratification), sexual efforts which exceed the subject's psychical capacity, etc.—all these agents, which occur only too frequently in modern life, seem to agree in the fact that they disturb the equilibrium of the psychical and somatic functions in sexual acts, and that they prevent the psychical participation necessary in order to free the nervous economy from sexual tension.

These remarks, which perhaps contain the germ of a theoretical explanation of the functional mechanism of the neurosis in question, give rise already to a suspicion that a complete and truly scientific exposition of the subject is not possible at the present time, and that it would be necessary to start off by approaching the physiological problem of sexual life from a fresh angle.

I will say finally that the pathogenesis of neurasthenia and anxiety neurosis can easily do without the co-operation of a hereditary disposition. That is the outcome of daily observation. But if heredity is present, the development of the neurosis will be affected by its powerful influence.

As regards the second class of major neuroses, hysteria and obsessional neurosis, the solution of the aetiological problem is of surprising simplicity and uniformity. I owe my results to a new method of psycho-analysis[1], Josef Breuer's exploratory procedure; it is a little intricate, but it is irreplaceable, so fertile has it shown itself to be in throwing light upon the obscure paths of unconscious ideation. By means of that procedure—this is not the place in which to describe it[2]—hysterical symptoms are traced back to their origin, which is always found in some event of the subject's sexual life appropriate for the production of a distressing emotion. Travelling backwards into the patient's past, step by step, and always guided by the organic train of symptoms and of memories and thoughts aroused, I finally reached the starting-point of the pathological process; and I was obliged to see that at bottom the same thing was present in

[1] [This was the word's first published appearance (cf. p. 47, n. 1).]
[2] See *Studies on Hysteria*, by Breuer and Freud, 1895.

all the cases submitted to analysis—the action of an agent which must be accepted as the specific cause of hysteria.

This agent is indeed a memory relating to sexual life; but it is one which presents two characteristics of the first importance. The event of which the subject has retained an unconscious memory is *a precocious experience of sexual relations with actual excitement of the genitals, resulting from sexual abuse committed by another person;* and *the period of life* at which this fatal event takes place is *earliest youth*—the years up to the age of eight to ten, before the child has reached sexual maturity.[1]

A passive sexual experience before puberty: this, then, is the specific aetiology of hysteria.

I will without delay add some factual details and some commentary to the result I have announced, in order to combat the scepticism with which I expect to meet. I have been able to carry out a complete psycho-analysis in thirteen cases of hysteria, three of that number being true combinations of hysteria and obsessional neurosis. (I do not speak of hysteria *with* obsessions.) In none of these cases was an event of the kind defined above missing. It was represented either by a brutal assault committed by an adult or by a seduction less rapid and less repulsive, but reaching the same conclusion. In seven out of the thirteen cases the intercourse was between children on both sides—sexual relations between a little girl and a boy a little older (most often her brother) who had himself been the victim of an earlier seduction. These relations sometimes continued for years, until the little guilty parties reached puberty; the boy would repeat the same practices with the little girl over and over again and without alteration—practices to which he himself had been subjected by some female servant or governess and which on account of their origin were often of a disgusting sort. In a few cases there was a combination of an assault and relations between children or a repetition of a brutal abuse.

The date of this precocious experience varied. In two cases the series started in the little creature's second year (?);[2] the commonest age in my observations is the fourth or fifth year. It

---

[1] [For this and what follows, compare the fuller discussion, accompanied by Freud's later critical comments, in his second paper on the neuro-psychoses of defence (1896b).]

[2] [The question-mark is in the original.]

may be somewhat by accident, but I have formed an impression from this that a passive sexual experience occurring only after the age of from eight to ten is no longer able to serve as the foundation of the neurosis.

How is it possible to remain convinced of the reality of these analytic confessions which claim to be memories preserved from the earliest childhood? and how is one to arm oneself against the tendency to lies and the facility of invention which are attributed to hysterical subjects? I should accuse myself of blameworthy credulity if I did not possess more conclusive evidence. But the fact is that these patients never repeat these stories spontaneously, nor do they ever in the course of a treatment suddenly present the physician with the complete recollection of a scene of this kind. One only succeeds in awakening the psychical trace of a precocious sexual event under the most energetic pressure of the analytic procedure, and against an enormous resistance. Moreover, the memory must be extracted from them piece by piece, and while it is being awakened in their consciousness they become the prey to an emotion which it would be hard to counterfeit.

Conviction will follow in the end, if one is not influenced by the patients' behaviour, provided that one can follow in detail the report of a psycho-analysis of a case of hysteria.

The precocious event has left an indelible imprint on the history of the case; it is represented in it by a host of symptoms and of special features which could be accounted for in no other way; it is peremptorily called for[1] by the subtle but solid interconnections of the intrinsic structure of the neurosis; the therapeutic effect of the analysis lags behind if one has not penetrated so far; and one is then left with no choice but to reject or to believe the whole.

Is it understandable that a precocious sexual experience of this kind, undergone by an individual whose sex is barely differentiated, can become the source of a persistent psychical abnormality like hysteria? And how would this supposition fit in

---

[1] [The original publication (1896) gives '*régi*' ('governed'). All the subsequent reprints from 1906 up to and including 1925 give '*exigé*' ('called for'); but the latest reprint (*G.W.*, 1952) returns to the original '*régi*'. Cf. the Editor's Note to 'Obsessions and Phobias', pp. 72-3 above.]

with our present ideas on the psychical mechanism of that neurosis? A satisfactory reply can be given to the first of these questions. It is precisely because the subject is in his infancy that the precocious sexual excitation produces little or no effect at the time; but its psychical trace is preserved. Later, when at puberty the reactions of the sexual organs have developed to a level incommensurable with their infantile condition, it comes about in one way or another that this unconscious psychical trace is awakened. Thanks to the change due to puberty, the memory will display a power which was completely lacking from the event itself. *The memory will operate as though it were a contemporary event.* What happens is, as it were, *a posthumous action by a sexual trauma.*

So far as I can see, this awakening of a sexual memory after puberty, when the event itself has happened at a time long before that period, forms the only psychological instance of the immediate effect of a *memory* surpassing that of an actual event. But the constellation is an abnormal one, which touches a weak side of the psychical mechanism and is bound to produce a pathological psychical effect.

I believe I can see that *this inverse relation between the psychical effect of the memory and of the event* contains the reason for *the memory remaining unconscious.*

In this way we arrive at a very complex psychical problem, but one which, properly appreciated, promises to throw a vivid light on the most delicate questions of psychical life.[1]

The ideas put forward here, which have as their starting-point the finding of psycho-analysis to the effect that a memory of a precocious sexual experience is always found as the specific cause of hysteria, are not in harmony with the psychological theory of neuroses held by M. Janet, nor with any other; but they agree perfectly with my own speculations on the '*Abwehr-neurosen*' [neuroses of defence], as I have developed them elsewhere.[2]

All the events subsequent to puberty to which an influence must be attributed upon the development of the hysterical

---

[1] [The subject of these last four paragraphs is discussed by Freud at greater length in a footnote to Section I of the second paper on the neuro-psychoses of defence, pp. 166-7 below.]

[2] [Cf. Freud's two papers on the subject, 1894*a* and 1896*b*.]

neurosis and upon the formation of its symptoms are in fact only concurrent causes—'*agents provocateurs*' as Charcot used to say, though for him nervous heredity occupied the place which I claim for the precocious sexual experience. These accessory agents are not subject to the strict conditions imposed on the specific causes; analysis demonstrates in an irrefutable fashion that they enjoy a pathogenic influence for hysteria only owing to their faculty for awakening the unconscious psychical trace of the childhood event. It is also thanks to their connection with the primary pathogenic impression, and inspired by it, that their memories will become unconscious in their turn and will be able to assist in the growth of a psychical activity withdrawn from the power of the conscious functions.

The obsessional neurosis (*Zwangsneurose*) arises from a specific cause very analogous to that of hysteria. Here too we find a precocious sexual event, occurring before puberty, the memory of which becomes active during or after that period; and the same remarks and arguments which I put forward in connection with hysteria will apply to my observations of the other neurosis (six cases, three of which were pure ones). There is only one difference which seems capital. At the basis of the aetiology of hysteria we found an event of passive sexuality, an experience submitted to with indifference or with a small degree of annoyance or fright. In obsessional neurosis it is a question on the other hand, of an event which has given *pleasure*, of an act of aggression inspired by desire (in the case of a boy) or of a participation in sexual relations accompanied by enjoyment (in the case of a little girl). The obsessional ideas, when their intimate meaning has been recognized by analysis, when they have been reduced, as it were, to their simplest expression, are nothing other than *reproaches addressed by the subject to himself on account of this anticipated sexual enjoyment*, but reproaches distorted by an unconscious psychical work of transformation and substitution.[1]

The very fact of sexual aggressions of this kind taking place at such a tender age seems to reveal the influence of a previous seduction of which the precocity of sexual desire would be the consequence. In the cases analysed by me analysis confirms

[1] [Cf. the fuller parallel account in the following paper, p. 168 ff. below.]

this suspicion. In this way an interesting fact is explained which is always found in these cases of obsessions: the regular complication of the framework of symptoms by a certain number of symptoms which are simply hysterical.

The importance of the active element in sexual life as a cause of obsessions, and of sexual passivity for the pathogenesis of hysteria, even seems to unveil the reason for the more intimate connection of hysteria with the female sex and the preference of men for obsessional neurosis.[1] One sometimes comes across a pair of neurotic patients who were a pair of little lovers in their earliest childhood—the man suffering from obsessions and the woman from hysteria. If they are a brother and sister, one might mistake for a result of nervous heredity what is in fact the consequence of precocious sexual experiences.

There are no doubt pure and isolated cases of hysteria or obsessions, independent of neurasthenia or anxiety neurosis; but this is not the rule. A psychoneurosis appears more often as an accessory to a neurasthenic neurosis, provoked by it and following its decline. This is because the specific causes of the latter, the contemporary disorders of sexual life, operate at the same time as auxiliary causes of the psychoneuroses, whose specific cause, the memory of the precocious sexual experience, they awaken and revive.[2]

As regards nervous heredity, I am far from being able to estimate correctly its influence in the aetiology of the psycho-neuroses. I admit that its presence is indispensable for severe cases; I doubt if it is necessary for slight ones; but I am convinced that nervous heredity by itself is unable to produce psychoneuroses if their specific aetiology, precocious sexual excitation, is missing. I even believe that the decision as to which of the neuroses, hysteria or obsessions, will develop in a given case, is not decided by heredity but a special characteristic of the sexual event in earliest childhood.[3]

[1] [Freud remarked upon this again thirty years later, at the end of Chapter VIII of Inhibitions, Symptoms and Anxiety (1926d), Standard Ed., 20, 143: 'There is no doubt that hysteria has a strong affinity with femininity, just as obsessional neurosis has with masculinity.']
[2] [This point, once more, is dealt with more fully below, p. 167 f.]
[3] [The problem of the 'choice of neurosis' was beginning to interest Freud. Cf. pp. 168–9 and 190 below.]

FURTHER REMARKS ON THE NEURO-PSYCHOSES OF DEFENCE
(1896)

EDITOR'S NOTE

WEITERE BEMERKUNGEN ÜBER DIE ABWEHR-NEUROPSYCHOSEN

(a) German Editions:

1896   *Neurol. Zbl.*, **15** (10), 434–48. (May 15.)
1906   *S.K.S.N.*, **1**, 112–34. (1911, 2nd ed.; 1920, 3rd ed.;
   1922, 4th ed.)
1925   *G.S.*, **1**, 363–87.
1952   *G.W.*, **1**, 379–403.

(b) English Translations:
'Further Observations on the Defense Neuropsychoses'
1909   *S.P.H.*, 155–74. (Tr. A. A. Brill.) (1912, 2nd ed.; 1920,
   3rd ed.)
   'Further Remarks on the Defence Neuro-Psychoses'
1924   *C.P.*, **1**, 155–82. (Tr. J. Rickman.)

Included (No. XXXV) in Freud's own collection of abstracts of his early works (1897*b*). The present translation, with a changed title, is based on that of 1924.

This paper, as explained above on p. 142, was sent off by Freud on the same day (February 5, 1896) as the French paper on 'Heredity and the Aetiology of the Neuroses' but was published some six weeks after it. When this paper came to be included in the *Gesammelte Schriften*, in 1925, Freud added two or three footnotes. He had previously made a substantial addition to a footnote in the English translation of 1924 (pp. 180–1 below); but this was not included in any German edition.

This second paper on the 'neuro-psychoses of defence' takes up the discussion at the point it had reached in the first paper (1894*a*) produced two years earlier. Many of the conclusions reached here had been very briefly anticipated in the contemporary French paper on heredity (1896a); the essential part of the work had been communicated a few weeks earlier to Fliess in a long document headed by Freud 'A Christmas Fairy Tale' and dated January 1, 1896 (Freud 1950a, Draft K). Like its predecessor of 1894, the present work is divided into three sections, dealing respectively with hysteria, obsessions, and psychotic states, and in each case we are presented with the results of two years of further investigation. In the earlier paper the stress was already on the concept of 'defence' or 'repression'; here there is a much closer examination of what it is against which the defence is brought into operation, and the conclusion is in every case that the responsible factor is a *sexual* experience of a traumatic nature—in the case of hysteria a *passive* experience, in that of obsessions an *active* one, though even here an earlier passive experience lay in the remoter background. In other words the ultimate cause was always the seduction of a child by an adult. (Cf. 'The Aetiology of Hysteria' (1896c, pp. 208–9 below.) Further, the actual traumatic event always occurred before the age of puberty, though the outbreak of the neurosis occurred *after* puberty.[1]

As will be seen from Freud's additional footnote on p. 168, this whole position was later abandoned by him, and its abandonment signalized a turning-point in his views that was of major importance. In a letter to Fliess of September 21, 1897 (Freud, 1950a, Letter 69), he revealed that for some months it had been dawning on him that it was hardly credible that perverse acts against children were so general—especially since in every case it was the father who had to be held responsible for them. But it was not for several years that he gave public expression to his changed opinions.[2] The important consequence of this realization, however, was that Freud became aware of the part played by phantasy in mental events, and this opened the door to the discovery of infantile sexuality and of the Oedipus complex. A more detailed account of the changes in

[1] These findings had been presented to Fliess in outline some months earlier (from October 8, 1895 onwards). Cf. also the long footnote on pp. 166–7 below.

[2] In his contribution to Löwenfeld's *Sexualleben und Nervenleiden* on the part played by sexuality in the neuroses (1906a), *Standard Ed.*, 7, 274–5.

his views on this subject is given in the Editor's Note to the *Three Essays on the Theory of Sexuality* (1905*d*), *Standard Ed.*, **7**, 126 ff., while a further development is recorded in Freud's late paper on 'Female Sexuality' (1931*b*), ibid., **21**, 238, where the girl's early phantasies of being seduced by her father are traced back to her even earlier relations with her mother.

Incidentally, the problem of how it could be that the *memory* of an infantile trauma could have so much greater an effect than the actual experience of it at the time—a problem discussed repeatedly by Freud at this period and elaborately accounted for in the long footnote on pp. 166–7—lost its meaning owing to the discovery of infantile sexuality and the recognition of the persistence of unconscious instinctual impulses.

It is perhaps of still greater interest to observe the emergence in this paper of several new psychological *mechanisms*, which were to play a very large part in Freud's subsequent accounts of mental processes. Especially remarkable is the elaborate analysis of obsessional mechanisms, which anticipates much that was to appear fifteen years later in the theoretical section of the 'Rat Man' analysis (1909*d*). Thus we find early allusions to the view of obsessions as self-reproaches (p. 169), to the notion of symptoms implying a failure of defence and a 'return of the repressed' (ibid.), and to the far-reaching theory that symptoms are compromises between repressed and repressing forces (p. 170). Finally, in the section on paranoia, the concept of 'projection' makes its first appearance (p. 184), and, in the concept of an 'alteration of the ego' at the very end of the paper (a concept already present in Draft K of the Fliess correspondence), we may see a foreshadowing of ideas which re-appear in some of Freud's very last writings, for instance in 'Analysis Terminable and Interminable' (1937*c*).

FURTHER REMARKS ON THE
NEURO-PSYCHOSES OF DEFENCE

[INTRODUCTION]

IN a short paper published in 1894, I grouped together hysteria, obsessions and certain cases of acute hallucinatory confusion under the name of 'neuro-psychoses of defence' [Freud, 1894a], because those affections turned out to have one aspect in common. This was that their symptoms arose through the psychical mechanism of (unconscious) *defence*—that is, in an attempt to repress an incompatible idea which had come into distressing opposition to the patient's ego. In some passages in a book which has since appeared by Dr. J. Breuer and myself (*Studies on Hysteria* [1895*d*]) I have been able to elucidate, and to illustrate from clinical observations, the sense in which this psychical process of 'defence' or 'repression' is to be understood. There, too, some information is to be found about the laborious but completely reliable method of psycho-analysis[1] used by me in making those investigations—investigations which also constitute a therapeutic procedure.

My observations during my last two years of work have strengthened me in the inclination to look on defence as the nuclear point in the psychical mechanism of the neuroses in question; and they have also enabled me to give this psychological theory a clinical foundation. To my own surprise, I have come upon a few simple, though narrowly circumscribed, solutions of the problems of neurosis, and in the following pages I shall give a preliminary and brief account of them. In this kind of communication it is not possible to bring forward the evidence needful to support my assertions, but I hope to be able to fulfil this obligation later in a detailed presentation.[2]

---

[1] [The first appearance of the term in German. Cf. above, p. 142.]

[2] [Very soon after writing this, on March 16, 1896, Freud reported to Fliess (Freud, 1950*a*, Letter 43): 'My scientific work is going forward

I

THE 'SPECIFIC' AETIOLOGY OF HYSTERIA[1]

In earlier publications, Breuer and I have already expressed
the opinion that the symptoms of hysteria can only be understood if they are traced back to experiences which have a
'traumatic' effect, and that these psychical traumas refer to the
patient's sexual life.[2] What I have to add here, as a uniform
outcome of the analyses carried out by me on thirteen cases of
hysteria, concerns on the one hand the *nature* of those sexual
traumas, and, on the other, the period of life in which they
occur. In order to cause hysteria, it is not enough that there
should occur at some period of the subject's life an event which
touches his sexual existence and becomes pathogenic through
the release and suppression of a distressing affect. On the
contrary, *these sexual traumas must have occurred in early childhood
(before puberty), and their content must consist of an actual irritation of
the genitals (of processes resembling copulation).*

I have found this specific determinant of hysteria—*sexual
passivity during the pre-sexual period*—in every case of hysteria
(including two male cases) which I have analysed. How greatly
the claims of hereditary disposition are diminished by the
establishment in this way of accidental aetiological factors as a
determinant needs no more than a mention. Furthermore, a
path is laid open to an understanding of why hysteria is far and
away more frequent in members of the female sex; for even in
childhood they are more liable to provoke sexual attacks.

gradually. To-day, like a budding poet, I wrote at the top of a sheet of
paper:
Lectures on the Major Neuroses
(Neurasthenia, Anxiety Neurosis, Hysteria, Obsessional Neurosis)
. . . Behind this there looms another and finer work:
Psychology and Psychotherapy of the Neuroses of Defence.
But, apart from a few unpublished lectures and the two or three papers
that follow in the present volume, nothing immediate was to come of
this. Other matters, Freud's self-analysis and the problem of dreams,
were soon to absorb his interest.]
[1] [Much of the material in this section is repeated or expanded in
the following paper (1896c), p. 202 ff. below.]
[2] [Cf. the Breuer and Freud 'Preliminary Communication' (1893a)
and Freud's first paper on the neuro-psychoses of defence (1894a).]

The most immediate objections to this conclusion will probably be that sexual assaults on small children happen too often
for them to have any aetiological importance, or that these sorts
of experiences are bound to be without effect precisely because
they happen to a person who is sexually undeveloped; and
further, that one must beware of forcing on patients supposed
reminiscences of this kind by questioning them, or of believing
in the romances which they themselves invent. In reply to the
latter objections we may ask that no one should form too certain
judgements in this obscure field until he has made use of the
only method which can throw light on it—of psycho-analysis
for the purpose of making conscious what has so far been unconscious.[1] What is essential in the first objections can be disposed of by pointing out that it is not the experiences themselves
which act traumatically but their revival as a *memory* after the
subject has entered on sexual maturity.

My thirteen cases were without exception of a severe kind; in
all of them the illness was of many years' duration, and a few
came to me after lengthy and unsuccessful institutional treatment. The childhood traumas which analysis uncovered in
these severe cases had all to be classed as grave sexual injuries;
some of them were positively revolting. Foremost among those
guilty of abuses like these, with their momentous consequences,
are nursemaids, governesses and domestic servants, to whose
care children are only too thoughtlessly entrusted; teachers,
moreover, figure with regrettable frequency.[2] In seven out of
these thirteen cases, however, it turned out that blameless
children were the assailants; these were mostly brothers who
for years on end had carried on sexual relations with sisters a
little younger than themselves. No doubt the course of events
was in every instance similar to what it was possible to trace
with certainty in a few individual cases: the boy, that is to say,

---

[1] I myself am inclined to think that the stories of being assaulted
which hysterics so frequently invent may be obsessional fictions which
arise from the memory-trace of a childhood trauma.

[2] [It may be remarked that in this published paper Freud does not
mention the fact that with female patients the apparent seducer was so
often their father, as he pointed out in the letter to Fliess quoted in the
Editor's Note on p. 160 above. In the 1925 edition of *Studies on Hysteria*
(1895*d*) Freud admitted to having suppressed this fact in two of the
cases reported there (*Standard Ed.*, 2, 134 *n*. and 170 *n*.).]

had been abused by someone of the female sex, so that his libido was prematurely aroused, and then, a few years later, he had committed an act of sexual aggression against his sister, in which he repeated precisely the same procedures to which he himself had been subjected.

Active masturbation must be excluded from my list of the sexual noxae in early childhood which are pathogenic for hysteria. Although it is found so very often side by side with hysteria, this is due to the circumstance that masturbation itself is a much more frequent consequence of abuse or seduction than is supposed.

It is not at all rare for both of the two children to fall ill later on of a defence neurosis—the brother with obsessions and the sister with hysteria. This naturally gives the appearance of a familial neurotic disposition. Occasionally, however, this pseudo-heredity is resolved in a surprising fashion. In one of my cases a brother, a sister, and a somewhat older male cousin were all of them ill. From the analysis which I carried out on the brother, I learnt that he was suffering from self-reproaches for being the cause of his sister's illness. He himself had been seduced by his cousin, and the latter, it was known in the family, had been the victim of his nursemaid.

I cannot say for certain what the upper age-limit is below which sexual injury plays a part in the aetiology of hysteria; but I doubt whether sexual passivity can bring on repression later than between the eighth and tenth years,[1] unless it is enabled to do so by previous experiences. The lower limit extends as far back as memory itself—that is, therefore, to the tender age of one and a half or two years! (I have had two cases of this.) In a number of my cases the sexual trauma (or series of traumas) occurred in the third and fourth years of life. I should not lend credence to these extraordinary findings myself if their complete reliability were not proved by the development of the subsequent neurosis. In every case a number of pathological symptoms, habits and phobias are only to be accounted for by going back to these experiences in childhood, and the logical structure of the neurotic manifestations makes it impossible to reject these faithfully preserved memories which emerge from childhood life. True, it would be useless to try to elicit these

[1] [See Editor's addition to the footnote on p. 167 below.]

childhood traumas from a hysteric by questioning him outside psycho-analysis; their traces are never present in conscious memory, only in the symptoms of the illness.

All the experiences and excitations which, in the period of life *after* puberty, prepare the way for, or precipitate, the outbreak of hysteria, *demonstrably* have their effect only because they arouse the memory-trace of these traumas in childhood, which do not thereupon become conscious but lead to a release of affect and to repression. This role of the later traumas tallies well with the fact that they are not subject to the strict conditions which govern the traumas in childhood but that they can vary in their intensity and nature, from actual sexual violation to mere sexual overtures or the witnessing of sexual acts in other people, or receiving information about sexual processes.[1]

In my first paper on the neuroses of defence [1894a] there was no explanation of how the efforts of the subject, who had hitherto been healthy, to forget a traumatic experience of this sort could have the result of actually effecting the intended repression and thus opening the door to the defence neurosis. It could not lie in the nature of the experiences, since other people remained healthy in spite of being exposed to the same precipitating causes. Hysteria, therefore, could not be fully explained from the effect of the trauma: it had to be acknowledged that the susceptibility to a hysterical reaction had already existed before the trauma.

The place of this indefinite hysterical disposition can now be taken, wholly or in part, by the posthumous operation of a sexual trauma in childhood. 'Repression' of the memory of a distressing sexual experience which occurs in maturer years is only possible for those in whom that experience can activate the memory-trace of a trauma in childhood.[2]

---

[1] In a paper on the anxiety neurosis [1895b, p. 99 f. above], I remarked that 'anxiety neurosis can be produced in girls who are approaching maturity by their first encounter with the problem of sex. ... Such an anxiety neurosis is combined with hysteria in an almost typical fashion.' I know now that the occasion on which this 'virginal anxiety' breaks out in young girls does not actually represent their *first* encounter with sexuality, but that an experience of sexual passivity had previously occurred in their childhood, the memory of which is aroused by this 'first encounter'.

[2] A psychological theory of repression ought also to throw light on the

Obsessions similarly presuppose a sexual experience in childhood (though one of a different nature from that found in hysteria). The aetiology of the two neuro-psychoses of defence is related as follows to the aetiology of the two simple neuroses,[1] neurasthenia and anxiety neurosis. Both the latter disorders are direct effects of the sexual noxae themselves, as I have shown in

question of why it is only ideas with a *sexual* content that can be repressed. Such an explanation might start out from the following indications. It is known that having ideas with a sexual content produces excitatory processes in the genitals which are similar to those produced by sexual experience itself. We may assume that this somatic excitation becomes transposed into the psychical sphere. As a rule the effect in question is much stronger in the case of the experience than in the case of the memory. But if the sexual experience occurs during the period of sexual immaturity and the memory of it is aroused during or after maturity, then the memory will have a far stronger excitatory effect than the experience did at the time it happened; and this is because in the meantime puberty has immensely increased the capacity of the sexual apparatus for reaction. An inverted relation of this sort between real experience and memory seems to contain the psychological precondition for the occurrence of a repression. Sexual life affords —through the retardation of pubertal maturity as compared with the psychical functions—the only possibility that occurs for this inversion of relative effectiveness. *The traumas of childhood operate in a deferred fashion as though they were fresh experiences; but they do so unconsciously.* I must postpone entering into any more far-reaching psychological discussion till another occasion. Let me add, however, that the period of 'sexual maturity' which is in question here does not coincide with puberty but falls earlier (from the eighth to the tenth year). [This whole question of the deferred operation of early traumas had been discussed by Freud at great length in Sections 4, 5 and 6 of Part II of his 'Project' of 1895 (Freud, 1950a). It is also mentioned above in the French paper on heredity (1896a), p. 153 f., and further discussed at greater length in the paper which follows the present one, on the aetiology of hysteria (1896c), p. 212 f. below, as well as in several letters in the Fliess correspondence of this period, e.g. on March 1, May 30 and December 6, 1896 (Letters 42, 46 and 52). The age of eight to ten, mentioned in this footnote and elsewhere (e.g. p. 165 above), is shown by the later passage below (p. 212) to refer to the period of the second dentition. At about this time Freud attached some particular importance to the part it played in sexual development, and it is repeatedly mentioned in the course of these discussions. Some elaborate chronological tables dealing with the age at which traumas and repression occurred and with the related problem of the 'choice of neurosis' will be found in the letters to Fliess referred to above. Cf. p. 161.]

[1] [I.e. the 'actual neuroses'. See p. 279, n. 1.]

my paper on anxiety neurosis (1895*b*); both the defence neuroses are indirect consequences of sexual noxae which have occurred before the advent of sexual maturity—are consequences, that is, of the psychical memory-traces of those noxae. The current causes which produce neurasthenia and anxiety neurosis often at the same time play the part of exciting causes of the neuroses of defence; on the other hand, the specific causes of a defence-neurosis—the traumas of childhood—can at the same time lay the foundations for a later development of neurasthenia. Finally, it not infrequently happens, too, that neurasthenia or anxiety neurosis is maintained, not by current sexual noxae, but, instead, solely by the persisting effect of a memory of childhood traumas.[1]

II

THE NATURE AND MECHANISM OF OBSESSIONAL NEUROSIS

Sexual experiences of early childhood have the same significance in the aetiology of obsessional neurosis as they have in that of hysteria. Here, however, it is no longer a question of sexual *passivity*, but of acts of aggression carried out with pleasure and of pleasurable participation in sexual acts—that is to say, of sexual *activity*. This difference in the aetiological circumstances is bound up with the fact that obsessional neurosis shows a visible preference for the male sex.

In all my cases of obsessional neurosis, moreover, I have found a *substratum of hysterical symptoms*[2] which could be traced

[1] (*Footnote added* 1924:) This section is dominated by an error which I have since repeatedly acknowledged and corrected. At that time I was not yet able to distinguish between my patients' phantasies about their childhood years and their real recollections. As a result, I attributed to the aetiological factor of seduction a significance and universality which it does not possess. When this error had been overcome, it became possible to obtain an insight into the spontaneous manifestations of the sexuality of children which I described in my *Three Essays on the Theory of Sexuality* (1905*d*). Nevertheless, we need not reject everything written in the text above. Seduction retains a certain aetiological importance, and even to-day I think some of these psychological comments are to the point.

[2] [Freud gave an example of this much later, in the 'Wolf Man' case history (1918*b*), *Standard Ed.*, **17**, 75, and he referred to the point again in *Inhibitions, Symptoms and Anxiety* (1926*d*), ibid., **20**, 113.]

back to a scene of sexual passivity that preceded the pleasurable action. I suspect that this coincidence is no fortuitous one, and that precocious sexual aggressivity always implies a previous experience of being seduced. However, I can as yet give no definitive account of the aetiology of obsessional neurosis; I only have an impression that the decision as to whether hysteria or obsessional neurosis will arise on the basis of traumas in childhood depends on *chronological* circumstances in the development of the libido.[1]

The nature of obsessional neurosis can be expressed in a simple formula. *Obsessional ideas* are invariably transformed *self-reproaches* which have re-emerged from *repression* and which always relate to some *sexual* act that was performed with pleasure *in childhood*.[2] In order to elucidate this statement it is necessary to describe the typical course taken by an obsessional neurosis.

In a first period—the period of childhood immorality—the events occur which contain the germ of the later neurosis. First of all, in earliest childhood, we have the experiences of sexual seduction that will later on make repression possible; and then come the acts of sexual aggression against the other sex, which will later appear in the form of acts involving self-reproach.

This period is brought to a close by the advent of sexual 'maturation', often itself unduly early. A self-reproach now becomes attached to the memory of these pleasurable actions; and the connection with the initial experience of passivity makes it possible [p. 166]—often only after conscious and remembered efforts—to repress them and to replace them by a *primary symptom of defence*. Conscientiousness, shame and self-distrust are symptoms of this kind, with which the third period begins—the period of *apparent* health, but actually, of successful defence.

The next period, that of the illness, is characterized by the *return of the repressed memories*—that is, therefore, by the failure of the defence. It is not certain whether the awakening of those memories occurs more often accidentally and spontaneously or

---

[1] [Cf. end of long footnote, p. 167 above.]

[2] [Freud re-examined this definition critically at the beginning of Chapter II of his 'Rat Man' case history (1909*d*), *Standard Ed.*, **10**, 221.]

as a result of current sexual disturbances, as a kind of by-product of them. The re-activated memories, however, and the self-reproaches formed from them never re-emerge into consciousness unchanged: what become conscious as obsessional ideas and affects, and take the place of the pathogenic memories so far as conscious life is concerned, are structures in the nature of a *compromise* between the repressed ideas and the repressing ones.[1]

In order to describe clearly and with probable accuracy the processes of repression, the return of the repressed[2] and the formation of pathological compromise-ideas, one would have to make up one's mind to quite definite assumptions about the substratum of psychical events and of consciousness.[3] So long as one seeks to avoid this, one must be content with the following remarks which are intended more or less figuratively. There are two forms of obsessional neurosis, according to whether what forces an entrance into consciousness is solely the *mnemic content* of the act involving self-reproach, or whether the self-reproachful *affect* connected with the act does so as well.

The first form includes the typical obsessional ideas, in which the content engages the patient's attention and, as an affect, he merely feels an indefinite unpleasure, whereas the only affect which would be suitable to the obsessional idea would be one of self-reproach. The content of the obsessional idea is distorted in two ways in relation to the obsessional act of childhood. First, something contemporary is put in the place of something past; and secondly, something sexual is replaced by something analogous to it that is not sexual. These two alterations are the effect of the inclination to repress, still in force, which we will ascribe to the 'ego'. The influence of the re-activated pathogenic memory is shown by the fact that the content of the obsessional idea is still in part identical with what has been repressed or follows from it by a logical train of thought. If, with the help of the psycho-analytic method, we reconstruct the origin of an individual obsessional idea, we find that from a single current impression two different trains of thought have been set going.

---

[1] [This last sentence, too, was quoted in a footnote to the passage in the 'Rat Man' case history referred to in the last footnote.]

[2] [The first appearance of the phrase.]

[3] [Another indication of Freud's concern with the problem of unconscious mental processes. Cf. footnote, p. 53 above.]

The one which has passed by way of the repressed memory proves to be as correctly logical in its structure as the other, although it is incapable of being conscious and insusceptible to correction. If the products of the two psychical operations do not tally, what takes place is not some sort of logical adjustment of the contradiction between them; instead, alongside of the *normal* intellectual outcome, there comes into consciousness, as a compromise between the resistance and the *pathological* intellectual product, an obsessional idea which appears absurd. If the two trains of thought lead to the *same* conclusion, they reinforce each other, so that an intellectual product that has been arrived at normally now behaves, psychologically, like an obsessional idea. *Wherever a neurotic obsession emerges in the psychical sphere, it comes from repression.* Obsessional ideas have, as it were, a compulsive [obsessional] psychical currency, not on account of their intrinsic value, but on account of the source from which they derive or which has added a contribution to their value.

A second form of obsessional neurosis comes about if what has forced its way to representation in conscious psychical life is not the repressed mnemic content but the likewise repressed self-reproach. The affect of self-reproach can, by means of some mental addition, be transformed into any other unpleasurable affect. When this has happened there is no longer anything to prevent the substituted affect from becoming conscious. Thus *self-reproach* (for having carried out the sexual act in childhood) can easily turn into *shame* (in case some one else should find out about it), into *hypochondriacal anxiety* (fear of the physical injuries resulting from the act involving the self-reproach), into *social anxiety* (fear of being punished by society for the misdeed), into *religious anxiety*, into *delusions of being noticed* (fear of betraying the act to other people), or into *fear of temptation* (a justified mistrust of one's own moral powers of resistance), and so on. In addition, the mnemic content of the act involving self-reproach may be represented in consciousness as well, or it may remain completely in the background—which makes diagnosis much more difficult. Many cases which, on a superficial examination, seem to be common (neurasthenic) hypochondria, belong to this group of *obsessional affects*; what is known as 'periodic neurasthenia' or 'periodic melancholia' seems in particular to resolve itself with unexpected frequency into obsessional affects and obsessional ideas—a discovery which is not a matter of indifference therapeutically.

Besides these compromise symptoms, which signify the return of the repressed and consequently a collapse of the defence that had been originally achieved, the obsessional neurosis constructs a set of further symptoms, whose origin is quite different. For the ego seeks to fend off the derivatives of the initially repressed memory, and in this defensive struggle it creates symptoms which might be classed together as '*secondary defence*'. These are all of them '*protective measures*', which have already done good service in the fight against obsessional ideas and obsessional affects. If these aids in the defensive struggle *genuinely* succeed in once more repressing the symptoms of the return [of the repressed] which have forced themselves on the ego, then the obsession is transferred to the protective measures themselves and creates a third form of 'obsessional neurosis'—*obsessional actions*. These actions are never primary; they never contain anything but a defence—never an aggression. A psychical analysis of them shows that, in spite of their peculiarity, they can always be fully explained by being traced back to the obsessional memories which they are fighting against.[1]

[1] To take a single example only. An eleven-year-old boy had in an obsessional way instituted the following ceremonial before going to bed. He did not go to sleep until he had told his mother in the minutest detail all the experiences he had had during the day; there must be no bits of paper or other rubbish on the carpet in his bedroom in the evening; his bed had to be pushed right up against the wall, three chairs had to be placed in front of it, and the pillows had to lie in a particular way. In order to go to sleep he was obliged first to kick both his legs out a certain number of times and then lie on his side. This was explained in the following manner. Years before, a servant-girl who put the nice-looking boy to bed had taken the opportunity of lying down on him and abusing him sexually. When, later on, this memory was aroused in him by a recent experience, it manifested itself in his consciousness in a compulsion to perform the ceremonial I have described above. The meaning of the ceremonial was easy to guess and was established point by point by psycho-analysis. The chairs were placed in front of the bed and the bed pushed against the wall in order that nobody else should be able to get at the bed; the pillows were arranged in a particular way so that they should be differently arranged from how they were on that evening; the movements with his legs were to kick away the person who was lying on him; sleeping on his side was because in the scene

Secondary defence against the obsessional ideas may be effected by a forcible diversion on to other thoughts with a content as contrary as possible. This is why *obsessional brooding*, if it succeeds, regularly deals with abstract and *suprasensual* things; because the ideas that have been repressed are always concerned with *sensuality*. Or else the patient tries to make himself master of each of his obsessional ideas singly by logical work and by having recourse to his conscious memories. This leads to *obsessional thinking*, to a *compulsion to test things* and to *doubting mania*. The advantage which perception has over memory in such tests at first causes the patient, and later compels him, to collect and store up all the objects with which he has come into contact. Secondary defence against obsessional *affects* leads to a still wider set of protective measures which are capable of being transformed into obsessional acts. These may be grouped according to their purpose: *penitential* measures (burdensome ceremonials, the observation of numbers), *precautionary* measures (all sorts of phobias, superstition, pedantry, increase of the primary symptom of conscientiousness); measures to do with *fear of betrayal* (collecting scraps of paper,[1] seclusiveness), or to ensure *numbing* [of the mind] (dipsomania). Among these obsessional acts and obsessional impulses, phobias, since they circumscribe the patient's existence, play the greatest part.

There are cases in which one can observe how the obsession is transferred from the idea or from the affect on to the protective measure; others in which the obsession oscillates periodically between the symptom of the return of the repressed and the symptom of the secondary defence; and yet other cases in which no obsessional idea is constructed at all, but, instead, the repressed memory is at once represented by what is apparently a primary measure of defence. Here we reach at one bound the

---

he had been lying on his back; his circumstantial confession to his mother was because, in obedience to a prohibition by his seductress, he had been silent to his mother about this and other sexual experiences; and, finally, the reason for his keeping his bedroom floor clean was that neglect to do so had been the chief reproach that he had so far had to hear from his mother. [A no less complicated sleep-ceremonial was analysed by Freud twenty years later in Lecture XVII of his *Introductory Lectures* (1916–17).]

[1] [An instance of this will be found in Case 10 in 'Obsessions and Phobias' (1895c), pp. 78–9 above.]

stage which elsewhere only completes the course run by the obsessional neurosis after the defensive struggle has taken place. Severe cases of this disorder end in the ceremonial actions becoming fixated, or in a general state of doubting mania, or in a life of eccentricity conditioned by phobias.

The fact that the obsessional ideas and everything derived from them meet with no belief [from the subject] is no doubt because at their first repression the defensive symptom of *conscientiousness* has been formed and that that symptom, too, acquires an obsessional force. The subject's certainty of having lived a moral life throughout the whole period of his successful defence makes it impossible for him to believe the self-reproach which his obsessional idea involves. Only transitorily, too, on the appearance of a new obsessional idea and occasionally in melancholic states of exhaustion of the ego, do the pathological symptoms of the return of the repressed compel belief. The 'obsessional' character of the psychical formations which I have described here has quite generally nothing to do with attaching belief to them. Nor is it to be confused with the factor which is described as the 'strength' or 'intensity' of an idea. Its essence is rather indissolubility by psychical activity that is capable of being conscious; and this attribute undergoes no change, whether the idea to which the obsession attaches is stronger or weaker, or less or more intensely 'illuminated', or 'cathected with energy' and so on.

The cause of this invulnerability of the obsessional idea and its derivatives is, however, nothing more than its connection with the repressed memory from early childhood. For if we can succeed in making that connection conscious—and psychotherapeutic methods already appear able to do so—the obsession, too, is resolved.

III

Analysis of a Case of Chronic Paranoia[1]

For a considerable time I have harboured a suspicion that paranoia, too—or classes of cases which fall under the heading of paranoia—is a psychosis of defence; that is to say, that, like hysteria and obsessions, it proceeds from the repression of dis-

---

[1] (*Footnote added* 1924:) More correctly, no doubt, *dementia paranoides.*

tressing memories and that its symptoms are determined in
their form by the content of what has been repressed. Paranoia
must, however, have a special method or mechanism of repression[1] which is peculiar to it, in the same way as hysteria
effects repression by the method of *conversion* into somatic
innervation, and obsessional neurosis by the method of *substitution* (viz. by displacement along the lines of certain categories
of associations). I had observed several cases which favoured
this interpretation, but had found none which proved it; until,
a few months ago, I had an opportunity, through the kindness
of Dr. Josef Breuer, of undertaking the psycho-analysis for
therapeutic purposes of an intelligent woman of thirty-two,
in whose case a diagnosis of chronic paranoia could not be
questioned. I am reporting in these pages, without waiting
further, some of the information I have been able to obtain
from this piece of work, because I have no prospect of studying
paranoia except in very isolated instances, and because I think
it possible that my remarks may encourage a psychiatrist better
placed than I am in this matter to give its rightful place to the
factor of 'defence' in the discussion as to the nature and
psychical mechanism of paranoia which is being carried on
so actively just now. I have, of course, on the strength of the
following single observation, no intention of saying more than:
'This case is a psychosis of defence and there are most probably
others in the class of "paranoia" which are equally so.'

Frau P., thirty-two years of age, has been married for three
years and is the mother of a child of two. Her parents were not
neurotic; but her brother and sister are to my knowledge, like
her, neurotic. It is doubtful whether she may not, at one time
in her middle twenties, have become temporarily depressed
and confused in her judgement. In recent years she was healthy
and capable, until, six months after the birth of her child, she
showed the first signs of her present illness. She became un-
communicative and distrustful, showed aversion to meeting

---

[1] [This passage offers a good example of Freud's changing use of the
terms 'defence' and 'repression'. He would have used the word 'defence'
instead of 'repression' after his discussion of the two terms in *Inhibitions,
Symptoms and Anxiety* (1926d), *Standard Ed.*, **20**, 163 f. But see also the
Editor's Appendix A to that work (ibid., 173 f.).]

her husband's brothers and sisters and complained that the neighbours in the small town in which she lived were behaving differently towards her from how they did before and were rude and inconsiderate to her. By degrees these complaints increased in intensity, although not in definiteness. She thought people had something against her, though she had no idea what; but there was no doubt that everyone—relatives and friends—had ceased to respect her and were doing all they could to slight her. She had racked her brains, she said, to find the reason for this, but had no idea. A little time later she complained that she was being watched and that people were reading her thoughts and knew everything that was going on in her house. One afternoon she suddenly had the idea that she was being watched while she was undressing in the evening. From that time on she took the most precautionary measures when she undressed; she got into bed in the dark and did not begin to take off her things till she was under the bedclothes. Since she avoided all contact with other people, ate poorly and was very depressed, she was sent in the summer of 1895 to a hydropathic establishment. There, fresh symptoms appeared and those she already had increased in strength. Already in the spring of that year, when she was alone one day with her housemaid, she had suddenly had a sensation in her lower abdomen, and had thought to herself that the girl had at that moment had an improper idea. This sensation grew more frequent during the summer and became almost continual. She felt her genitals 'as one feels a heavy hand'. Then she began to see images which horrified her—hallucinations of naked women, especially of the lower part of a woman's abdomen with pubic hairs, and occasionally of male genitals as well. The image of the abdomen with hair and the physical sensation in her own abdomen usually occurred together. The images became very tormenting, for they happened regularly when she was in the company of a woman, and it made her think that she was seeing the woman in an indecent state of nakedness, but that simultaneously the woman was having the same picture of her (!). At the same time as these visual hallucinations—which vanished again for several months after their first appearance in the hydropathic establishment—she began to be pestered by voices which she did not recognize and which she could not account

for. When she was in the street, they said: 'That's Frau P.—
There she goes! Where's she going to?' Every one of her movements and actions was commented on; and at times she heard
threats and reproaches. All these symptoms became worse when
she was in company or in the street. For that reason she refused
to go out; she said that eating disgusted her; and her state of
health rapidly deteriorated.

I gathered all this from her when she came to Vienna for
treatment with me in the winter of 1895. I have set it out at
length because I want to convey the impression that what we
are dealing with here really is a quite frequent form of chronic
paranoia—a conclusion with which the details of her symptoms
and behaviour which I have still to describe will be found to
tally. At that time she concealed from me the delusions which
served to interpret her hallucinations, or else the delusions
had in fact not yet occurred to her. Her intelligence was undiminished; the only unusual thing I learnt was that she had
repeatedly made appointments with her brother, who lived
in the neighbourhood, in order to confide something important
to him, but had never told him anything. She never spoke about
her hallucinations, and towards the end she no longer said
much either about the slights and persecutions to which she
was subjected.

What I have to report about this patient concerns the
aetiology of the case and the mechanism of the hallucinations.
I discovered the aetiology when I applied Breuer's method,
exactly as in a case of hysteria—in the first instance for the
investigation and removal of the hallucinations. In doing so,
I started out from the assumption that in this case of paranoia,
just as in the two other defence neuroses with which I was
familiar, there must be unconscious thoughts and repressed
memories which could be brought into consciousness in the
same way as they were in those neuroses, by overcoming a
certain resistance. The patient at once confirmed my expectation, for she behaved in analysis exactly like, for instance, a
hysterical patient; with her attention on the pressure of my
hand,[1] she produced thoughts which she could not remember

[1] Cf. my *Studies on Hysteria* [1895d. Freud had described this technique
at several points in that work. See, for instance, *Standard Ed.*, **2**, 109–11
and 271.]

having had, which at first she did not understand and which were contrary to her expectations. The presence of significant unconscious ideas was thus demonstrated in a case of paranoia as well, and I was able to hope that I might trace the compulsion of paranoia, too, to repression. The only peculiarity was that the thoughts which arose from the unconscious were for the most part heard inwardly or hallucinated by the patient, in the same way as her voices.

Concerning the origin of the visual hallucinations, or at least of the vivid images, I learned the following. The image of the lower part of a woman's abdomen almost always coincided with the physical sensation in her own abdomen; but the latter was much more constant and often occurred without the image. The first images of a woman's abdomen had appeared in the hydropathic establishment a few hours after she had in fact seen a number of naked women at the baths; so they turned out to be simple reproductions of a real impression. It was therefore to be presumed that these impressions had been repeated only because great interest was attached to them. She told me that she had felt ashamed for these women; she herself had been ashamed to be seen naked for as long as she could remember. Since I was obliged to regard the shame as something obsessional, I concluded, in accordance with the mechanism of defence, that an experience must have been repressed here about which she had *not* felt ashamed. So I requested her to let the memories emerge which belonged to the theme of feeling ashamed. She promptly reproduced a series of scenes going back from her seventeenth to her eighth year, in which she had felt ashamed of being naked in her bath in front of her mother, her sister and the doctor; but the series ended in a scene at the age of six, in which she was undressing in the nursery before going to bed, without feeling any shame in front of her brother who was there. On my questioning her, it transpired that scenes like this had occurred often and that the brother and sister had for years been in the habit of showing themselves to one another naked before going to bed. I now understood the meaning of her sudden idea that she was being watched as she was going to bed. It was an unaltered piece of the old memory which involved self-reproach, and she was now making up for the shame which she had omitted to feel as a child.

My conjecture that we had to do with an affair between children, as is so often found in the aetiology of hysteria, was strengthened by the further progress of the analysis, which at the same time yielded solutions of individual details that frequently recurred in the clinical picture of the paranoia. The patient's depression began at the time of a quarrel between her husband and her brother, as a result of which the latter no longer came to the house. She had always been very fond of this brother and she missed him very much at that time. Besides this she spoke of a certain moment in her illness at which for the first time 'everything became clear to her'—that is, at which she became convinced of the truth of her suspicion that she was despised by everyone and deliberately slighted. This certainty came to her during a visit from her sister-in-law who, in the course of conversation, let fall the words: 'If anything of that sort happens to me, I treat it in a light vein.' At first Frau P. took this remark unsuspectingly; but later, after the visitor had left, it seemed to her that the words had contained a reproach, as if *she* was in the habit of taking serious things lightly; and from that moment on she was certain that she was the victim of general slander. When I questioned her as to what made her feel justified in applying the words to herself, she answered that it was the tone of voice in which her sister-in-law had spoken that had (although, it is true, only subsequently) convinced her of it. This is a detail which is characteristic of paranoia. I now obliged her to remember what her sister-in-law had been saying *before* the remark she complained of, and it emerged that the sister-in-law had related how in her parents' home there had been all sorts of difficulties with her *brothers*, and had added the wise comment: 'In every family all sorts of things happen that one would like to draw a veil over. But if anything of the kind happens to *me*, I take it lightly.' Frau P. now had to admit that her depression was attached to the statements made by her sister-in-law *before* her last remark. Since she had repressed both the statements which might have awakened a memory of her relations with her brother, and had only retained the insignificant last one, it was with it that she was obliged to connect her feeling that her sister-in-law was making a reproach against her; and since its *content* offered no basis for this, she turned from the content to the *tone* in which the words had been spoken. This is probably a typical piece of evidence that the misinterpretations of paranoia are based on a repression.

My patient's singular conduct, too, in making appointments with her brother, and then having nothing to tell him, was solved in a surprising fashion. Her explanation was that she had thought that if she could only look at him he would be bound to understand her sufferings, since he knew the cause of them. Now, as this brother was in fact the only person who could know about the aetiology of her illness, it was clear that she had been acting in accordance with a motive which, although she herself did not understand it consciously, could be seen to be perfectly justified as soon as it was supplied with a meaning derived from the unconscious.

I then succeeded in getting her to reproduce the various scenes in which her sexual relationship with her brother (which had certainly lasted at least from her sixth to her tenth year) had culminated. During this work of reproduction, the physical sensation in her abdomen 'joined in the conversation' [1] as it were, as is regularly observed to happen in the analysis of hysterical mnemic residues. The image of the lower part of a woman's naked abdomen (but now reduced to childish proportions and without hair on it) appeared with the sensation or stayed away, according as the scene in question had occurred in full light or in the dark. Her disgust at eating, too, found an explanation in a repulsive detail of these proceedings. After we had gone through this series of scenes, the hallucinatory sensations and images had disappeared, and (up to the present, at any rate) they have not returned.[2]

[1] [This phenomenon observed during psycho-analyses had been discussed and explained by Freud in his technical contribution to *Studies on Hysteria* (1895*d*), *Standard Ed.*, **2**, 296-7.]

[2] Later on, when an exacerbation of her illness undid the successful results of the treatment—which were in any case meagre—the patient no longer saw the offensive images of other people's genitals but had the idea that other people saw *her* genitals whenever they were *behind* her.

[The following addition appears in the 1924 edition of the English translation. It is not included in any of the German editions, and no German text is extant. It is therefore printed here without alteration. The note is dated 1922.]

The fragmentary account of this analysis in the text above was written

I had found, therefore, that these hallucinations were nothing else than parts of the content of repressed childhood experiences, symptoms of the return of the repressed.

I now turned to the analysis of the voices. First and foremost what had to be explained was why such an indifferent content as 'Here comes Frau P.', 'She's looking for a house now', and so on, could have been so distressing to her; next, how it was that precisely these innocent phrases had managed to be marked out by hallucinatory reinforcement. From the first it was clear that the 'voices' could not be *memories* that were being produced in a hallucinatory way, like the images and sensations, but were rather *thoughts* that were being 'said aloud'.

The first time she heard the voices was in the following circumstances. She had been reading Otto Ludwig's fine story, *Die Heiterethei*,[1] with eager interest, and she noticed that while she was reading, thoughts were emerging which claimed her attention. Immediately afterwards, she went for a walk along a country road, and, as she was passing a small peasant's house, the voices suddenly said to her 'That's what the Heiterethei's cottage looked like! There's the spring and there are the bushes! How happy she was in spite of all her poverty!' The voices then repeated to her whole paragraphs from what she had just been

---

while the patient was still undergoing treatment. Very shortly after, her condition became so much more serious that the treatment had to be broken off. She was transferred to an institution and there went through a period of severe hallucinations which had all the signs of dementia praecox. [An editorial comment in the English translation of 1924 explains that the original German footnote applied to this period.] Contrary to expectation, however, she recovered and returned home, had another child which was quite healthy, and was able for a long period (12 to 15 years) to carry out all her duties in a satisfactory manner. The only sign of her earlier psychosis was said to be that she avoided the company of all relatives, whether of her own family or of her husband's. At the end of this period, affected by very adverse changes in her circumstances, she again became ill. Her husband had become unable to work and the relatives she had avoided were obliged to support the family. She was again sent to an institution, and died there soon after, of a pneumonia which rapidly supervened.

[1] [Otto Ludwig (1813–65) was a very well-known German dramatist and novelist. *Die Heiterethei und ihr Widerspiel* (1857) was a novel of which the heroine was a Thuringian peasant-girl. Freud referred back to this episode in his paper on 'Screen Memories' (1899a), p. 308 below.]

reading. But it remained unintelligible why the Heiterethei's
cottage and bushes and spring, and precisely the most trivial
and irrelevant passages of the story, should be forced on her
attention with pathological strength. However, the solution of
the puzzle was not difficult. Her analysis showed that while she
was reading, she had had other thoughts as well and that she
had been excited by quite different passages in the book. Against
this material—analogies between the couple in the story and
herself and her husband, memories of intimacies in her married
life, and of family secrets—against all this a repressing resistance
had arisen because it was connected, by easily demonstrable
trains of thought, with her aversion to sexuality and thus
ultimately went back to the awakening of her old childhood
experience. In consequence of this censorship[1] exercised by the
repression, the innocuous and idyllic passages, which were connected with the proscribed ones by contrast and also by pro-
pinquity, acquired the additional strength in their relation to
consciousness which made it possible for them to be spoken
aloud. The first of the repressed ideas, for instance, related to
the slander to which the heroine, who lived alone, was exposed
from her neighbours. My patient easily discovered the analogy
with her own self. She, too, lived in a small place, met no one,
and thought she was despised by her neighbours. This distrust
of her neighbours had a real foundation. She had been obliged
at first to be content with a small apartment, and the bedroom
wall against which the young couple's double bed stood ad-
joined a room belonging to their neighbours. With the beginning of her marriage—obviously through an unconscious
awakening of her childhood affair, in which she and her brother
had played at husband and wife—she had developed a great
aversion to sexuality. She was constantly worried in case her
neighbours might hear words and noises through the party
wall, and this shame turned into suspiciousness towards the
neighbours.

Thus the voices owed their origin to the repression of thoughts
which, in the last analysis, were in fact self-reproaches about
experiences that were analogous to her childhood trauma. The
voices were accordingly symptoms of the return of the repressed.
But they were at the same time consequences of a compromise

[1] [Cf. *Studies on Hysteria* (1895d), *Standard Ed.*, **2**, 269 and 282.]

between the resistance of the ego and the power of the returning repressed—a compromise which in this instance had brought about a distortion that went beyond recognition. In other instances in which I had occasion to analyse Frau P.'s voices, the distortion was less great. Nevertheless, the words she heard always had a quality of diplomatic indefiniteness: the insulting allusion was generally deeply hidden; the connection between the separate sentences was disguised by a strange mode of expression, unusual forms of speech and so on—characteristics which are common to the auditory hallucinations of paranoics in general and in which I see the traces of distortion through compromise. For instance, the remark, 'there goes Frau P.; she's looking for a house in the street', meant a threat that she would never recover; for I had promised her that after her treatment she would be able to go back to the small town in which her husband worked. (She had provisionally taken rooms in Vienna for a few months.)

In isolated instances Frau P. also received more definite threats—for example, in regard to her husband's relatives; yet there was still a contrast between the reserved manner in which they were expressed and the torment which the voices caused her. In view of what is known of paranoia apart from this, I am inclined to suppose that there is a gradual impairment of the resistances which weaken the self-reproaches; so that finally the defence fails altogether and the original self-reproach, the actual term of abuse, from which the subject was trying to spare himself, returns in its unaltered form. I do not know, however, whether this course of events is a constant one, or whether the censorship of the words involving the self-reproach may be absent from the beginning or may persist to the end.

It only remains for me now to employ what has been learned from this case of paranoia for making a comparison between paranoia and obsessional neurosis. In each of them, repression has been shown to be the nucleus of the psychical mechanism, and in each what has been repressed is a sexual experience in childhood. In this case of paranoia, too, every obsession sprang from repression; the symptoms of paranoia allow of a classification similar to the one which has proved justified for obsessional neurosis. Part of the symptoms, once again, arise from primary defence—namely, all the delusional ideas which are characterized by distrust and suspicion and which are concerned with ideas of being persecuted by others. In obsessional neurosis the initial self-reproach has been repressed by the formation of the primary symptom of defence: *self-distrust*. With this, the self-reproach is acknowledged as justified; and, to weigh against this, the conscientiousness which the subject has acquired during his healthy interval now protects him from giving credence to the self-reproaches which return in the form of obsessional ideas. In paranoia, the self-reproach is repressed in a manner which may be described as *projection*.[1] It is repressed by erecting the defensive symptom of *distrust of other people*. In this way the subject withdraws his acknowledgement of the self-reproach; and, as if to make up for this, he is deprived of a protection against the self-reproaches which return in his delusional ideas.

Other symptoms of my case of paranoia are to be described as symptoms of the return of the repressed, and they, too, like those of obsessional neurosis, bear the traces of the compromise which alone allows them to enter consciousness. Such are, for instance, my patient's delusional idea of being watched while she was undressing, her visual hallucinations, her hallucinations of sensation and her hearing of voices. In the delusional idea which I have just mentioned there is a mnemic content which is almost unaltered and has only been made indefinite through omission. The return of the repressed in visual images approaches the character of hysteria rather than of obsessional neurosis; but hysteria is in the habit of repeating its mnemic symbols without modification, whereas mnemic hallucinations in paranoia undergo a distortion similar to that in obsessional neurosis: an analogous modern image takes the place of the repressed one. (E.g., the abdomen of an adult woman appears instead of a child's, and an abdomen on which the hairs are especially distinct, because they were absent in the original impression.) A thing which is quite peculiar to paranoia and on which no further light can be shed by this comparison, is that the re-

---

[1] [This seems to be the first published use made by Freud of this term. It occurs in his earlier study of paranoia which was sent to Fliess on January 24, 1895 (Freud, 1950*a*, Draft H), and which examines the concept more fully than the present passage.]

pressed self-reproaches return in the form of thoughts spoken aloud. In the course of this process, they are obliged to submit to twofold distortion: they are subjected to a censorship, which leads to their being replaced by other, associated, thoughts or to their being concealed by an indefinite mode of expression, and they are referred to recent experiences which are no more than analogous to the old ones.

The third group of symptoms that are found in obsessional neurosis, the symptoms of secondary defence, cannot be present as such in paranoia, because no defence can avail against the returning symptoms[1] to which, as we know, belief is attached. In place of this, we find in paranoia another source for the formation of symptoms. The delusional ideas which have arrived in consciousness by means of a compromise (the symptoms of the return [of the repressed]) make demands on the thought-activity of the ego until they can be accepted without contradiction. Since they are not themselves open to influence, the ego must adapt itself to them; and thus what corresponds here to the symptoms of secondary defence in obsessional neurosis is a combinatory delusional formation[2]— *interpretative delusions* which end in an *alteration of the ego*.[3] In this respect, the case under discussion was not complete; at that time my patient did not as yet exhibit any signs of the attempts at interpretation which appeared later. But I have no doubt that if we apply psycho-analysis to this stage of paranoia as well, we shall be able to arrive at a further important result. It should then turn out that the so-called *weakness of memory* of paranoics is also a tendentious one—that is to say, that it is based on repression and serves the ends of repression. A subsequent repression and replacement takes place of memories which are not in the least pathogenic, but which are in contradiction to the alteration of the ego which the symptoms of the return of the repressed so insistently demand.

[1] [I.e. the symptoms of the return of the repressed.]
[2] [I.e. one which attempts to bring the different parts of the material into harmony with each other. In Draft K (see above p. 160 *n.*) Freud used the term 'assimilatory delusions'.]
[3] [See the Editor's Note, p. 161 above.]

THE AETIOLOGY OF HYSTERIA

(1896)

EDITOR'S NOTE

ZUR ÄTIOLOGIE DER HYSTERIE

(a) German Editions:
1896   *Wien. klin. Rdsch.*, **10** (22), 379–81, (23), 395–7, (24),
       413–15, (25), 432–3, and (26), 450–2. (May 31, June
       7, 14, 21 and 28.)
1906   *S.K.S.N.*, **1**, 149–180. (1911, 2nd ed.; 1920, 3rd ed.;
       1922, 4th ed.)
1925   *G.S.*, **1**, 404–38.
1952   *G.W.*, **1**, 425–59.

(b) English Translations:
                     'The Aetiology of Hysteria'
1924   *C.P.*, **1**, 183–219. (Tr. C. M. Baines.)

Included (No. XXXVI) in Freud's own collection of abstracts of his early works (1897*b*). The present translation is a modified version of that of 1924.

According to a footnote in the *Wiener klinische Rundschau* of May 31, 1896, this paper is based on a lecture delivered by Freud before the 'Verein für Psychiatrie und Neurologie' on May 2. The correctness of this date is, however, questionable. In an unpublished letter to Fliess of Thursday, April 16, Freud wrote that on the following Tuesday [April 21] he was due to give a lecture before the 'Psychiatrischer Verein'. He does not specify the topic, but in another unpublished letter, dated April 26 and 28, 1896, he reported having given a lecture before that society on the aetiology of hysteria. He went on to remark that 'the donkeys gave it an icy reception' and that Krafft-Ebing, who was in the chair, said it sounded like a scientific fairy tale. In yet another letter, dated May 30, this time included in the Fliess correspondence (Freud, 1950*a*, Letter 46), he wrote: 'In defiance of my colleagues, I have written out my lecture on the aetiology of hysteria in full for Paschkis [the

editor of the *Rundschau*].' And its publication in fact started in
that paper on the next day. It seems to follow from all this that
the lecture was actually given on April 21, 1896.

The present work may be regarded as an amplified repetition
of the first section of its predecessor, the second paper on the
neuro-psychoses of defence (1896*b*). Freud's findings on the
causes of hysteria are given in fuller detail, with some account
of the difficulties he had to overcome in reaching them. Much
more space is given, especially in the last part of the paper, to
the sexual experiences in childhood which Freud believed to
lie behind the later symptoms. As in the previous papers, these
experiences are regarded as invariably initiated by adults: the
realization of the existence of infantile sexuality still lay in the
future. There is nevertheless a hint (on pp. 214–15) of what was
to be described in the *Three Essays* (1905*d*), *Standard Ed.*, 7, 191,
as the 'polymorphously perverse' character of infantile sexuality.
Among other points of interest, we may note an increasing
tendency to prefer psychological to neurological explanations
(p. 203), and an early attempt at solving the problem of 'choice
of neurosis' (pp. 219–20), which was to be a constantly returning subject of discussion. Freud's varying views on this are
traced in the Editor's Note to 'The Disposition to Obsessional
Neurosis' (1913*i*), *Standard Ed.*, 12, 313 ff.; the subject had in
fact been approached already in the two papers preceding the
present one (pp. 156 and 168–9 above).

THE AETIOLOGY OF HYSTERIA

[I]

GENTLEMEN,—When we set out to form an opinion about the causation of a pathological state such as hysteria, we begin by adopting the method of anamnestic investigation: we question the patient or those about him in order to find out to what harmful influences they themselves attribute his having fallen ill and developed these neurotic symptoms. What we discover in this way is, of course, falsified by all the factors which commonly hide the knowledge of his own state from a patient —by his lack of scientific understanding of aetiological influences, by the fallacy of *post hoc, propter hoc*, by his reluctance to think about or mention certain noxae and traumas. Thus in making an anamnestic investigation of this sort, we keep to the principle of not adopting the patients' belief without a thorough critical examination, of not allowing them to lay down our scientific opinion for us on the aetiology of the neurosis. Although we do, on the one hand, acknowledge the truth of certain constantly repeated assertions, such as that the hysterical state is a long-persisting after-effect of an emotion experienced in the past, we have, on the other hand, introduced into the aetiology of hysteria a factor which the patient himself never brings forward and whose validity he only reluctantly admits —namely, the hereditary disposition derived from his pro- genitors. As you know, in the view of the influential school of Charcot heredity alone deserves to be recognized as the true cause of hysteria, while all other noxae of the most various nature and intensity only play the part of incidental causes, of 'agents provocateurs'.

You will readily admit that it would be a good thing to have a second method of arriving at the aetiology of hysteria, one in which we should feel less dependent on the assertions of the patients themselves. A dermatologist, for instance, is able to recognize a sore as luetic from the character of its margins, of the crust on it and of its shape, without being misled by the

191

protestations of his patient, who denies any source of infection for it; and a forensic physician can arrive at the cause of an injury, even if he has to do without any information from the injured person. In hysteria, too, there exists a similar possibility of penetrating from the symptoms to a knowledge of their causes. But in order to explain the relationship between the method which we have to employ for this purpose and the older method of anamnestic enquiry, I should like to bring before you an analogy taken from an advance that has in fact been made in another field of work.

Imagine that an explorer arrives in a little-known region where his interest is aroused by an expanse of ruins, with remains of walls, fragments of columns, and tablets with half-effaced and unreadable inscriptions. He may content himself with inspecting what lies exposed to view, with questioning the inhabitants—perhaps semi-barbaric people—who live in the vicinity, about what tradition tells them of the history and meaning of these archaeological remains, and with noting down what they tell him—and he may then proceed on his journey. But he may act differently. He may have brought picks, shovels and spades with him, and he may set the inhabitants to work with these implements. Together with them he may start upon the ruins, clear away the rubbish, and, beginning from the visible remains, uncover what is buried. If his work is crowned with success, the discoveries are self-explanatory: the ruined walls are part of the ramparts of a palace or a treasure-house; the fragments of columns can be filled out into a temple; the numerous inscriptions, which, by good luck, may be bilingual, reveal an alphabet and a language, and, when they have been deciphered and translated, yield undreamed-of information about the events of the remote past, to commemorate which the monuments were built. *Saxa loquuntur!*[1]

If we try, in an approximately similar way, to induce the symptoms of a hysteria to make themselves heard as witnesses to the history of the origin of the illness, we must take our start from Josef Breuer's momentous discovery: *the symptoms of hysteria* (apart from the stigmata[2]) *are determined by certain*

---

[1] ['Stones talk!']

[2] [These, defined by Charcot (1887, 255) as 'the permanent symptoms of hysteria', had been described by Freud as non-psychogenic in *Studies*

experiences of the patient's which have operated in a traumatic fashion and which are being reproduced in his psychical life in the form of mnemic symbols.[1] What we have to do is to apply Breuer's method —or one which is essentially the same—so as to lead the patient's attention back from his symptom to the scene in which and through which that symptom arose; and, having thus located the scene, we remove the symptom by bringing about, during the reproduction of the traumatic scene, a subsequent correction of the psychical course of events which took place at the time.

It is no part of my intention to-day to discuss the difficult technique of this therapeutic procedure or the psychological discoveries which have been obtained by its means. I have been obliged to start from this point only because the analyses conducted on Breuer's lines seem at the same time to open up the path to the causes of hysteria. If we subject a fairly large number of symptoms in a great number of subjects to such an analysis, we shall, of course, arrive at a knowledge of a correspondingly large number of traumatically operative scenes. It was in these experiences that the efficient causes of hysteria came into action. Hence we may hope to discover from the study of these traumatic scenes what the influences are which produce hysterical symptoms and in what way they do so.

This expectation proves true; and it cannot fail to, since Breuer's theses, when put to the test in a considerable number of cases, have turned out to be correct. But the path from the symptoms of hysteria to its aetiology is more laborious and leads through other connections than one would have imagined.

For let us be clear on this point. Tracing a hysterical symptom back to a traumatic scene assists our understanding only if the scene satisfies two conditions; if it possesses the relevant *suitability to serve as a determinant* and if it recognizably possesses the necessary *traumatic force*. Instead of a verbal explanation, here is an example. Let us suppose that the symptom under consideration is hysterical vomiting; in that case we shall feel that

on Hysteria (1895*d*), *Standard Ed.*, **2**, 265. They had also been discussed by Breuer, ibid., 244 f. (See also ibid., 15.) In a very early letter to Breuer of June 29, 1892, Freud (1941*a*) had described the origin of these symptoms as 'highly obscure'.]

[1] [See footnote 3, above, p. 49.]

we have been able to understand its causation (except for a
certain residue) if the analysis traces the symptom back to
an experience which *justifiably produced a high amount of disgust*—
for instance, the sight of a decomposing dead body. But if,
instead of this, the analysis shows us that the vomiting arose
from a great fright, e.g. from a railway accident, we shall feel
dissatisfied and will have to ask ourselves how it is that the
fright has led to the particular symptom of vomiting. This
derivation lacks *suitability as a determinant*. We shall have another
instance of an insufficient explanation if the vomiting is supposed
to have arisen from, let us say, eating a fruit which had partly
gone bad. Here, it is true, the vomiting *is* determined by disgust,
but we cannot understand how, in this instance, the disgust
could have become so powerful as to be perpetuated in a
hysterical symptom; the experience lacks *traumatic force*.

Let us now consider how far the traumatic scenes of hysteria
which are uncovered by analysis fulfil, in a fairly large number
of symptoms and cases, the two requirements which I have
named. Here we meet with our first great disappointment. It is
true, indeed, that the traumatic scene in which the symptom
originated does in fact occasionally possess both the qualities
—suitability as a determinant and traumatic force—which we
require for an understanding of the symptom. But far more
frequently, incomparably more frequently, we find one of the
three other possibilities realized, which are so unfavourable to
an understanding. Either the scene to which we are led by
analysis and in which the symptom first appeared seems to us
unsuited for determining the symptom, in that its content bears
no relation to the nature of the symptom; or the allegedly
traumatic experience, though it *does* have a relation to the
symptom, proves to be an impression which is normally
innocuous and incapable as a rule of producing any effect; or,
lastly, the 'traumatic scene' leaves us in the lurch in both
respects, appearing at once innocuous and unrelated to the
character of the hysterical symptom.

(Here I may remark in passing that Breuer's view of the
origin of hysterical symptoms is not shaken by the discovery
of traumatic scenes which correspond to experiences that are
insignificant in themselves. For Breuer assumed—following
Charcot—that even an innocuous experience can be heightened

into a trauma and can develop determining force if it happens
to the subject when he is in a special psychical condition—in
what is described as a *hypnoid state*.[1] I find, however, that there
are often no grounds whatever for presupposing the presence
of such hypnoid states. What remains decisive is that the theory
of hypnoid states contributes nothing to the solution of the
other difficulties, namely that the traumatic scenes so often
lack suitability as determinants.)

Moreover, Gentlemen, this first disappointment we meet
with in following Breuer's method is immediately succeeded
by another, and one that must be especially painful to us as
physicians. When our procedure leads, as in the cases described
above, to findings which are insufficient as an explanation both
in respect to their suitability as determinants and to their
traumatic effectiveness, we also fail to secure any therapeutic
gain; the patient retains his symptoms unaltered, in spite of
the initial result yielded by the analysis. You can understand
how great the temptation is at this point to proceed no further
with what is in any case a laborious piece of work.

But perhaps all we need is a new idea in order to help us out
of our dilemma and lead to valuable results. The idea is this.
As we know from Breuer, hysterical symptoms can be resolved
if, starting from them, we are able to find the path back to the
memory of a traumatic experience. If the memory which we
have uncovered does not answer our expectations, it may be
that we ought to pursue the same path a little further; perhaps
behind the first traumatic scene there may be concealed the
memory of a second, which satisfies our requirements better
and whose reproduction has a greater therapeutic effect; so
that the scene that was first discovered only has the significance
of a connecting link in the chain of associations. And perhaps
this situation may repeat itself; inoperative scenes may be interpolated more than once, as necessary transitions in the process
of reproduction, until we finally make our way from the hysterical
symptom to the scene which is really operative traumatically
and which is satisfactory in every respect, both therapeutically
and analytically. Well, Gentlemen, this supposition is correct.
If the first-discovered scene is unsatisfactory, we tell our patient
that this experience explains nothing, but that behind it there

[1] [See p. 46 above.]

must be hidden a more significant, earlier, experience; and we direct his attention by the same technique to the associative thread which connects the two memories—the one that has been discovered and the one that has still to be discovered.[1] A continuation of the analysis then leads in every instance to the reproduction of new scenes of the character we expect. For example, let us take once again the case of hysterical vomiting which I selected before, and in which the analysis first led back to a fright from a railway accident—a scene which lacked suitability as a determinant. Further analysis showed that this accident had aroused in the patient the memory of another, earlier accident, which, it is true, he had not himself experienced but which had been the occasion of his having a ghastly and revolting sight of a dead body. It is as though the combined operation of the two scenes made the fulfilment of our postulates possible, the one experience supplying, through fright, the traumatic force and the other, from its content, the determining effect. The other case, in which the vomiting was traced back to eating an apple which had partly gone bad, was amplified by the analysis somewhat in the following way. The bad apple reminded the patient of an earlier experience: while he was picking up windfalls in an orchard he had accidentally come upon a dead animal in a revolting state.

I shall not return any further to these examples, for I have to confess that they are not derived from any case in my experience but are inventions of mine. Most probably, too, they are bad inventions. I even regard such solutions of hysterical symptoms as impossible. But I was obliged to make up fictitious examples for several reasons, one of which I can state at once. The real examples are all incomparably more complicated: to relate a single one of them in detail would occupy the whole period of this lecture. The chain of associations always has more than two links; and the traumatic scenes do not form a simple row, like a string of pearls, but ramify and are interconnected like genealogical trees, so that in any new experience two or

---

[1] I purposely leave out of this discussion the question of what the category is to which the association between the two memories belongs (whether it is an association by simultaneity, or by causal connection, or by similarity of content), and of what psychological character is to be attributed to the various 'memories' (conscious or unconscious).

more earlier ones come into operation as memories. In short, giving an account of the resolution of a single symptom would in fact amount to the task of relating an entire case history.

But we must not fail to lay special emphasis on one conclusion to which analytic work along these chains of memory has unexpectedly led. We have learned that *no hysterical symptom can arise from a real experience alone, but that in every case the memory of earlier experiences awakened in association to it plays a part in causing the symptom.* If—as I believe—this proposition holds good *without exception*, it furthermore shows us the basis on which a psychological theory of hysteria must be built.

You might suppose that the rare instances in which analysis is able to trace the symptom back direct to a traumatic scene that is thoroughly suitable as a determinant and possesses traumatic force, and is able, by thus tracing it back, at the same time to remove it (in the way described in Breuer's case history of Anna O.[1])—you might suppose that such instances must, after all, constitute powerful objections to the general validity of the proposition I have just put forward. It certainly looks so. But I must assure you that I have the best grounds for assuming that even in such instances there exists a chain of operative memories which stretches far back behind the first traumatic scene, *even though* the reproduction of the latter alone may have the result of removing the symptom.

It seems to me really astonishing that hysterical symptoms can only arise with the co-operation of memories, especially when we reflect that, according to the unanimous accounts of the patients themselves, these memories did not come into their consciousness at the moment when the symptom first made its appearance. Here is much food for thought; but these problems must not distract us at this point from our discussion of the aetiology of hysteria.[2] We must rather ask ourselves: where shall we get to if we follow the chains of associated memories which the analysis has uncovered? How far do they extend? Do they come anywhere to a natural end? Do they perhaps lead to experiences which are in some way alike, either in their

---

[1] [See p. 29 f. above.]

[2] [Freud takes up the postponed problem below, on p. 212 ff. He had already touched on it in a footnote to Section I of his second paper on the neuro-psychoses of defence (1896*b*), pp. 166–7 *n*. above.]

content or the time of life at which they occur, so that we may discern in these universally similar factors the aetiology of hysteria of which we are in search?

The knowledge I have so far gained already enables me to answer these questions. If we take a case which presents several symptoms, we arrive by means of the analysis, starting from each symptom, at a series of experiences the memories of which are linked together in association. To begin with, the chains of memories lead backwards separately from one another; but, as I have said, they ramify. From a single scene two or more memories are reached at the same time, and from these again side-chains proceed whose individual links may once more be associatively connected with links belonging to the main chain. Indeed, a comparison with the genealogical tree of a family whose members have also intermarried, is not at all a bad one. Other complications in the linkage of the chains arise from the circumstance that a single scene may be called up several times in the same chain, so that it has multiple relationships to a later scene, and exhibits both a direct connection with it and a connection established through intermediate links. In short, the concatenation is far from being a simple one; and the fact that the scenes are uncovered in a reversed chronological order (a fact which justifies our comparison of the work with the excavation of a stratified ruined site) certainly contributes nothing to a more rapid understanding of what has taken place.

If the analysis is carried further, new complications arise. The associative chains belonging to the different symptoms begin to enter into relation with one another; the genealogical trees become intertwined. Thus a particular symptom in, for instance, the chain of memories relating to the symptom of vomiting, calls up not only the earlier links in its own chain but also a memory from another chain, relating to another symptom, such as a headache. This experience accordingly belongs to both series, and in this way it constitutes a *nodal point*[1] Several such nodal points are to be found in every

---

[1] ['Nodal points' had been described by Freud in his technical contribution to *Studies on Hysteria* (1895*d*), *Standard Ed.*, **2**, 290 and 295. It is worth comparing the account of the chains of associations given there (ibid., 288 ff.) with the present much shorter one. An actual instance of a 'nodal point'—the word 'wet'—is described in the analysis of the first dream in the 'Dora' case history (1905*e*), ibid., **7**, 90 f.]

analysis. Their correlate in the clinical picture may perhaps
be that from a certain time onwards both symptoms have
appeared together, symbiotically, without in fact having any
internal dependence on each other. Going still further back,
we come upon nodal points of a different kind. Here the separate
associative chains converge.[1] We find experiences from which
two or more symptoms have proceeded; one chain has attached
itself to one detail of the scene, the second chain to another
detail.

But the most important finding that is arrived at if an analysis
is thus consistently pursued is this. Whatever case and whatever
symptom we take as our point of departure, *in the end we in-
fallibly come to the field of sexual experience.* So here for the first
time we seem to have discovered an aetiological precondition
for hysterical symptoms.

From previous experience I can foresee that it is precisely
against this assertion or against its universal validity that your
contradiction, Gentlemen, will be directed. Perhaps it would
be better to say, your *inclination* to contradict; for none of you,
no doubt, have as yet any investigations at your disposal which,
based upon the same procedure, might have yielded a different
result. As regards the controversial matter itself, I will only
remark that the singling out of the sexual factor in the aetiology
of hysteria springs at least from no preconceived opinion on
my part. The two investigators as whose pupil I began my
studies of hysteria, Charcot and Breuer, were far from having
any such presupposition; in fact they had a personal disinclina-
tion to it which I originally shared. Only the most laborious
and detailed investigations have converted me, and that slowly
enough, to the view I hold to-day. If you submit my assertion
that the aetiology of hysteria lies in sexual life to the strictest
examination, you will find that it is supported by the fact that
in some eighteen[2] cases of hysteria I have been able to discover
this connection in every single symptom, and, where the circumstances allowed, to confirm it by therapeutic success. No

[1] [The regular occurrence first of divergence and then of convergence
in chains of associations is also mentioned by Freud as characteristic
of dream-analysis. Cf. Section II of 'Remarks on the Theory and
Practice of Dream Interpretation' (1923c), *Standard Ed.*, **19**, 110.]
[2] [Cf. the earlier figure of thirteen (pp. 152 and 163 above.)]

doubt you may raise the objection that the nineteenth or the twentieth analysis will perhaps show that hysterical symptoms are derived from other sources as well, and thus reduce the universal validity of the sexual aetiology to one of eighty per cent. By all means let us wait and see; but, since these eighteen cases are at the same time *all* the cases on which I have been able to carry out the work of analysis and since they were not picked out by anyone for my convenience, you will find it understandable that I do not share such an expectation but am prepared to let my belief run ahead of the evidential force of the observations I have so far made. Besides, I am influenced by another motive as well, which for the moment is of merely subjective value. In the sole attempt to explain the physiological and psychical mechanism of hysteria which I have been able to make in order to correlate my observations, I have come to regard the participation of sexual motive forces as an indispensable premiss.

Eventually, then, after the chains of memories have converged, we come to the field of sexuality and to a small number of experiences which occur for the most part at the same period of life—namely, at puberty. It is in these experiences, it seems, that we are to look for the aetiology of hysteria, and through them that we are to learn to understand the origin of hysterical symptoms. But here we meet with a fresh disappointment and a very serious one. It is true that these experiences, which have been discovered with so much trouble and extracted out of all the mnemic material, and which seemed to be the ultimate traumatic experiences, have in common the two characteristics of being sexual and of occurring at puberty; but in every other respect they are very different from each other both in *kind* and in *importance*. In some cases, no doubt, we are concerned with experiences which must be regarded as severe traumas—an attempted rape, perhaps, which reveals to the immature girl at a blow all the brutality of sexual desire, or the involuntary witnessing of sexual acts between parents, which at one and the same time uncovers unsuspected ugliness and wounds childish and moral sensibilities alike, and so on. But in other cases the experiences are astonishingly trivial. In one of my women patients it turned out that her neurosis was based on the experience of a boy of her acquaintance stroking her hand tenderly and, at another time, pressing his knee against her dress as they sat side by side at table, while his expression let her see that he was doing something forbidden. For another young lady, simply hearing a riddle which suggested an obscene answer had been enough to provoke the first anxiety attack and with it to start the illness. Such findings are clearly not favourable to an understanding of the causation of hysterical symptoms. If serious and trifling events alike, and if not only experiences affecting the subject's own body but visual impressions too and information received through the ears are to be recognized as the ultimate traumas of hysteria, then we may be tempted to hazard the explanation that hysterics are peculiarly constituted creatures—probably on account of some hereditary disposition or degenerative atrophy—in whom a shrinking from sexuality, which normally plays some part at puberty, is raised to a pathological pitch and is permanently retained; that they are, as it were, people who are psychically inadequate to meeting the demands of sexuality. This view, of course, leaves hysteria in men out of account. But even without blatant objections such as that, we should scarcely be tempted to be satisfied with this solution. We are only too distinctly conscious of an intellectual sense of something half-understood, unclear and insufficient.

Luckily for our explanation, some of these sexual experiences at puberty exhibit a further inadequacy, which is calculated to stimulate us into continuing our analytic work. For it sometimes happens that they, too, lack suitability as determinants— although this is much more rarely so than with the traumatic scenes belonging to later life. Thus, for instance, let us take the two women patients whom I have just spoken of as cases in which the experiences at puberty were actually innocent ones. As a result of those experiences the patients had become subject to peculiar painful sensations in the genitals which had established themselves as the main symptoms of the neurosis. I was unable to find indications that they had been determined either by the scenes at puberty or by later scenes; but they were certainly not normal organic sensations nor signs of sexual excitement. It seemed an obvious thing, then, to say to ourselves that we must look for the determinants of these symptoms in yet other experiences, in experiences which went still further back—and that we must, for the second time, follow the saving notion which had earlier led us from the first traumatic scenes to the chains of memories behind them. In doing so, to be sure, we arrive at the period of earliest childhood, a period before the development of sexual life; and this would seem to involve the abandonment of a sexual aetiology. But have we not a right to assume that even the age of childhood is not wanting in slight sexual excitations, that later sexual development may perhaps be decisively influenced by childhood experiences? Injuries sustained by an organ which is as yet immature, or by a function which is in process of developing, often cause more severe and lasting effects than they could do in maturer years. Perhaps the abnormal reaction to sexual impressions which surprises us in hysterical subjects at the age of puberty is quite generally based on sexual experiences of this sort in childhood, in which case those experiences must be of a similar nature to one another, and must be of an important kind. If this is so, the prospect is opened up that what has hitherto had to be laid at the door of a still unexplained hereditary pre-disposition may be accounted for as having been acquired at an early age. And since infantile experiences with a sexual content could after all only exert a psychical effect through their *memory-traces*, would not this view be a welcome amplification of the finding of psycho-analysis which tells *us that hysterical symptoms can only arise with the co-operation of memories?* [P. 197 above.]

II

You will no doubt have guessed, Gentlemen, that I should not have carried this last line of thought so far if I had not wanted to prepare you for the idea that it is this line alone which, after so many delays, will lead us to our goal. For now we are really at the end of our wearisome and laborious analytic work, and here we find the fulfilment of all the claims and expectations upon which we have so far insisted. If we have the perseverance to press on with the analysis into early childhood, as far back as a human memory is capable of reaching, we invariably bring the patient to reproduce experiences which, on account both of their peculiar features and of their relations to the symptoms of his later illness, must be regarded as the aetiology of his neurosis for which we have been looking. These *infantile* experiences are once more *sexual* in content, but they are of a far more uniform kind than the scenes at puberty that had been discovered earlier. It is now no longer a question of sexual topics having been aroused by some sense impression or other, but of sexual experiences affecting the subject's own body —of *sexual intercourse* (in the wider sense). You will admit that the *importance* of such scenes needs no further proof; to this may now be added that, in every instance, you will be able to discover in the details of the scenes the *determining* factors which you may have found lacking in the other scenes—the scenes which occurred later and were reproduced earlier. [Cf. p. 193.]

I therefore put forward the thesis that at the bottom of every case of hysteria there are *one or more occurrences of premature sexual experience,* occurrences which belong to the earliest years of childhood but which can be reproduced through the work of psycho-analysis in spite of the intervening decades.[1] I believe that this is an important finding, the discovery of a *caput Nili*[2] in neuropathology; but I hardly know what to take as a starting-point for a continuation of my discussion of this subject. Shall I put before you the actual material I have obtained from my analyses? Or shall I rather try first to meet the mass of objections and doubts which, as I am surely correct in supposing, have now taken possession of your attention? I shall choose the latter course; perhaps we shall then be able to go over the facts more calmly.

(*a*) No one who is altogether opposed to a psychological view of hysteria, who is unwilling to give up the hope that some day it will be possible to trace back its symptoms to 'finer anatomical changes' and who has rejected the view that the material foundations of hysterical changes are bound to be of the same kind as those of our normal mental processes—no one who adopts this attitude will, of course, put any faith in the results of our analyses; however, the difference in principle between his premises and ours absolves us from the obligation of convincing him on individual points.

[1] (*Footnote added* 1924:) Cf. my remark on p. 204.
[2] [Source of the Nile.]

But other people, too, although they may be less averse to psychological theories of hysteria, will be tempted, when considering our analytic findings, to ask what degree of certainty the application of psycho-analysis offers. Is it not very possible either that the physician forces such scenes upon his docile patients, alleging that they are memories, or else that the patients tell the physician things which they have deliberately invented or have imagined and that he accepts those things as true? Well, my answer to this is that the general doubt about the reliability of the psycho-analytic method can be appraised and removed only when a complete presentation of its technique and results is available. Doubts about the genuineness of the infantile sexual scenes can, however, be deprived of their force here and now by more than one argument. In the first place, the behaviour of patients while they are reproducing these infantile experiences is in every respect incompatible with the assumption that the scenes are anything else than a reality which is being felt with distress and reproduced with the greatest reluctance. Before they come for analysis the patients know nothing about these scenes. They are indignant as a rule if we warn them that such scenes are going to emerge. Only the strongest compulsion of the treatment can induce them to embark on a reproduction of them. While they are recalling these infantile experiences to consciousness, they suffer under the most violent sensations, of which they are ashamed and which they try to conceal; and, even after they have gone through them once more in such a convincing manner, they still attempt to withhold belief from them, by emphasizing the fact that, unlike what happens in the case of other forgotten material, they have no feeling of remembering the scenes.[1]

This latter piece of behaviour seems to provide conclusive proof. Why should patients assure me so emphatically of their unbelief, if what they want to discredit is something which—from whatever motive—they themselves have invented?

It is less easy to refute the idea that the doctor forces reminiscences of this sort on the patient, that he influences him

---

[1] (*Footnote added* 1924:) All this is true; but it must be remembered that at the time I wrote it I had not yet freed myself from my *overvaluation* of reality and my *low valuation* of phantasy. [Cf. the additional footnote to the previous paper, p. 168 above.]

by suggestion to imagine and reproduce them. Nevertheless it appears to me equally untenable. I have never yet succeeded in forcing on a patient a scene I was expecting to find, in such a way that he seemed to be living through it with all the appropriate feelings. Perhaps others may be more successful in this.

There are, however, a whole number of other things that vouch for the reality of infantile sexual scenes. In the first place there is the uniformity which they exhibit in certain details, which is a necessary consequence if the preconditions of these experiences are always of the same kind, but which would otherwise lead us to believe that there were secret understandings between the various patients. In the second place, patients sometimes describe as harmless events whose significance they obviously do not understand, since they would be bound otherwise to be horrified by them. Or again, they mention details, without laying any stress on them, which only someone of experience in life can understand and appreciate as subtle traits of reality.

Events of this sort strengthen our impression that the patients must really have experienced what they reproduce under the compulsion of analysis as scenes from their childhood. But another and stronger proof of this is furnished by the relationship of the infantile scenes to the content of the whole of the rest of the case history. It is exactly like putting together a child's picture-puzzle: after many attempts, we become absolutely certain in the end which piece belongs in the empty gap; for only that one piece fills out the picture and at the same time allows its irregular edges to be fitted into the edges of the other pieces in such a manner as to leave no free space and to entail no overlapping.[1] In the same way, the contents of the infantile scenes turn out to be indispensable supplements to the associative and logical framework of the neurosis, whose insertion makes its course of development for the first time evident, or even, as we might often say, self-evident.

Without wishing to lay special stress on the point, I will add

---

[1] [This analogy was used by Freud again more than a quarter of a century later, in a period when 'jig-saw' puzzles had become an adult pastime. See 'Remarks on the Theory and Practice of Dream Interpretation' (1923c), *Standard Ed.*, **19**, 116.]

that in a number of cases therapeutic evidence of the genuineness of the infantile scenes can also be brought forward. There are cases in which a complete or partial cure can be obtained without our having to go as deep as the infantile experiences. And there are others in which no success at all is obtained until the analysis has come to its natural end with the uncovering of the earliest traumas. In the former cases we are not, I believe, secure against relapses; and my expectation is that a complete psycho-analysis implies a radical cure of the hysteria.[1] We must not, however, be led into forestalling the lessons of observation.

There would be one other proof, and a really unassailable one, of the genuineness of childhood sexual experiences—namely, if the statements of someone who is being analysed were to be confirmed by someone else, whether under treatment or not. These two people will have had to have taken part in the same experience in their childhood—perhaps to have stood in some sexual relationship to each other. Such relations between children are, as you will hear in a moment [p. 208], by no means rare. Moreover, it quite often happens that both of those concerned subsequently fall ill of neuroses; yet I regard it as a fortunate accident that, out of eighteen cases, I have been able to obtain an objective confirmation of this sort in two. In one instance, it was the brother (who had remained well) who of his own accord confirmed—not, it is true, his earliest sexual experiences with his sister (who was the patient)—but at least scenes of that kind from later childhood, and the fact that there had been sexual relations dating further back. In the other instance, it happened that two women whom I was treating had as children had sexual relations with the same man, in the course of which certain scenes had taken place à trois. A particular symptom, which was derived from these childhood events, had developed in both women, as evidence of what they had experienced in common.

(b) Sexual experiences in childhood consisting in stimulation of the genitals, coitus-like acts, and so on, must therefore be

---

[1] [It is of interest to compare this with the less sanguine views expressed by Freud in his very late paper, 'Analysis Terminable and Interminable' (1937c).]

recognized, in the last analysis, as being the traumas which lead to a hysterical reaction to events at puberty and to the development of hysterical symptoms. This statement is certain to be met from different directions by two mutually contradictory objections. Some people will say that sexual abuses of this kind, whether practised upon children or between them, happen too seldom for it to be possible to regard them as the determinant of such a common neurosis as hysteria. Others will perhaps argue that, on the contrary, such experiences are very frequent—much too frequent for us to be able to attribute an aetiological significance to the fact of their occurrence. They will further maintain that it is easy, by making a few enquiries, to find people who remember scenes of sexual seduction and sexual abuse in their childhood years, and yet who have never been hysterical. Finally we shall be told, as a weighty argument, that in the lower strata of the population hysteria is certainly no more common than in the highest ones, whereas everything goes to show that the injunction for the sexual safeguarding of childhood is far more frequently transgressed in the case of the children of the proletariat.

Let us begin our defence with the easier part of the task. It seems to me certain that our children are far more often exposed to sexual assaults than the few precautions taken by parents in this connection would lead us to expect. When I first made enquiries about what was known on the subject, I learnt from colleagues that there are several publications by paediatricians which stigmatize the frequency of sexual practices by nurses and nursery maids, carried out even on infants in arms; and in the last few weeks I have come across a discussion of 'Coitus in Childhood' by Dr. Stekel (1895)[1] in Vienna. I have not had time to collect other published evidence; but even if it were only scanty, it is to be expected that increased attention to the subject will very soon confirm the great frequency of sexual experiences and sexual activity in childhood.

Lastly, the findings of my analysis are in a position to speak for themselves. In all eighteen cases (cases of pure hysteria and of hysteria combined with obsessions, and comprising six men

[1] [This date is wrongly given as '1896' in the German editions. Incidentally, Stekel only came to hear of Freud some five years after this. Cf. Jones, 1955, 8.]

and twelve women) I have, as I have said, come to learn of
sexual experiences of this kind in childhood. I can divide my
cases into three groups, according to the origin of the sexual
stimulation. In the first group it is a question of assaults—of
single, or at any rate isolated, instances of abuse, mostly
practised on female children, by adults who were strangers,
and who, incidentally, knew how to avoid inflicting gross,
mechanical injury. In these assaults there was no question of
the child's consent, and the first effect of the experience was
preponderantly one of fright. The second group consists of the
much more numerous cases in which some adult looking after
the child—a nursery maid or governess or tutor, or, unhappily
all too often, a close relative[1]—has initiated the child into
sexual intercourse and has maintained a regular love relationship with it—a love relationship, moreover, with its mental side
developed—which has often lasted for years. The third group,
finally, contains child-relationships proper—sexual relations
between two children of different sexes, mostly a brother and
sister, which are often prolonged beyond puberty and which
have the most far-reaching consequences for the pair. In most
of my cases I found that two or more of these aetiologies were
in operation together; in a few instances the accumulation of
sexual experiences coming from different quarters was truly
amazing. You will easily understand this peculiar feature of
my observations, however, when you consider that the patients
I was treating were all cases of severe neurotic illness which
threatened to make life impossible.

Where there had been a relation between two children I
was sometimes able to prove that the boy—who, here too,
played the part of the aggressor—had previously been seduced
by an adult of the female sex, and that afterwards, under the
pressure of his prematurely awakened libido and compelled by
his memory, he tried to repeat with the little girl exactly the
same practices that he had learned from the adult woman,
without making any modification of his own in the character
of the sexual activity.

In view of this, I am inclined to suppose that children cannot
find their way to acts of sexual aggression unless they have been
seduced previously. The foundation for a neurosis would

---

[1] [Cf. an Editor's footnote to the previous paper, p. 164 above.]

accordingly always be laid in childhood by adults, and the children themselves would transfer to one another the disposition to fall ill of hysteria later. I will ask you to consider a moment longer the special frequency with which sexual relations in childhood occur precisely between brothers and sisters and cousins, as a result of their opportunities for being together so often; supposing, then, ten or fifteen years later several members of the younger generation of the family are found to be ill, might not this appearance of a family neurosis naturally lead to the false supposition that a hereditary disposition is present where there is only a *pseudo-heredity* and where in fact what has taken place is a handing-on, an infection in childhood?

Now let us turn to the other objection [p. 207], which is based precisely on an acknowledgement of the frequency of infantile sexual experiences and on the observed fact that many people who remember scenes of that kind have *not* become hysterics. Our first reply is that the excessive frequency of an aetiological factor cannot possibly be used as an objection to its aetiological significance.[1] Is not the tubercle bacillus ubiquitous and is it not inhaled by far more people than are found to fall ill of tuberculosis? And is its aetiological significance impaired by the fact that other factors must obviously be at work too before the tuberculosis, which is its specific effect, can be evoked? In order to establish the bacillus as the specific aetiology it is enough to show that tuberculosis cannot possibly occur without its playing a part. The same doubtless applies to our problem. It does not matter if many people experience infantile sexual scenes without becoming hysterics, provided only that all the people who become hysterics have experienced scenes of that kind. The area of occurrence of an aetiological factor may be freely allowed to be wider than that of its effect, but it must not be narrower. Not everyone who touches or comes near a smallpox patient develops smallpox; nevertheless infection from a smallpox patient is almost the only known aetiology of the disease.

It is true that if infantile sexual activity were an almost

[1] [The whole question of 'specific aetiology' had been discussed by Freud more fully in his second paper on anxiety neurosis (1895f), p. 135 ff. above.]

universal occurrence the demonstration of its presence in every case would carry no weight. But, to begin with, to assert such a thing would certainly be a gross exaggeration; and secondly, the aetiological pretensions of the infantile scenes rest not only on the regularity of their appearance in the anamneses of hysterics, but, above all, on the evidence of there being associative and logical ties between those scenes and the hysterical symptoms—evidence which, if you were given the complete history of a case, would be as clear as daylight to you.

What can the other factors be which the 'specific aetiology' of hysteria still needs in order actually to produce the neurosis? That, Gentlemen, is a theme in itself, which I do not propose to enter upon. To-day I need only indicate the point of contact at which the two parts of the topic—the specific and the auxiliary aetiology—fit into one another. No doubt a considerable quantity of factors will have to be taken into account. There will be the subject's inherited and personal constitution, the inherent importance of the infantile sexual experiences, and, above all, their number: a brief relationship with a strange boy, who afterwards becomes indifferent, will leave a less powerful effect on a girl than intimate sexual relations of several years' standing with her own brother. In the aetiology of the neuroses quantitative preconditions are as important as qualitative ones: there are threshold-values which have to be crossed before the illness can become manifest. Moreover, I do not myself regard this aetiological series as complete; nor does it solve the riddle of why hysteria is not more common among the lower classes.[1] (You will remember, by the way, what a surprisingly large incidence of hysteria was reported by Charcot among working-class *men*). I may also remind you that a few years ago I myself pointed out a factor, hitherto little considered, to which I attribute the leading role in provoking hysteria after puberty. I then[2] put forward the view that the outbreak of hysteria may almost invariably be traced to a *psychical conflict* arising through an incompatible idea setting in action a *defence* on the part of the ego and calling up a demand

[1] [Cf. above, p. 207.]
[2] [See Freud's first paper on the neuro-psychoses of defence (1894*a*), p. 47 f. above.]

for repression. What the circumstances are in which a defensive endeavour of this kind has the pathological effect of actually thrusting the memory which is distressing to the ego into the unconscious and of creating a hysterical symptom in its place I was not able to say at that time. But to-day I can repair the omission. *The defence achieves its purpose of thrusting the incompatible idea out of consciousness if there are infantile sexual scenes present in the (hitherto normal) subject in the form of unconscious memories, and if the idea that is to be repressed can be brought into logical or associative connection with an infantile experience of that kind.*

Since the ego's efforts at defence depend upon the subject's total moral and intellectual development, the fact that hysteria is so much rarer in the lower classes than its specific aetiology would warrant is no longer entirely incomprehensible.

Let us return once again, Gentlemen, to the last group of objections, the answering of which has led us such a long way. We have heard and have acknowledged that there are numerous people who have a very clear recollection of infantile sexual experiences and who nevertheless do not suffer from hysteria. This objection has no weight; but it provides an occasion for making a valuable comment. According to our understanding of the neurosis, people of this kind *ought* not to be hysterical at all, or at any rate, not hysterical as a result of the scenes which they consciously remember. With our patients, those memories are never conscious; but we cure them of their hysteria by transforming their unconscious memories of the infantile scenes into conscious ones. There was nothing that we could have done or needed to do about the fact that they have had such experiences. From this you will perceive that the matter is not merely one of the existence of the sexual experiences, but that a psychological precondition enters in as well. The scenes must be present as *unconscious memories*; only so long as, and in so far as, they are unconscious are they able to create and maintain hysterical symptoms. But what decides whether those experiences produce conscious or unconscious memories—whether that is conditioned by the content of the experiences, or by the time at which they occur, or by later influences—that is a fresh problem, which we shall prudently avoid. Let me merely remind you that, as its first conclusion, analysis has arrived at the proposition that *hysterical symptoms are derivatives of memories which are operating unconsciously.*

(*c*) Our view then is that infantile sexual experiences are the fundamental precondition for hysteria, are, as it were, the *disposition* for it and that it is they which create the hysterical symptoms, but that they do not do so immediately, but remain without effect to begin with and only exercise a pathogenic action later, when they have been aroused after puberty in the form of unconscious memories. If we maintain this view, we shall have to come to terms with the numerous observations which show that a hysterical illness may already make its appearance in childhood and before puberty. This difficulty, however, is cleared up as soon as we examine more closely the data gathered from analyses concerning the chronology of the infantile experiences. We then learn that in our severe cases the formation of hysterical symptoms begins—not in exceptional instances, but, rather, as a regular thing—at the age of eight, and that the sexual experiences which show no immediate effect invariably date further back, into the third or fourth, or even the second year of life. Since in no single instance does the chain of effective experiences[1] break off at the age of eight, I must assume that this time of life, the period of growth in which the second dentition takes place, forms a boundary line for hysteria, after which the illness cannot be caused. From then on, a person who has not had sexual experiences earlier can no longer become disposed to hysteria; and a person who *has* had experiences earlier, is already able to develop hysterical symptoms. Isolated instances of the occurrence of hysteria on the other side of this boundary line (that is, *before* the age of eight) may be interpreted as a phenomenon of precocious maturity. The existence of this boundary-line is very probably connected with developmental processes in the sexual system. Precocity of somatic sexual development may often be observed, and it is even possible that it can be promoted by too early sexual stimulation.[2]

[1] [The sense would appear to suggest that this is a condensed way of saying 'experiences that might be expected to be effective'.]
[2] [Cf. the long footnote in Section I of the previous paper (1896*b*), pp. 166–7 above.]

In this way we obtain an indication that a certain *infantile* state of the psychical functions, as well as of the sexual system, is required in order that a sexual experience occurring during this period shall later on, in the form of a memory, produce a pathogenic effect. I do not venture as yet, however, to make any more precise statement on the nature of this psychical infantilism or on its chronological limits.

(*d*) Another objection might arise from exception being taken to the supposition that the *memory* of infantile sexual experiences produces such an enormous pathogenic effect, while the actual experience itself has none. And it is true that we are not accustomed to the notion of powers emanating from a mnemic image which were absent from the real impression. You will moreover notice the consistency with which the proposition that symptoms can only proceed from memories is carried through in hysteria. None of the later scenes, in which the symptoms arise, are the effective ones; and the experiences which *are* effective have at first no result. But here we are faced with a problem which we may very justifiably keep separate from our theme. It is true that we feel impelled to make a synthesis, when we survey the number of striking conditions that we have come to know: the fact that in order to form a hysterical symptom a defensive effort against a distressing idea must be present, that this idea must exhibit a logical or associative connection with an unconscious memory through a few or many intermediate links, which themselves, too, remain unconscious at the moment, that this unconscious memory must have a sexual content, that its content must be an experience which occurred during a certain infantile period of life. It is true that we cannot help asking ourselves how it comes about that this memory of an experience that was innocuous at the time it happened, should posthumously produce the abnormal effect of leading a psychical process like defence to a pathological result, while it itself remains unconscious.

But we shall have to tell ourselves that this is a purely psychological problem, whose solution may perhaps necessitate certain hypotheses about normal psychical processes and about the part played in them by consciousness, but that this problem may be allowed to remain unsolved for the time being, without detracting from the value of the insight we have so far gained into the aetiology of hysterical phenomena.

III

Gentlemen, the problem, the approaches to which I have just formulated, concerns the *mechanism* of the formation of hysterical symptoms. We find ourselves obliged, however, to describe the *causation* of those symptoms without taking that mechanism into account, and this involves an inevitable loss of completeness and clarity in our discussion. Let us go back to the part played by the infantile sexual scenes. I am afraid that I may have misled you into over-estimating their power to form symptoms. Let me, therefore, once more stress the fact that every case of hysteria exhibits symptoms which are determined, not by infantile but by later, often by recent, experiences. Other symptoms, it is true, go back to the very earliest experiences and belong, so to speak, to the most ancient nobility. Among these latter are above all to be found the numerous and diverse sensations and paraesthesias of the genital organs and other parts of the body, these sensations and paraesthesias being phenomena which simply correspond to the sensory content of the infantile scenes, reproduced in a hallucinatory fashion, often painfully intensified.

Another set of exceedingly common hysterical phenomena—painful need to urinate, the sensation accompanying defaecation, intestinal disturbances, choking and vomiting, indigestion and disgust at food—were also shown in my analyses (and with surprising regularity) to be derivatives of the same childhood experiences and were explained without difficulty by certain invariable peculiarities of those experiences. For the idea of these infantile sexual scenes is very repellent to the feelings of a sexually normal individual; they include all the abuses known to debauched and impotent persons, among whom the buccal cavity and the rectum are misused for sexual purposes. For physicians, astonishment at this soon gives way to a complete understanding. People who have no hesitation in satisfying their sexual desires upon children cannot be expected to jib a finer shades in the methods of obtaining that satisfaction; and the sexual impotence which is inherent in children inevitably forces them into the same substitutive actions as those to which adults descend if they become impotent. All the singular conditions under which the ill-matched pair conduct their love-relations—on the one hand the adult, who cannot escape his share in the mutual dependence necessarily entailed by a sexual relationship, and who is yet armed with complete authority and the right to punish, and can exchange the one role for the other to the uninhibited satisfaction of his moods, and on the other hand the child, who in his helplessness is at the mercy of this arbitrary will, who is prematurely aroused to every kind of sensibility and exposed to every sort of disappointment, and whose performance of the sexual activities assigned to him is often interrupted by his imperfect control of his natural needs —all these grotesque and yet tragic incongruities reveal themselves as stamped upon the later development of the individual and of his neurosis, in countless permanent effects which deserve to be traced in the greatest detail. Where the relation is between two children, the character of the sexual scenes is none the less of the same repulsive sort, since every such relationship between children postulates a previous seduction of one of them by an adult. The psychical consequences of these child-relations are quite extraordinarily far-reaching; the two individuals remain linked by an invisible bond throughout the whole of their lives.

Sometimes it is the accidental circumstances of these infantile sexual scenes which in later years acquire a determining power over the symptoms of the neurosis. Thus, in one of my cases the circumstance that the child was required to stimulate the genitals of a grown-up woman with his foot was enough to fixate his neurotic attention for years on to his legs and to their function, and finally to produce a hysterical paraplegia. In another case, a woman patient suffering from anxiety attacks which tended to come on at certain hours of the day could not be calmed unless a particular one of her many sisters stayed by her side all the time. Why this was so would have remained a riddle if analysis had not shown that the man who had committed the assaults on her used to enquire at every visit whether this sister, who he was afraid might interrupt him, was at home.

It may happen that the determining power of the infantile scenes is so much concealed that, in a superficial analysis, it is bound to be overlooked. In such instances we imagine that we have found the explanation of some particular symptom in the content of one of the later scenes—until, in the course of our work, we come upon the same content in one of the *infantile* scenes, so that in the end we are obliged to recognize that, after all, the later scene only owes its power of determining symptoms to its agreement with the earlier one. I do not wish because of this to represent the later scene as being unimportant; if it was my task to put before you the rules that govern the formation of hysterical symptoms, I should have to include as one of them that the idea which is selected for the production of a symptom is one which has been called up by a combination of several factors and which has been aroused from various directions simultaneously. I have elsewhere tried to express this in the formula: *hysterical symptoms are overdetermined.*[1]

One thing more, Gentlemen. It is true that earlier [p. 213 f.] I put the relation between recent and infantile aetiology aside as a separate theme. Nevertheless, I cannot leave the subject without overstepping this resolution at least with one remark. You will agree with me that there is *one* fact above all which leads us astray in the psychological understanding of hysterical phenomena, and which seems to warn us against measuring psychical acts in hysterics and in normal people with the same yardstick. That fact is the discrepancy between psychically exciting stimuli and psychical reactions which we come upon in hysterical subjects. We try to account for it by assuming the presence in them of a general abnormal sensitivity to stimuli, and we often endeavour to explain it on a physiological basis, as if in such patients certain organs of the brain which serve to transmit stimuli were in a peculiar chemical state (like the spinal centres of a frog, perhaps, which has been injected with strychnine) or as if these cerebral organs had withdrawn from the influence of higher inhibiting centres (as in animals being experimented on under vivisection). Occasionally one or other of these concepts may be perfectly valid as an explanation of hysterical phenomena; I do not dispute this. But the main part

[1] [See Freud's technical contribution to *Studies on Hysteria* (1895*d*), *Standard Ed.*, **2**, 263 and 290.]

of the phenomenon—of the abnormal, exaggerated, hysterical reaction to psychical stimuli—admits of another explanation, an explanation which is supported by countless examples from the analyses of patients. And this is as follows: *The reaction of hysterics is only apparently exaggerated; it is bound to appear exaggerated to us because we only know a small part of the motives from which it arises.*

In reality, this reaction is proportionate to the exciting stimulus; thus it is normal and psychologically understandable. We see this at once when the analysis has added to the manifest motives, of which the patient is conscious, those other motives, which have been operative without his knowing about them, so that he could not tell us of them.

I could spend hours demonstrating the validity of this important assertion for the whole range of psychical activity in hysteria, but I must confine myself here to a few examples. You will remember the mental 'sensitiveness' which is so frequent among hysterical patients and which leads them to react to the least sign of being depreciated as though they had received a deadly insult. What would you think, now, if you were to observe this high degree of readiness to feel hurt on the slightest occasion, if you came across it between two normal people, a husband and wife, perhaps? You would certainly infer that the conjugal scene you had witnessed was not solely the result of this latest trifling occasion, but that inflammable material had been piling up for a long time and that the whole heap of it had been set alight by the final provocation.

I would ask you to carry this line of thought over on to hysterical patients. It is not the latest slight—which, in itself, is minimal—that produces the fit of crying, the outburst of despair or the attempt at suicide, in disregard of the axiom that an effect must be proportionate to its cause; the small slight of the present moment has aroused and set working the memories of very many, more intense, earlier slights, behind all of which there lies in addition the memory of a serious slight in childhood which has never been overcome. Or again, let us take the instance of a young girl who blames herself most frightfully for having allowed a boy to stroke her hand in secret, and who from that time on has been overtaken by a neurosis. You can, of course, answer the puzzle by pronouncing her an abnormal, eccentrically disposed and over-sensitive person; but you will think differently when analysis shows you that the touching of her hand reminded her of another, similar touching, which had happened very early in her childhood and which formed part of a less innocent whole, so that her self-reproaches were actually reproaches about that old occasion. Finally, the problem of the hysterogenic points[1] is of the same kind. If you touch a particular spot, you do something you did not intend: you awaken a memory which may start off a convulsive attack, and since you know nothing of this psychical intermediate link you refer the attack directly to the operation of your touch. The patients are in the same state of ignorance and therefore fall into similar errors. They constantly establish 'false connections'[2] between the most recent cause, which they are conscious of, and the effect, which depends on so many intermediate links. If, however, the physician has been able to bring together the conscious and unconscious motives for the purpose of explaining a hysterical reaction, he is almost always obliged to recognize that the seemingly exaggerated reaction is appropriate and is abnormal only in its form.

You may, however, rightly object to this justification of the hysterical reaction to psychical stimuli and say that nevertheless the reaction is not a normal one. For why do healthy people behave differently? Why do not all *their* excitations of long ago come into operation once more when a new, present-day, excitation takes place? One has an impression, indeed, that with hysterical patients it is as if all their old experiences—to which they have already reacted so often and, moreover, so violently—had retained their effective power; as if such people were incapable of disposing of their psychical stimuli. Quite true, Gentlemen, something of the sort must really be assumed. You must not forget that in hysterical people when there is a present-day precipitating cause, the old experiences come into operation in the form of *unconscious memories*. It looks as though the difficulty of disposing of a present impression, the im-

----

[1] [The term used by Charcot, e.g. 1887, 85 ff., is 'hysterogenic zones'; but the present word appears also in Freud's contribution to *Studies on Hysteria*, Standard Ed., **2**, 261.]

[2] [See Section II of the first paper on the neuro-psychoses of defence (1894*a*), p. 52 above.]

possibility of transforming it into a powerless memory, is attached precisely to the character of the psychical unconscious.[1] You see that the remainder of the problem lies once more in the field of psychology—and, what is more, a psychology of a kind for which philosophers have done little to prepare the way for us.

To this psychology, which has yet to be created to meet our needs—to this future *psychology of the neuroses*—I must also refer you when, in conclusion, I tell you something which will at first make you afraid that it may disturb our dawning comprehension of the aetiology of hysteria. For I must affirm that the aetiological role of infantile sexual experience is not confined to hysteria but holds good equally for the remarkable neurosis of obsessions, and perhaps also, indeed, for the various forms of chronic paranoia and other functional psychoses. I express myself on this with less definiteness, because I have as yet analysed far fewer cases of obsessional neurosis than of hysteria; and as regards paranoia, I have at my disposal only a single full analysis and a few fragmentary ones. But what I discovered in these cases seemed to be reliable and filled me with confident expectations for other cases. You will perhaps remember that already, at an earlier date,[2] I recommended that hysteria and obsessions should be grouped together under the name of '*neuroses of defence*', even before I had come to know of their common infantile aetiology. I must now add that—although this need not be expected to happen in general—every one of my cases of obsessions revealed a substratum of hysterical symptoms,[3] mostly sensations and pains, which went back precisely to the earliest childhood experiences. What, then, determines whether the infantile sexual scenes which have remained unconscious will later on, when the other pathogenic factors are super-added, give rise to hysterical or to obsessional neurosis or even to paranoia? This increase in our knowledge seems, as you see, to prejudice the aetiological value of these scenes, since it removes the specificity of the aetiological relation.

---

[1] [This is an early hint of Freud's later view of the 'timelessness' of the unconscious. See Section V of the metapsychological paper on 'The Unconscious' (1915e), *Standard Ed.*, **14**, 187 *n*.]

[2] [I.e. in the first paper on the neuro-psychoses of defence (1894a).]

[3] [See p. 168 above.]

I am not yet in a position, Gentlemen, to give a reliable answer to this question. The number of cases I have analysed is not large enough nor have the determining factors in them been sufficiently various. So far, I have observed that obsessions can be regularly shown by analysis to be disguised and transformed *self-reproaches about acts of sexual aggression in childhood*, and are therefore more often met with in men than in women, and that men develop obsessions more often than hysteria. From this I might conclude that the character of the infantile scenes— whether they were experienced with pleasure or only passively —has a determining influence on the choice of the later neurosis; but I do not want to underestimate the significance of the age at which these childhood actions occur, and other factors as well. Only a discussion of further analyses can throw light on these points. But when it becomes clear which are the decisive factors in the choice between the possible forms of the neuro-psychoses of defence, the question of what the mechanism is in virtue of which that particular form takes shape will once again be a purely psychological problem.

I have now come to the end of what I have to say to-day. Prepared as I am to meet with contradiction and disbelief, I should like to say one thing more in support of my position. Whatever you may think about the conclusions I have come to, I must ask you not to regard them as the fruit of idle specula- tion. They are based on a laborious individual examination of patients which has in most cases taken up a hundred or more hours of work. What is even more important to me than the value you put on my results is the attention you give to the procedure I have employed. This procedure is new and difficult to handle, but it is nevertheless irreplaceable for scientific and therapeutic purposes. You will realize, I am sure, that one cannot properly deny the findings which follow from this modi- fication of Breuer's procedure so long as one puts it aside and uses only the customary method of questioning patients. To do so would be like trying to refute the findings of histological technique by relying upon macroscopic examination. The new method of research gives wide access to a new element in the psychical field of events, namely, to processes of thought which have remained unconscious—which, to use Breuer's expression, are 'inadmissible to consciousness'.[1] Thus it inspires us with the hope of a new and better understanding of all functional psychical disturbances. I cannot believe that psychiatry will long hold back from making use of this new pathway to knowledge.

[1] [See Part 5 of Breuer's theoretical contribution to *Studies on Hysteria* (1895*d*), *Standard Ed.*, **2**, 225.]

ABSTRACTS OF THE SCIENTIFIC WRITINGS OF DR. SIGM. FREUD 1877–1897

(1897)

EDITOR'S NOTE

INHALTSANGABEN DER WISSENSCHAFTLICHEN
ARBEITEN DES PRIVATDOCENTEN DR. SIGM. FREUD
1877–1897

(*a*) GERMAN EDITIONS:
1897 Vienna: Deuticke. Pp. 24. (Privately printed.)
1940 *Int. Z. Psychoanal. Imago*, **25** (1), 69–93.
      (With the title 'Bibliographie und Inhaltsangaben der
      Arbeiten Freuds bis zu den Anfängen der Psycho-
      analyse' ['Bibliography and Abstracts of Freud's
      Works up to the Beginnings of Psycho-Analysis'].)
1952 *G.W.*, **1**, 463–88.

(*b*) ENGLISH TRANSLATION:
'Abstracts of the Scientific Writings of Dr. Sigm. Freud
(1877–1897)'

This translation, the first into English, is by James Strachey.

Freud had been appointed a Privatdozent at the Vienna
University in 1885. (This was a post comparable, not quite
accurately, with a Lectureship in an English university.) The
next step would be an appointment as 'Professor Extraordinarius' (roughly equivalent to an Assistant Professor), but
there were long delays over this, and it was twelve years later
that Freud heard that his name was to be put forward to the
Council of the Faculty by two very eminent men, Nothnagel
and Krafft-Ebing. This is reported in a letter to Fliess of
February 8, 1897 (Freud, 1950*a*, Letter 58).[1] The necessary
preliminaries included a 'Curriculum Vitae' (ibid., Letter 59
of April 6), and a bibliographical abstract of publications,
which is reprinted here. It had been finished before May 16

---

[1] The episode figured prominently in one of Freud's dreams reported
in *The Interpretation of Dreams* (1900*a*), *Standard Ed.*, **4**, 136 ff.

(ibid., Letter 62), and was evidently in print by May 25 (ibid., Letter 63), when Freud sent a copy of it to Fliess, describing it, in a phrase borrowed from Leporello, as a 'List of all the beauties, etc. . . .' All these preparations were, however, in vain; for though the Council of the Faculty, by a majority vote, recommended the appointment, the higher Ministerial consent was withheld, largely, no doubt, for anti-semitic reasons. It was not for another five years, in 1902, that Freud was made a Professor.

It will be noticed, if a comparison is made with the complete bibliography in the last volume of this edition, that a few items have been omitted by Freud from the present list. These absentees are for the most part reviews, very minor papers and some unsigned contributions to collective works. Only a single work of any importance seems to have been overlooked—a lecture on cocaine (1885*b*), and it seems possible that unconscious factors had a share in the omission (Jones, 1953, 106).

The inclusion of these abstracts in the *Standard Edition* offers a fortunate reminder to its readers that Freud's 'complete psychological works' are very far from coinciding with Freud's 'complete works', and that the first fifteen prolific years of his activity were concerned entirely with the physical sciences. It may be remarked that Freud himself was sometimes a little inclined to make rather contemptuous remarks about his neurological writings, and some of these are quoted below. But other and more recent neurologists have been far from echoing Freud in this. (Cf. a discussion by the Swiss neurologist Brun, 1936.)

It will be noted that the order in which Freud arranges the items, though roughly chronological, is exactly so neither in respect of writing nor of publication.

We are greatly indebted to Dr. Sabine Strich, of the Department of Neuropathology in the Institute of Psychiatry, University of London, for reading through these abstracts and advising on the translation of the neurological material.

ABSTRACTS OF THE SCIENTIFIC WRITINGS OF DR. SIGM. FREUD
1877–1897

A

BEFORE APPOINTMENT AS PRIVATDOZENT

I

'Observations on the configuration and finer structure of the lobed organs in eels described as testes.' [1877b.][1]

Dr. Syrski had recently recognized a paired, lobulated, grooved organ occurring in the abdominal cavity of the eel as the animal's male sexual organ which had long been looked for. At Professor Claus's suggestion I investigated the occurrence and tissue components of these lobed organs at the zoological station in Trieste.

[1] [This paper was the report on Freud's first work of scientific research, carried out while he was still a student at the University during two visits to Trieste in 1876, in the course of which he dissected some 400 eels. The present paper was in fact published three months after the following one (1877a, II) though written before it. Professor Claus was head of the Institute of Comparative Anatomy in Vienna.]

II

'On the origin of the posterior nerve-roots in the spinal cord of Ammocoetes (Petromyzon planeri).'[1] [1877a.][2]
(From the Institute of Physiology of the University of Vienna. With one plate.)

Investigation of the spinal cord of Ammocoetes showed that the large nerve-cells described by Reissner as occurring in the posterior grey matter (posterior cells) give rise to the root-fibres of the posterior roots.—The anterior and posterior spinal roots of the Petromyzon, at all events in the caudal region, are displaced relatively to each other in their origins and remain distinct from each other in their peripheral course.

III

'On the spinal ganglia and spinal cord of Petromyzon.' [1878a.][3]
(From the Institute of Physiology of the University of Vienna. With four plates and two woodcuts.)

The spinal ganglion cells of fish were long regarded as *bipolar*, and those of the higher animals were considered to be *unipolar*. As regards the latter elements Ranvier had shown that their single process branched in a T-shape after a short course. —By the use of a gold maceration technique it was possible to

---

[1] [The larval form of the brook lamprey.]
[2] [This was Freud's first published work, though the study upon eels (1877b, I) was written before it. The present paper and the following one (1878a, III) were the outcome of a piece of research suggested to him by Brücke, head of the Institute of Physiology, to which Freud had been admitted in the autumn of 1876.—Some forty years later Freud summarized these two papers in Lecture XXII of his *Introductory Lectures* (1916–17) in an attempt at finding an analogy for the psychological processes of fixation and regression.]
[3] [This was a much more elaborate piece of work than its predecessor —eighty-six pages long, including an eighteen page bibliography, compared with the thirteen pages of the earlier paper.]

make a complete survey of the spinal ganglia of Petromyzon; their nerve cells exhibit every transition between bipolarity and unipolarity with T-shaped branching of the fibres; the number of fibres of the posterior root is regularly greater than the number of nerve cells in the ganglion; thus there are 'fibres of passage' and 'subsidiary' nerve fibres, of which the latter merely mingle with the elements of the roots.—A link between the spinal ganglion cells and the posterior cells in the spinal cord which have been described [by Reissner, see II above] is provided in Petromyzon by cellular elements which are exposed on the surface of the spinal cord between the posterior root and ganglion. These scattered cells indicate the path taken by the spinal ganglion cells in the course of evolution.—In relation to the spinal cord of Petromyzon, the paper further describes the branching of the fibres in the central pathway of the posterior root fibres, and the forked ramification of the anterior commissural fibres, the intercalation of nerve cells in the spinal portions of the anterior roots, and a very fine nerve-net (which can be stained by gold chloride) in the pia mater.

IV

'Note upon a method for anatomical preparations of the nervous system.' [1879a.]

A modification of a method recommended by Reichert.—A mixture of 1 part concentrated nitric acid, 3 parts water, and 1 part concentrated glycerine, since it destroys connective tissue and makes it easy to remove bones and muscles, is useful for laying bare the central nervous system with its peripheral branches, particularly in small mammals.

V

'On the structure of the nerve fibres and nerve cells of the river crayfish.' [1882a.]

The nerve fibres of the river crayfish, when the tissues are examined live, exhibit without exception a fibrillary structure. The nerve cells, whose survival can be recognized from the granules in their nucleus, seem to be composed of two substances. One of these is reticular and is continued into the fibrils of the nerve fibres, and the other is homogeneous and is continued in their ground substance.

VI

'The structure of the elements of the nervous system.' [1884f.][1]
(Lecture delivered before the Psychiatric Society, 1882.)

Contents as in V.

---

[1] [There is some doubt as to the date of delivery of the lecture, but it seems highly probable that it was given on the occasion described in great detail by Freud to his fiancée in a letter written the same day, February 14, 1884 (Freud 1960a). In that case the date of 1882 given by Freud must be a slip or misprint. In his letter, however, Freud speaks of the lecture as being based on one of his earlier works, which may well have been No. V above, actually written in 1882. Although Freud deals with its contents so cursorily, according to Ernest Jones the lecture was of very great importance. It summarized Freud's researches on the structure of the nervous system (as reported in Nos. I, II, III and V above), and was feeling its way towards the neurone theory, which was to be enunciated by Waldeyer in 1891. For all this see the first volume of Jones's biography (1953, 53-6).]

VII

'A new method for the study of nerve-tracts in the central nervous system.' [1884d.][1]

If fine sections of the central organ, hardened in chromate, are treated with gold chloride, a strong solution of soda and a 10% solution of calcium iodide, a red to blue stain is obtained which affects either the medullary sheaths or only the axis cylinders. The method is no more reliable than other methods of gold staining.

VII a

'A new histological method for the study of nerve-tracts in the brain and spinal chord.' [1884c.][2]

Contents as in VII.

[1] [Freud had previously published a much shorter description of this method (not included in this list) under the same title in *Zbl. med. Wiss.* (1884b), which he finished writing on February 6, 1884. On the following day he completed the English translation of this shorter version (1884c, VII a below) with the help of an American, Bernard Sachs, who later became well-known as a neurologist in New York. It was the first work by Freud to appear in English. The present, longer version (VII), was written later and not published till April.]

[2] [This paper was in English. See preceding footnote.]

VIII

'A case of cerebral haemorrhage with indirect basal focal symptoms in a patient suffering from scurvy.' [1884a.][1]

A report of a case of cerebral haemorrhage in a patient suffering from scurvy, which ran a rapid course under continuous observation. The symptoms are explained with reference to Wernicke's theory of the indirect effect of focal lesions.

---

[1] [A sixteen-year-old cobbler's apprentice was admitted to hospital on January 17, 1884 and died the next day. Freud's diagnosis was confirmed in every detail by the autopsy. He finished writing this report of the case on January 28. This and two other clinical studies published later (XIII and XII below) all date from 1884, while Freud was working under Franz Scholz in the department for nervous diseases in the Vienna General Hospital. They were no doubt written largely with a view to Freud's appointment as Privatdozent, which was made in September, 1885, just before he started on his visit to Paris.]

IX

'On Coca.' [1884e.][1]

The alkaloid of the coca plant which was described by Niemann [in 1860] received little attention for medical purposes at the time. My work included botanical and historical notes on the coca plant based on statements in the literature; it confirmed by experiments on normal subjects the remarkable stimulating effects of cocaine and its action in preventing hunger, thirst and sleep; and it endeavoured to lay down indications for the therapeutic use of the drug.

Among these indications the reference to the possible employment of cocaine during withdrawal of morphine became of importance later. The expectation voiced at the end of the work that the property of cocaine for producing local anaesthesia would find further applications was soon afterwards fulfilled by K. Koller's experiments in anaesthetizing the cornea.

---

[1] [This monograph was completed by Freud on June 18, 1884, and published in July. An abridged English translation of it appeared in December in the *St. Louis Medical and Surgical Journal* (**47**, 502). In January, 1885, Freud published a paper (1885a, X below) on the effect of cocaine on muscular strength. In the middle of February the original monograph was reprinted, with some additions, in pamphlet form. Then came a lecture 'On the general effects of cocaine', delivered on March 5 at the Psychiatrischer Verein, and published on August 7 (1885b). This publication is not included in the present list; nor is a 'Report on Parke's cocaine' (a comparison of an American preparation with the German one, Merck's, which Freud had been using earlier), which appeared in June (1885e). It was soon after this, in July, that criticisms of Freud's favourable attitude to the drug began to appear, especially from Erlenmeyer (1885, 1886 and 1887). Finally, in July 1887 Freud published a reply to the criticisms (1887d, XVII below). A very full account of Freud's interest in cocaine is given by Ernest Jones in Chapter VI of the first volume of his biography (Jones, 1953).]

X

'Contribution to our knowledge of the effects of coca.'
[1885a.]¹

Dynamometric demonstration of the increase in motor
strength during cocaine euphoria. Motor strength (measured
by the strength of the grip) shows a regular daily oscillation
(similar to that of body temperature).

XI

'A note upon the inter-olivary tract.' [1885d.]²

Short notes on the connections of the roots of the auditory
nerve and the connection between the inter-olivary tract and
the crossed trapezoid body, based upon incompletely myelinated human preparations.

¹ [See preceding footnote. The experiments reported here were begun
by Freud in November, 1884.]
² [This was completed on May 17, 1885. It is the first of three papers
on the medulla oblongata (the others being XIV and XV below).
The manuscript of this paper is dated 'Vienna, mid-May, 1885'. Freud
commented on this early interest in the medulla oblongata in his
Autobiographical Study (1925d), Standard Ed., 20, 10–11. Again, in Lecture
XXV of his Introductory Lectures (1916–17), speaking of the light thrown
by academic medicine on the problem of anxiety, he wrote: 'Interest
there seems mainly to be centred on tracing the anatomical paths along
which the state of anxiety is brought about. We are told that the
medulla oblongata is stimulated, and the patient learns that he is
suffering from a neurosis of the vagus nerve. The medulla oblongata
is a very serious and lovely object. I remember quite clearly how much
time and trouble I devoted to its study many years ago. To-day, however, I must remark that I know nothing that could be of less interest
to me for the psychological understanding of anxiety than a knowledge
of the path of the nerves along which its excitations pass.']

XII

'A case of muscular atrophy with extensive disturbances of sensibility (syringomyelia).' [1885c.][1]

The combination of bilateral muscular atrophy, of bilateral disturbance of sensibility in the nature of a 'partial', dissociated paralysis of sensation, and of trophic disturbances in the left hand (which also exhibited the most intense anaesthesia), taken together with the restriction of the pathological symptoms to the upper part of the body, permitted a diagnosis *in vivo* in a 36-year-old man of syringomyelia, an affection which at that time was regarded as rare and hard to recognize.

[1] [The patient was a weaver who was under Freud's observation and treatment for six weeks from November 10, 1884, and was then discharged from hospital. Cf. footnote p. 232.]

B

AFTER APPOINTMENT AS PRIVATDOZENT

XIII

'Acute multiple neuritis of the spinal and cranial nerves.'
[1886a.][1]

An eighteen-year-old man fell ill without fever but with
general symptoms and dragging pains in his chest and legs. At
first he showed symptoms of endocarditis, but later the pains
increased and sensitiveness to pressure developed in the verte-
bral column and regionally in the skin, muscles and nerve-
trunks as the affection involved one extremity after the other:
heightening of the reflexes, outbreaks of sweating, local wasting,
and lastly diplopia, disturbances of swallowing, facial paresis,
and hoarseness. Finally fever, extreme acceleration of the pulse
and pulmonary affection. The diagnosis of acute multiple
neuritis made during the course of the illness was confirmed by
the post-mortem findings, which showed that all the spinal
nerves in their sheaths were injected, greyish-red, and, as it
were, bunched up. Similar changes in the cranial nerves.
Endocarditis.—According to the pathologist [Kundrat],[2] this
was the first post-mortem finding of polyneuritis to be made in
Vienna.

[1] [The patient, a baker, was under Freud's observation from
October 3, 1884, until his death on December 17. Cf. footnote, p. 232
above. Freud refers to this successful diagnosis in his *Autobiographical
Study* (1925d), *Standard Ed.*, 20, 12.]
[2] [Hans Kundrat (1845-93), Professor of Pathological Anatomy in
Vienna.]

XIV

'On the relation of the restiform body to the posterior column and its nucleus with some remarks on two fields of the medulla oblongata.' [1886b.][1]
Jointly with Dr. L. Darkschewitsch (Moscow).

By studying preparations with incompletely myelinated medulla the restiform body can be divided into two components: a 'nucleus' (primary restiform body) and a 'fringe' (secondary restiform body). The latter contains the olivary fibre system which becomes medullated later. The primary restiform body, which is medullated earlier, is divided into a 'head portion' and a 'tail portion'. The head of the primary restiform body arises from the nucleus of the column of Burdach and thus represents a (for the most part uncrossed) continuation to the cerebellum of the centripetal tract from the extremities. The corresponding continuation to the cerebrum is provided by means of the arcuate fibres originating from this same nucleus. The tail portion of the primary restiform body is a direct continuation of the spinal lateral cerebellar tract.—The lateral field of the medulla oblongata allows of a uniform interpretation of its components. It contains four grey substances with the systems of fibres proceeding from them, which are to be considered homologous to one another as substances in which the sensory nerves from the extremities, and the trigeminal, vagal, and auditory nerves have their origin.

---

[1] [This was the second of the group of three histological papers mentioned above, p. 234, n. 2. The manuscript is dated 'Paris, January 23, 1886'. His collaborator was a Russian neurologist whom he had known two years earlier in Vienna and met again in Paris. We are told that in fact he was responsible only for the drawings which accompanied Freud's text. He later became well known in Russia. (It may be remarked that his writings are usually indexed in England under the spelling 'Darkshevich'.)]

XV

'On the origin of the auditory nerve.' [1886c.][1]

A description of the origin of the auditory nerve, based on preparations of the human foetus, illustrated by four drawings of cross-sections and a diagram. The auditory nerve falls into three portions, of which the lowest (most spinal) terminates in the auditory ganglion and has continuations through the cornu trapezoides and the tracts of the superior olivary body; the second can be traced as the 'ascending' auditory root of Roller into what is known as Deiters' nucleus; and the third runs into the inner auditory field of the medulla oblongata, from which continuations into the cerebellum arise. Details are given of the further course of these tracts so far as it has been possible to follow them.

XVI

'Observation of a severe case of hemi-anaesthesia in a hysterical male.' [1886d.][2]
(The organ of vision was examined by Dr. Königstein.)

The case history of a 29-year-old engraver with a bad family history, who fell ill after a dispute with his brother. The case afforded a demonstration of the symptom of sensible and sensorial hemi-anaesthesia in its classical form.—The disturbance in the field of vision and in the sense of colour is reported by Dr. Königstein.

[1] [The third of the series of papers mentioned on p. 234, n. 2 above.]
[2] [On October 15, 1886, not long after his return from Paris, Freud had read a paper before the Vienna 'Gesellschaft der Aerzte' on male hysteria, of which the full text has not survived. It was received with something like derision, and Freud was challenged to produce a case of male hysteria in Vienna. The present lecture before the same Society was the result: the case was demonstrated by him and his friend Königstein, the ophthalmic surgeon, on November 26, 1886. We have here the first published indication of the shift in Freud's field of interest since his contact with Charcot.
It may be remarked that the paper was headed 'Contributions to the Clinical Study of Hysteria, No. 1'; but the series was never continued further.]

XVII

'Remarks on addiction to cocaine and the fear of cocaine.'
[1887d.][1]
(With reference to a lecture by W. A. Hammond.)

The employment of cocaine for the relief of abstinence from
morphine resulted in the misuse of cocaine and gave physicians
an opportunity of observing the new clinical picture of chronic
cocaine addiction. My essay, supported by a pronouncement
from an American neuropathologist, seeks to show that this
addiction to cocaine comes about only in addicts to other drugs
(such as morphine) and that cocaine itself cannot be blamed
for it.

XVIII

'On hemianopsia in earliest childhood.' [1888a.][2]

An observation of disturbance in one half of the visual field
in two children, aged 26 months and three and a quarter
years, an age at which the symptom had not previously been
medically recorded. A discussion on the lateral inclination of
the head and eyes which was to be observed in one of the cases
and on the localization of the suspected lesion. Both cases are to
be classed among the 'unilateral cerebral palsies of children'.

---

[1] [This is Freud's last paper on the subject of cocaine; see above,
p. 233 n.]

[2] [This was the first of a series of studies on the cerebral palsies of
children, which was to include three works of considerable size. (Cf.
below Nos. XX, XXV, XXVI, XXVII and XXXVIII.) From 1886,
after his return to Vienna from Paris, Freud was attached for several
years to the newly opened neurological department in an Institute for
Children's Diseases, which had recently been founded by Max
Kassowitz (1842-1913). These works are all the outcome of this
appointment.]

XIX

On the Interpretation of the Aphasias, a critical study. [1891*b*.]¹

After a firm basis for the understanding of cerebral disturbances of speech had been established by the discovery and
definite localization of a motor and a sensory aphasia (Broca
and Wernicke), the authorities set about tracing the more
subtle symptoms of aphasia as well to factors of localization.
In this way they arrived at the hypothesis of a *conduction* aphasia,
with subcortical and transcortical, and motor and sensory
forms. This critical study is directed against this view of speech-
disorders and it seeks to introduce for their explanation functional factors in place of the topographical ones. The forms
described as subcortical and transcortical are not to be explained by a particular localization of the lesion but by conditions of reduced capacity for conduction in the apparatus of
speech. In fact there are no aphasias caused by subcortical
lesion. The justification for distinguishing a central aphasia
from a conduction aphasia is also disputed. The speech area of
the cortex is seen rather as a continuous region of the cortex
inserted between the motor fields of the cortex and those of the
optic and auditory nerves—a region within which all communication and association subserving speech function takes
place. The so-called speech-centres revealed by the pathology
of the brain correspond merely to the corners of this field of
speech; they are not distinguished functionally from the interior
regions; it is only on account of their position in relation to the
contiguous cortical centres that they produce more obvious
signs when they become disordered.

The nature of the subject treated here called at many points
for a closer investigation of the delimitation between the
physiological and the psychological approach. Meynert's and
Wernicke's views on the localization of ideas in nervous elements have had to be rejected and Meynert's account of a

¹ [This book is generally regarded as Freud's most important contribution to neurology. (An English translation by Professor E. Stengel
appeared in 1953.) Freud had lectured on aphasia some years before (in
1886 and 1887) and contributed an article on it to Villaret's encyclopaedia of medicine (1888*b*).]

representation of the body in the cerebral cortex has required revision. Two facts of cerebral anatomy, namely (1) that
the masses of fibres entering the spinal cord are constantly
diminished on passing upwards, owing to the interposition of
grey matter, and (2) that there are no direct paths from the
periphery of the body to the cortex—these two facts lead to
the conclusion that a really complete representation of the body
is present only in the grey matter of the cord (as a 'projection'),
whereas in the cortex the periphery of the body is only 'represented' in less detail through selected fibres arranged according
to function.

XX

Clinical Study of the Unilateral Cerebral Palsies of Children.
[1891*a*.][1]
(In collaboration with Dr. O. Rie.)
(No. III of *Beiträge zur Kinderheilkunde* [Contributions to
Paediatrics] edited by Dr. M. Kassowitz.)

A monograph describing this affection, based on studies of
material in the First Public Institute for Children's Diseases in
Vienna, directed by Kassowitz. In ten sections it deals with
(1) the history and literature of the cerebral palsies of children;
(2) 35 observations of the authors' own, which are then summarized in tabular form and described individually; (3) the
analysis of the individual symptoms of the clinical picture;
(4) the pathological anatomy; (5) the relations of cerebral palsy to
epilepsy and, (6) to infantile poliomyelitis; (7) differential
diagnosis and (8) therapy. A 'choreatic paresis' is described by
the authors for the first time; it is distinguished by peculiar
characteristics in its onset and course, and in it the unilateral
paresis is from the beginning represented by hemichorea. There
is further an account of the findings of an autopsy (lobar
sclerosis as a result of an embolism of the middle cerebral
artery) on a woman patient described in the *Iconographie de la*

---

[1] [This is a volume of over two hundred pages. Freud's collaborator,
his friend Oscar Rie, was a paediatrician also attached to the Kassowitz
Institute (see above p. 239, *n*. 2).]

Salpêtrière [**3**, 22–30].[1] Emphasis is laid on the close relations between epilepsy and the cerebral palsies of children, in consequence of which some cases of apparent epilepsy might deserve to be described as 'cerebral palsy without palsy'. In connection with the much discussed question as to the existence of a *polio-encephalitis acuta*, which is supposed to constitute the anatomical basis of unilateral cerebral palsy and to offer a complete analogy with *poliomyelitis infantilis*, the authors argue against this hypothesis of Strümpell's; but they hold firmly to the expectation that a modified view of *poliomyelitis acuta infantilis* will allow of its being equated with cerebral palsy on another basis. In the therapeutic section are collected the hitherto published reports on the intervention by brain surgeons directed to the cure of genuine or traumatic epilepsy.

XXI

'A case of successful treatment by hypnotism with some remarks on the origin of hysterical symptoms through "counter-will".' [1892–93.][2]

A young woman after the birth of her first child was compelled to give up breast-feeding it owing to a complex of hysterical symptoms (loss of appetite, sleeplessness, pains in her breasts, failure of milk-secretion, agitation). When, after the birth of a second child, these obstacles recurred, deep hypnosis on two occasions, accompanied by counter-suggestions, succeeded in removing the obstacles, so that the patient became an excellent nursing mother. The same result was brought about a year later in similar circumstances after two more hypnoses. Some remarks are appended on the fact that it is possible in hysterical patients for distressing antithetic or anxious ideas to

---

[1] [This was a case entrusted to Freud by Charcot; the patient had been in the Salpêtrière since 1853. Cf. Freud's obituary of Charcot, p. 14 *n*. above.]

[2] [This paper may be considered as Freud's first one on psychopathology, since the first half of it was published before the 'Preliminary Communication' (1893*a*). His interest in hypnotism goes back, of course, to his Paris visit, and he was using it himself from 1887. The paper is included in the first volume of the *Standard Edition*.]

be realized[1] which normal people are able to inhibit; several observations of *tic* are traced back to this mechanism of 'counter-will'.

XXII

'Charcot.' [1893*f.*][2]

An obituary of the master of neuropathology who died in 1893 and among whose pupils the present writer numbers himself.

XXIII

'On a symptom which often accompanies *enuresis nocturna* in children.' [1893*g.*][3]

In perhaps half the cases of children suffering from enuresis we find a hypertonia of the lower extremities the significance and implications of which are unexplained.

---

[1] ['*Realisierung.*' In the paper itself the term used throughout is '*Objektivierung*', which is there rendered 'putting into effect'.]

[2] [See above, p. 7.]

[3] [There is no trace in this paper of any possible psychological determinants of the disorder. In sending a copy to Fliess on November 17, 1893, Freud (1950*a*, Letter 15) speaks of it contemptuously as '*ein Schmarren*' ('a rubbishy trifle').]

XXIV

'On the psychical mechanism of hysterical phenomena.'
(Preliminary communication in collaboration with Dr. J.
Breuer.) [1893a.][1]

The mechanism to which Charcot traced back hystero-traumatic paralyses, and the assumption of which enabled him to provoke them deliberately in hypnotized hysterical patients, can also be made responsible for numerous symptoms of what is described as non-traumatic hysteria. If we put the hysteric under hypnosis and lead his thoughts back to the time at which the symptom in question first appeared, a memory of a psychical trauma (or series of traumas) belonging to that time awakens in him with hallucinatory vividness, the symptom having persisted as a mnemic symbol of the trauma. Thus hysterics suffer mainly from reminiscences. If the traumatic scene which has been arrived at in this way is reproduced vividly, accompanied by a generation of affect, the symptom which has hitherto been obstinately maintained disappears. We must therefore suppose that the forgotten memory has been acting like a foreign body in the mind, with the removal of which the irritating phenomena cease. This discovery, first made by Breuer in 1881, can be made the basis of a therapy of hysterical phenomena which deserves to be described as 'cathartic'.

The memories which are revealed as 'pathogenic', as the roots of hysterical symptoms, are regularly 'unconscious' to the patient. It seems that by thus remaining unconscious they escape the wearing-away process to which psychical material is normally subject. A wearing-away of this sort is brought about by the method of 'abreaction'. Pathogenic memories avoid being dealt with by abreaction either because the experiences concerned have occurred in special psychical states to which hysterical persons are inherently inclined, or because those experiences have been accompanied by an affect which brings about a special psychical state in hysterical persons. A tendency to a 'splitting of consciousness' is accordingly the basic psychical phenomenon in cases of hysteria.

[1] [This was included in Studies on Hysteria (1895d) and will be found in Standard Ed., 2. Cf. also the lecture, p. 25 above.]

XXV

An Account of the Cerebral Diplegias of Childhood (in Connection with Little's Disease.) [1893b.][1]
(No. III, New Series, of *Beiträge zur Kinderheilkunde* [Contributions to Paediatrics] edited by Dr. M. Kassowitz.)

A supplement to the *Clinical Study of the Unilateral Cerebral Palsies of Children* summarized under XX above [p. 241]. The history, pathological anatomy and physiology of the affection are treated here in the same order as in the earlier monograph, and the relevant clinical pictures are illustrated by 53 observations made by the author himself. It was, however, necessary in addition to take into account the range of forms that must be described as 'cerebral diplegias' and to point out their clinical similarity. In face of the differences of opinion that prevail in the literature of these disorders, the author has adopted the standpoint of an earlier authority, Little,[2] and has thus arrived at the erection of four principal types, which are described as general spasticity, paraplegic spasticity, general chorea and bilateral athetosis, and bilateral spastic hemiplegia (spastic diplegia).

General spasticity includes the forms which are usually referred to as 'Little's disease'. Paraplegic spasticity is the name given to what was earlier regarded as a spinal affection, *tabes spastica infantilis.* The spastic diplegias correspond most easily to a doubling of unilateral cerebral palsies, but are characterized by a superfluity of symptoms which finds its

[1] [This monograph is comparable in dimensions to its pendant, No. XX. Freud sent a copy of it to Fliess on May 30, 1893, with the comment that 'it is not very interesting' (Freud, 1950a, Letter 12). In another letter, dealing with the psychoneuroses, a year later (May 21, 1894) he wrote: 'There is something comic in the disparity between one's own and other people's estimate of one's intellectual work. Take that book on the diplegias, which I knocked together with a minimum of interest and effort—almost as a lark. It has had a tremendous success. The critics say the nicest things about it. The French reviews in particular are overflowing with praise. . . . But for really good things, like my aphasia, or the paper on obsessions that is soon coming out, or like my future aetiology and theory of the neuroses, I can expect nothing better than respectful failure.' (Ibid., Letter 18.)]
[2] [W. J. Little (1810-94).]

explanation in the bilateral nature of the cerebral affection. The justification for including general chorea and bilateral athetosis among these types is provided by numerous characteristics of the clinical picture and by the existence of many mixed and transitional forms which link all these types together.

A discussion follows of the relations of these clinical types to the aetiological factors which are here assumed to be operative and to the insufficient number of post-mortem findings that have been reported. The following conclusions are reached:

Cerebral diplegias can be divided according to their origin into (a) those congenitally determined, (b) those arising at the time of birth and (c) those acquired after birth. But it is extremely rarely that this distinction can be drawn from the clinical peculiarities of the case, and not always possible from the anamnesis. All the aetiological factors of the diplegias are enumerated: prenatal (trauma, illness, or shock affecting the mother, place of the child in the family); operative at the time of birth (the factors stressed by Little, namely premature birth, difficult labour, asphyxia); and after birth (infectious diseases, trauma or shock affecting the child). Convulsions cannot be regarded as causes but only as symptoms of the affection. The aetiological part played by inherited syphilis is recognized as important. There is no exclusive relation between any one of these aetiologies and any one type of cerebral diplegia, but preferential relations are often apparent. The view that cerebral diplegias are affections with a single aetiology is untenable.

The pathological findings in the diplegias are of many kinds, and in general the same as in the hemiplegias; for the most part they are in the nature of end stages, from which it is not invariably possible to infer back to the initial lesions. They do not as a rule allow of a decision as to the aetiological category to which a case is to be referred. Nor is it usually possible to deduce the clinical picture from the post-mortem findings; so that the assumption that there are intimate and exclusive relations between clinical types and anatomical changes must also be rejected.

The pathological physiology of cerebral diplegias has an essential connection with the two characteristics by which both general and paraplegic spasticity are distinguished from other manifestations of organic disease of the cerebrum. For in both these clinical forms contracture predominates over paralysis and the lower extremities are affected more severely than the upper ones. The discussion in this paper reaches the conclusion that ·the more intense affection of the lower extremities in general and paraplegic spasticity must be connected with the localization of the lesion (meningeal haemorrhage along the median fissure) and the preponderance of contracture with the superficiality of the lesion. The strabismus of diplegic children, which is particularly common in paraplegic spasticity and where premature birth is the aetiology, is traceable to the retinal haemorrhages in new-born children described by Königstein.

A special section directs attention to the numerous instances of the familial and hereditary occurrence of children's diseases which show a clinical affinity with cerebral diplegias.

XXVI

'On familial forms of cerebral diplegias.' [1893d.]

An observation of two brothers, one six and a half and the other five years old, whose parents were blood relations, and who present a complicated clinical picture which has gradually developed, in the one case since birth and in the other since the second year. The symptoms of this familial disorder (lateral nystagmus, atrophy of the optic nerve, alternating convergent strabismus, monotonous and, as it were, scanning speech, intention tremor of the arms, spastic weakness of the legs, accompanied by high intelligence) give grounds for constructing a new affection which is to be regarded as a spastic counterpart to Friedreich's disease. Emphasis is laid on the far-reaching similarity of these cases to those described as multiple sclerosis by Pelizaeus in 1885.

XXVII

'The cerebral diplegias of children.' [1893e.][1]

A summary of the findings in the monograph abstracted above, No. XXV.

[1] [In French, contributed to a periodical edited by Pierre Marie (Charcot's successor at the Salpêtrière), who had written a highly laudatory review of the monograph (cf. footnote 1, p. 245 above) and no doubt asked Freud for this summary.]

XXVIII

'Some points for a comparative study of organic and hysterical motor paralyses.' [1893*c.*]¹

A comparison between organic and hysterical paralyses made under the influence of Charcot in order to arrive at a line of approach to the nature of hysteria. Organic paralysis is either periphero-spinal or cerebral. On the basis of discussions in my critical study on the aphasias [No. XIX above], the former is described as *projection* paralysis and is paralysis *en détail*, and the latter is described as *representation* paralysis and is paralysis *en masse*.² Hysteria imitates only the latter category of paralyses but has freedom to specialize which makes it resemble projection paralysis; it can dissociate the areas of paralysis which regularly occur in cerebral affections. Hysterical paralysis has a tendency to excessive development; it can be extremely intense and yet strictly confined to a small area, while cortical paralysis regularly increases its extent with an increase in its intensity. Sensibility behaves in a directly contrary manner in the two kinds of paralysis.

The special characteristics of cortical paralysis are determined by the peculiarities of cerebral structure, and allow us to infer back to the anatomy of the brain. Hysterical paralysis on the contrary behaves as though there were no such thing as cerebral anatomy. Hysteria knows nothing of the anatomy of the brain. The alteration which underlies hysterical paralysis can have no resemblance to organic lesions but must be looked for in the conditions governing the accessibility of some particular circle of ideas.

¹ [The original of this paper is in French. It is included in Volume I of the *Standard Edition*.]
² [Cf. the last paragraph of No. XIX. The point is fully explained in the present paper itself, in *Standard Ed.*, **1**.]

XXIX

'The neuro-psychoses of defence: an attempt at a psychological theory of acquired hysteria, of many phobias and obsessions and of certain hallucinatory psychoses.' [1894a.][1]

The first of a series of short papers which now follow and which are directed to the task of preparing a general exposition of the neuroses on a new basis which is now in hand.

The splitting of consciousness in hysteria is not a primary characteristic of this neurosis, based on degenerative weakness, as Janet insists. It is the consequence of a peculiar psychical process known as 'defence' which is shown by some short reports of analyses to be present not only in hysteria but in numerous other neuroses and psychoses. Defence comes into operation when an instance of incompatibility arises in ideational life between a particular idea and the 'ego'. The process of defence may be figuratively represented as though the quota of excitation were torn away from the idea that is to be repressed and put to some other use. This can occur in a variety of ways: in hysteria the liberated sum of excitation is transformed into somatic innervation (*conversion hysteria*); in obsessional neurosis it remains in the psychical field and attaches itself to other ideas which are not incompatible in themselves and which are thus *substituted* for the repressed idea. The source of the incompatible ideas which are subjected to defence is solely and exclusively sexual life. An analysis of a case of hallucinatory psychosis shows that this psychosis too represents a method of achieving defence.

[1] [See above, p. 41.]

XXX

'Obsessions and phobias: their psychical mechanism and aetiology.' [1895c.][1]

Obsessions and phobias are to be distinguished from neurasthenia as independent neurotic affections. In both [obsessions and phobias] it is a question of the linkage between an idea and an affective state. In phobias the latter is always the same, namely anxiety; in true obsessions it can be of various kinds (self-reproach, sense of guilt, doubt, etc.). The affective state emerges as the essential element of the obsession, since it remains unaltered in the individual case, whereas the idea attached to it is changed. Psychical analysis shows that the affect of the obsession is justified in every instance, but that the idea attached to it represents a substitute for an idea derived from sexual life which is more appropriate to the affect and which has succumbed to repression. This state of affairs is illustrated by numerous short analyses of cases of *folie du doute*, washing mania, arithmomania, etc., in which the reinstatement of the repressed idea was successful and accompanied by useful therapeutic effects. The phobias in the strict sense are reserved for the paper on anxiety neurosis (No. XXXII).

XXXI

Studies on Hysteria. [1895d.]
(In collaboration with Dr. J. Breuer.)[2]

This volume contains the carrying-through of the subject raised in the 'Preliminary Communication' (No. XXIV) dealing with the psychical mechanism of hysterical phenomena. Although it proceeds from the joint work of the two authors, it is divided into separate sections, of which four detailed case histories together with discussions and an attempt at a 'Psychotherapy of Hysteria' represent my share. The aetiological part played by the sexual factor is stressed with greater emphasis in

---

[1] [The present paper is in French. See above, p. 69.]
[2] [This book is translated in Volume II of the *Standard Edition*.]

this book than in the 'Preliminary Communication', and the concept of 'conversion' is used to throw light on the formation of hysterical symptoms. The essay on psychotherapy seeks to give some insight into the technique of the psycho-analytic procedure, which is alone able to lead to the investigation of the unconscious content of the mind, and the employment of which may also be expected to lead to important psychological discoveries.

XXXII

'On the grounds for detaching a particular syndrome from neurasthenia under the description "anxiety neurosis".' [1895*b*.][1]

The concurrence of a constant grouping of symptoms with a particular aetiological determinant makes it possible to pick out from the composite province of 'neurasthenia' a syndrome which deserves the name of 'anxiety neurosis', because all of its constituents arise from the symptoms of anxiety. These are either to be regarded as immediate manifestations of anxiety or as rudiments and equivalents of them (E. Hecker), and they are often in complete opposition to the symptoms which constitute neurasthenia proper. The aetiology of the two neuroses also points to an opposition of this kind. Whereas true neurasthenia arises from spontaneous emissions or is acquired through masturbation, the factors belonging to the aetiology of anxiety neurosis are such as correspond to a holding back of sexual excitation—such as abstinence when libido is present, unconsummated excitation and, above all, coitus interruptus. In actual life the neuroses here distinguished usually appear in combination, though pure cases can also be demonstrated. When a mixed neurosis of this kind is subjected to analysis, it is possible to indicate a mixture of several specific aetiologies.

An attempt to arrive at a theory of anxiety neurosis leads to a formula to the effect that its mechanism lies in *the deflection of somatic sexual excitation from the psychical field* and a consequent abnormal employment of that excitation. *Neurotic anxiety is transformed sexual libido.*

[1] [See p. 85 above.]

XXXIII

'A reply to criticisms of my paper on anxiety neurosis.'
[1895*f*.]¹

A reply to objections made by Löwenfeld to the content of
No. XXXII. The problem of the aetiology of the pathology of
the neuroses is dealt with here, to justify the division into three
categories of the aetiological factors that appear: (*a*) preconditions, (*b*) specific causes and (*c*) concurrent or auxiliary
causes. What are called preconditions are the factors which,
though they are indispensable for producing the effect, cannot
by themselves produce it but need in addition the specific
causes. The specific causes are distinguished from the preconditions by the fact that they figure in only a few aetiological
formulas, while the preconditions play the same part in numerous affections. Auxiliary causes are such as neither need invariably be present nor are able by themselves to produce the
effect in question.—In the case of neuroses it is possible that the
precondition may be heredity; the specific cause lies in sexual
factors; everything else that is brought up apart from these as
forming the aetiology of the neuroses (overwork, emotion,
physical illness) is an auxiliary cause and can never entirely
take the place of the specific factor, though it can no doubt
serve as a substitute for it in the matter of *quantity*. The form of
a neurosis depends on the nature of the specific sexual cause;
whether there shall be a neurotic illness *at all* is determined by
factors operating quantitatively; heredity works like a multiplier
inserted in an electric circuit.

¹ [See above, p. 119.]

XXXIV

'On Bernhardt's disturbance of sensibility in the thigh.' [1895*e*.][1]

A self-observation of this harmless affection, which is probably traceable to local neuritis; and a report of some other cases, including bilateral ones.

XXXV

'Further remarks on the neuro-psychoses of defence.' [1896*b*.][2]

(1) *The specific aetiology of hysteria.* A continuation of psycho-analytic work with hysterical subjects has had the uniform result of showing that the suspected traumatic events (as mnemic symbols of which hysterical symptoms persist) occur in the patients' *earliest childhood* and are to be described as sexual abuses in the narrowest sense.

(2) *The nature and mechanism of obsessional neurosis.* Obsessional ideas are invariably transformed self-reproaches which have re-emerged from repression and which always relate to some sexual act that was performed with pleasure in childhood. The course taken by this return of the repressed is traced, as are the results of a primary and secondary work of defence.

(3) *Analysis of a case of chronic paranoia.* This analysis, which is reported in detail, indicates that the aetiology of paranoia is to be found in the same sexual experiences of early childhood in which the aetiology of hysteria and of obsessional neurosis has already been discovered. The symptoms of this case of paranoia are traced in detail to the activities of defence.

---

[1] [A disorder from which Freud suffered for a year or two at this time.]

[2] [See above, p. 157.]

XXXVI

'The aetiology of hysteria.' [1896*c*.][1]

More detailed reports of the infantile sexual experiences which have been shown to constitute the aetiology of the psychoneuroses. In their content these experiences must be described as 'perversions', and those responsible are as a rule to be looked for among the patient's nearest relatives. A discussion of the difficulties which have to be surmounted in uncovering these repressed memories and of the objections that may be raised against the results thus arrived at. Hysterical symptoms are shown to be derivatives of memories operating unconsciously; they appear only in collaboration with such memories. The presence of infantile sexual experiences is an indispensable condition if the efforts of defence (which occur in normal people as well) are to result in producing pathogenic effects—that is to say, neuroses.

[1] [See above, p. 187.]

XXXVII

'Heredity and the aetiology of the neuroses.' [1896a.][1]

The findings hitherto arrived at by psycho-analysis on the aetiology of the neuroses are here employed to criticize the current theories of the omnipotence of heredity in neuro-pathology. The part played by heredity has been over-estimated in several directions. Firstly, by including among the inheritable neuropathic illnesses conditions such as headaches, neuralgias, etc., which are very probably attributable as a rule to organic affections of the cranial cavities (the nose). Secondly, by regarding every discoverable nervous ailment among relatives as evidence of hereditary taint and by thus from the first leaving no room for *acquired* neuropathic illnesses which can possess no similar evidential weight. Thirdly, the aetiological role of syphilis has been misunderstood and the nervous ailments deriving from it have been put down to the account of heredity. But in addition, a general objection is permissible against a form of heredity which is described as 'dissimilar inheritance' (or inheritance with a change in the form of the illness), and to which a far more important part is allotted than to 'similar' inheritance. But when the fact of hereditary taint in a family is demonstrated in its members being affected alternatively by every sort of nervous complaint—chorea, epilepsy, hysteria, apoplexy, etc.—without any more precise determinants, then either we need a knowledge of the laws according to which these complaints replace one another or else room is left for the individual aetiologies which determine precisely the choice of the neuropathic state which in fact results from them. If such particular aetiologies exist, they are the specific causes, so much sought after, of the various different clinical forms, and heredity is pushed back into the role of a requirement or precondition.

[1] [This paper was written by Freud in French. It appears above, on p. 141.]

XXXVIII

Infantile Cerebral Palsies. [1897a.][1]

This is a summary of the two works on the same theme published in 1891 and 1893 [Nos. XX and XXV], together with the additions and alterations which have since become necessary. These affect the chapter on *poliomyelitis acuta*, which has meantime been recognized as a non-systematic disease, on encephalitis as an initial process of spastic hemiplegia, and on the interpretation of cases of paraplegic spasticity, the cerebral nature of which affection may recently have been placed in doubt. A special discussion is concerned with the attempts to split up the content of the cerebral diplegias into several clearly divided clinical entities, or at least to separate what is known as 'Little's disease' as a clinical individual from among the medley of forms of similar affections. The difficulties which meet such attempts are pointed out, and it is maintained as the only justifiable view that 'infantile cerebral palsy' shall be retained at present as a collective clinical concept for a whole number of similar affections with an exogenous aetiology. The rapid increase in observations of familial and hereditary nervous disorders of children, which resemble infantile cerebral palsies clinically at many points, has made it a pressing matter to collect these new forms and to attempt to draw a fundamental distinction between them and infantile cerebral palsies.

---

[1] [This was Freud's last publication on a neurological subject. It was prepared at Nothnagel's request for his great encyclopaedia of medicine, of which it forms Part II, Section II of Volume IX. This is the bulkiest of all Freud's neurological works, well over three hundred pages long and with over four hundred entries in the bibliography. He was engaged on it for some years, and seems quite to have lost interest in it, to judge from his caustic letters on the subject to Fliess (see p. 262 below).]

APPENDIX

A. *Works written under my influence.*

E. Rosenthal, *Contribution à l'étude des diplégies cérébrales de l'enfance.* Thèse de Lyon. (Médaille d'argent.) (1892.)

L. Rosenberg, *Casuistische Beiträge zur Kenntnis der cerebralen Kinderlähmungen und der Epilepsie.* (No. IV, New Series, of *Beiträge zur Kinderheilkunde,* edited by Kassowitz.) (1893.)

B. *Translations from the French.*

J.-M. Charcot, *Neue Vorlesungen über die Krankheiten des Nervensystems, insbesondere über Hysterie.* (Toeplitz & Deuticke, Vienna.) [1886*f*.]

H. Bernheim, *Die Suggestion und ihre Heilwirkung.* (Fr. Deuticke, Vienna.) [1888–89.] (Second edition, 1896.)

H. Bernheim, *Neue Studien über Hypnotismus, Suggestion und Psychotherapie.* (Fr. Deuticke, Vienna.) [1892*a*.]

J.-M. Charcot, *Poliklinische Vorträge.* Vol. I. (*Leçons du Mardi.*) With notes by the translator. (Fr. Deuticke, Vienna.) [1892–94.]

SEXUALITY IN THE AETIOLOGY OF THE NEUROSES

(1898)

EDITOR'S NOTE

DIE SEXUALITÄT IN DER ÄTIOLOGIE DER NEUROSEN

(a) German Editions:

1898 *Wien. klin. Rdsch.*, **12** (2), 21–2, (4), 55–7, (5), 70–2, (7), 103–5. (January 9, 23, 30 and February 13.)
1906 *S.K.S.N.*, **1**, 181–204. (1911, 2nd ed.; 1920, 3rd ed.; 1922, 4th ed.)
1925 *G.S.*, **1**, 439–64.
1952 *G.W.*, **1**, 491–516.

(b) English Translation:
'Sexuality in the Aetiology of the Neuroses'
1924 *C.P.*, **1**, 220–48. (Tr. J. Bernays.)

The present translation is a modified version of that published in 1924.

This paper was finished, as we learn from a letter to Fliess (Freud, 1950*a*, Letter 83), on February 9, 1898. It had been begun already a month earlier (ibid., Letter 81), and in both these letters Freud speaks of it contemptuously as a *'Gartenlaube'* article. This was the title (literally 'garden arbour') of a family magazine whose name had become proverbial for its sentimental stories. But he adds that the paper 'is fairly impudent and chiefly designed to cause trouble—which it will succeed in doing. Breuer will say that I have done myself a lot of harm.'

Two years had elapsed since Freud's last paper on psychopathology, 'The Aetiology of Hysteria' (1896*c*), and during those two years a very great deal had happened to occupy his mind. Perhaps the least important thing (at any rate from our point of view) was his completion by the beginning of 1897 of his three-hundred-page treatise on children's palsies for Nothnagel's great encyclopaedia of medicine, on which he had been most unwillingly engaged for several years past, and which was his last neurological work. Cf., for instance, letters to Fliess of October 20, 31 and November 8, 1895, June 4 and November 2, 1896, and January 24, 1897 (Freud, 1950*a*, Letters 32, 33, 35, 47, 50 and 57). Once this task was out of the way, he was able to devote himself more completely to psychology, and he was soon involved in what was to prove an epoch-making event —his own self-analysis. This began in the summer of 1897, and already by the autumn had led to some fundamental discoveries: the abandonment of the traumatic theory of the aetiology of the neuroses (September 21, Letter 69), the discovery of the Oedipus complex (October 15, Letter 71) and the gradual recognition of infantile sexuality as a normal and universal fact (e.g. November 14, Letter 75).

Of all these developments (and of the parallel advances in Freud's understanding of dream-psychology) there is scarcely a trace to be found in the present paper; and this no doubt accounts for its author's contempt for it. As regards fundamentals it carries things no further than the point at which they stood two years before: Freud was reserving himself for his next major effort which was to follow in still another two years in *The Interpretation of Dreams* (1900*a*).

But if the first part of the paper contains little more than a restatement of Freud's earlier views on the aetiology of the neuroses, the argument also presents us with something new— an approach to sociological problems. The outspoken criticism here of the attitude of the medical profession to matters of sex, and in particular to masturbation, to the use of contraceptives and to the difficulties of married life, foreshadows a whole series of Freud's later animadversions against the social conventions of civilization—beginning with the paper on ' "Civilized" Sexual Morality' (1908*d*) and ending with *Civilization and its Discontents* (1930*a*).

SEXUALITY IN THE AETIOLOGY
OF THE NEUROSES

EXHAUSTIVE researches during the last few years have led me to recognize that the most immediate and, for practical purposes, the most significant causes of every case of neurotic illness are to be found in factors arising from sexual life. This theory is not entirely new. A certain amount of importance has been allowed to sexual factors in the aetiology of the neuroses from time immemorial and by every writer on the subject. In certain marginal regions of medicine a cure for 'sexual complaints' and for 'nervous weakness' has always been promised in the same breath. When once the validity of the theory ceases to be denied, therefore, it will not be hard to dispute its originality.

In a few short papers which have appeared during the last years in the *Neurologisches Zentralblatt* [1894*a*, 1895*b* and 1896*b*], the *Revue Neurologique* [1895*c* and 1896*a*] and the *Wiener klinische Rundschau* [1895*f* and 1896*c*],[1] I have tried to give an indication of the material and the points of view which offer scientific support for the theory of the 'sexual aetiology of the neuroses'. A full presentation is, however, still wanting, mainly because, in endeavouring to throw light on what is recognized as the actual state of affairs, we come upon ever fresh problems for the solution of which the necessary preliminary work has not been done. It does not seem to me at all premature, however, to attempt to direct the attention of medical practitioners to what I believe to be the facts, so that they may convince themselves of the truth of my assertions and at the same time of the benefits they may derive in their practice from a knowledge of them.

I am aware that efforts will be made, by the use of arguments with an ethical colouring, to prevent the physician from pursuing the matter further. Anyone who wants to make certain whether or not his patients' neuroses are really connected with their sexual life cannot avoid asking them about their sexual life and insisting upon receiving a true account of it. But in this, it is

---

[1] [All of them in the present volume.]

asserted, lies the danger both for the individual and society. A doctor, I hear it being said, has no right to intrude upon his patients' sexual secrets and grossly injure their modesty (especially with women patients) by an interrogation of this sort. His clumsy hand can only ruin family happiness, offend the innocence of young people and encroach upon the authority of parents; and where adults are concerned he will come to share uncomfortable knowledge and destroy his own relations to his patients. It is therefore his ethical duty, the conclusion is, to keep away from the whole business of sex.

To this one may well reply that it is the expression of a prudery which is unworthy of a physician and which inadequately conceals its weakness behind bad arguments. If factors arising out of sexual life must really be acknowledged to be causes of illness, then, for that very reason, investigation and discussion of them automatically falls within the sphere of a physician's duty. The injury to modesty of which he is guilty in this is no different and no worse, one would imagine, than when he insists on examining a woman's genital organs in order to cure a local affection—a demand on which he is pledged to insist by his medical training itself. Even now one often hears elderly women who have spent their youth in the provinces tell of how at one time they were reduced to a state of exhaustion by excessive genital haemorrhages, because they could not make up their minds to allow a doctor to see their nakedness. The educative influence which has been exercised on the public by the medical world has, in the course of one generation, so altered things that an objection of this sort is an extremely rare occurrence among the young women of to-day. If it were to occur, it would be condemned as unreasonable prudery, as modesty in the wrong place. Are we living in Turkey, a husband would ask, where all that a sick woman may show to the physician is her arm through a hole in the wall?

It is not true that interrogation of his patients and knowledge about their sexual concerns give the physician a dangerous degree of power over them. It was possible in earlier times for the same objection to be made against the uses of anaesthetics, which deprive the patient of his consciousness and of the exercise of his will and leave it to the doctor to decide whether and when he shall regain them. And yet to-day anaesthetics have become indispensable to us because they are able, better than anything else, to assist the doctor in his medical work; and, among his many other serious obligations, he has taken over the responsibility for their use.

A doctor can always do harm if he is unskilful or unscrupulous, and this is no more and no less true where it is a question of investigating his patients' sexual life than it is in other things. Naturally, if someone, after an honest self-examination, feels that he does not possess the tact, seriousness and discretion which are necessary for questioning neurotic patients, and if he is aware that revelations of a sexual character would provoke lascivious thrills in him rather than scientific interest, then he will be right to avoid the topic of the aetiology of the neuroses. All we ask, in addition, is that he should also refrain from treating nervous patients.

Nor is it true that patients put insuperable obstacles in the way of an investigation into their sexual life. After some slight hesitation, adults usually adjust themselves to the situation by saying: 'After all, I'm at the doctor's; I can say anything to him.' A great many women who find it difficult enough to go through life concealing their sexual feelings, are relieved to find that with the doctor no other consideration outweighs that of their recovery, and they are grateful to him that for once they are allowed to behave quite humanly about sexual things. A dim knowledge of the overwhelming importance of sexual factors in the production of neuroses (a knowledge which I am trying to capture afresh for science) seems never to have been lost in the consciousness of laymen. How often do we witness scenes like this: A married couple, one of whom is suffering from a neurosis, comes to us for consultation. After we have made a great many introductory remarks and apologies to the effect that no conventional barriers should exist between them and the doctor who wants to be of use in such cases, and so on, we tell them that we suspect that the cause of the illness lies in the unnatural and detrimental form of sexual intercourse which they must have chosen since the wife's last confinement. We tell them that doctors do not as a rule concern themselves with such matters, but that that is reprehensible of them, even though the patients do not want to be told about things like that, etc. Thereupon one of the couple nudges the other and says: 'You see! I told you all along it would make me ill.' And the other answers: 'Well, I know, I thought so too; but what is one to do?'

In certain other circumstances, such as when one is dealing with young girls, who, after all, are systematically brought up to conceal their sexual life, one will have to be content with a very small measure of sincere response on the part of the patient. But an important consideration comes into play here—namely that a doctor who is experienced in these things does not meet his patients unprepared and as a rule does not have to ask them for information but only for a confirmation of his surmises. Anyone who will follow my indications as to how to elucidate the morphology of the neuroses and translate it into aetiological terms, will need the addition of very few further admissions from his patients; in the very description of their symptoms, which they are only too ready to give, they have usually acquainted him at the same time with the sexual factors that are hidden behind.

It would be a great advantage if sick people had a better knowledge of the certainty with which a doctor is now in a position to interpret their neurotic complaints and to infer from them their operative sexual aetiology. It would undoubtedly spur such people on to abandon their secretiveness from the moment they have made up their minds to seek help for their sufferings. Moreover, it is in the interest of all of us that a higher degree of honesty about sexual things should become a duty among men and women than has hitherto been expected of them. This cannot be anything but a gain for sexual morality. In matters of sexuality we are at present, every one of us, ill or well, nothing but hypocrites. It will be all to our good if, as a result of such general honesty, a certain amount of toleration in sexual concerns should be attained.

Doctors usually take very little interest in a good many of the questions which are discussed among neuropathologists in connection with the neuroses: whether, for instance, one is justified in making a strict differentiation between hysteria and neurasthenia, whether one may distinguish hystero-neurasthenia alongside of them, whether obsessions should be classed with neurasthenia or recognized as a separate neurosis, and so on. And, indeed, such distinctions may well be a matter of indifference to a practitioner, so long as no further consequences follow from the decisions arrived at—no deeper insight and no pointers for therapeutic treatment—and so long as the patient will in every instance be sent off to a hydropathic establishment, and be told that there is nothing the matter with him. But it will be a different thing if our point of view about the causative relations between sexuality and the neuroses is adopted. Fresh interest is then aroused in the symptomatology of the different neurotic cases, and it becomes of practical importance that one should be able correctly to break down the complicated picture into its components and correctly to name them. For the morphology of the neuroses can with little difficulty be translated into aetiology and a knowledge of the latter leads on quite naturally to new indications for methods of cure.

Now the important decision we have to make—and this can be done with certainty in every instance if the symptoms are carefully assessed—is whether the case bears the characteristics of neurasthenia or of a psychoneurosis (hysteria, obsessions). (Mixed cases in which signs of neurasthenia are combined with signs of a psychoneurosis are of very frequent occurrence; but we will leave consideration of them till later.) It is only in neurasthenias that questioning the patient succeeds in disclosing the aetiological factors in his sexual life. These factors are, of course, known to him and belong to the present time, or, more properly, to the period of his life since sexual maturity (though this delimitation does not cover every case). In psychoneuroses questioning of this kind has little result. It may perhaps give us a knowledge of the factors which have to be recognized as precipitating ones, and these may or may not be connected with sexual life. If they are, they show themselves to be no different in kind from the aetiological factors of neurasthenia; that is, they entirely lack any specific relation to the causation of the psychoneurosis. And yet, in every instance, the aetiology of the psychoneuroses, too, lies in the field of sexuality. By a curious circuitous path, of which I shall speak later, it is possible to arrive at a knowledge of this aetiology and to understand why the patient was unable to tell us anything about it. For the events and influences which lie at the root of every psychoneurosis belong, not to the present day, but to an epoch of life which is long past and which is, as it were, a prehistoric one—to the time of early childhood; and that is why the patient, too, knows nothing of them. He has—though only in a particular sense—forgotten them.

Thus, in every case of neurosis there is a sexual aetiology; but in neurasthenia it is an aetiology of a present-day kind, whereas in the psychoneuroses the factors are of an infantile nature. This is the first great contrast in the aetiology of the neuroses. A second one emerges when we take account of a difference in the symptomatology of neurasthenia itself. Here, on the one hand, we find cases in which certain complaints characteristic of neurasthenia (intracranial pressure, proneness to fatigue, dyspepsia, constipation, spinal irritation, etc.) are prominent; in other cases these signs play a minor part and the clinical picture is composed of other symptoms, all of which exhibit a relation to the nuclear symptom, that of anxiety (free anxiousness, unrest, expectant anxiety, complete, rudimentary or supplementary anxiety attacks, locomotor vertigo, agoraphobia, insomnia, increased sensitivity to pain, and so on). I have left the name of neurasthenia to the first type, but have distinguished the second type as 'anxiety neurosis'; and I have given reasons for this separation in another place,[1] where I have also taken account of the fact that as a rule both neuroses appear together.[2] For the present purpose it is enough to emphasize that parallel to the difference in the symptoms of these two forms of illness there goes a difference in their aetiology. Neurasthenia can always be traced back to a condition of the nervous system such as is acquired by excessive masturbation or arises spontaneously from frequent emissions; anxiety neurosis regularly discloses sexual influences which have in common the factor of reservation or of incomplete satisfaction—such as coitus interruptus, abstinence together with a lively libido, so-called unconsummated excitation, and so on. In my short paper intended to introduce anxiety neurosis I put forward the formula that anxiety is always libido which has been deflected from its [normal] employment.[3]

Where there is a case in which symptoms of neurasthenia and of anxiety neurosis are combined—where, that is, we have a mixed case—we have only to keep to our proposition, empirically arrived at, that a mingling of neuroses implies the col-

[1] [See Freud's first paper on anxiety neurosis (1895b), p. 85 ff. above.]
[2] [P. 112 ff.]   [3] [P. 108.]

laboration of several aetiological factors, and we shall find our expectation confirmed in every instance. How often these aetiological factors are linked with one another organically, through the interplay of sexual processes—for instance, coitus interruptus or insufficient potency in the man, going along with masturbation—would well deserve separate discussion.

Having diagnosed a case of neurasthenic neurosis with certainty and having classified its symptoms correctly, we are in a position to translate the symptomatology into aetiology; and we may then boldly demand confirmation of our suspicions from the patient. We must not be led astray by initial denials. If we keep firmly to what we have inferred, we shall in the end conquer every resistance by emphasizing the unshakeable nature of our convictions. In this way we learn all sorts of things about the sexual life of men and women, which might well fill a useful and instructive volume; and we learn, too, to regret from every point of view that sexual science is even to-day still regarded as disreputable. Since minor deviations from a normal *vita sexualis* are much too common for us to attach any value to their discovery, we shall only allow a serious and long-continued abnormality in the sexual life of a neurotic patient to carry weight as an explanation. Moreover, the idea that one might, by one's insistence, cause a patient who is psychically normal to accuse himself falsely of sexual misdemeanours—such an idea may safely be disregarded as an imaginary danger.

If one proceeds in this manner with one's patients, one also gains the conviction that, so far as the theory of the sexual aetiology of neurasthenia is concerned, there are no negative cases. In my mind, at least, the conviction has become so certain that where an interrogation has shown a negative result, I have turned this to account too for diagnostic purposes. I have told myself, that is, that such a case cannot be one of neurasthenia. In this way I have been led in several instances to assume the presence of progressive paralysis instead of neurasthenia, because I had not succeeded in establishing the fact—a fact that was necessary for my theory—that the patient indulged very freely in masturbation; and the further course of those cases later confirmed my view. In another instance the patient, who exhibited no clear organic changes, complained of intracranial pressure, headaches and dyspepsia, but countered my

suspicions about his sexual life straightforwardly and with un-
shaken certainty; and the possibility occurred to me that he
might have a latent suppuration in one of his nasal sinuses. A
specialist colleague of mine confirmed this inference I had made
from the negative sexual results of my interrogation, by removing the pus from the patient's antrum and relieving him of
his ailments.

The appearance of there nevertheless being 'negative cases'
can arise in another way as well. Sometimes an interrogation
discloses the presence of a normal sexual life in a patient whose
neurosis, on a superficial view, does in fact closely resemble
neurasthenia or anxiety neurosis. But a more deep-going investigation regularly reveals the true state of affairs. Behind such
cases, which have been taken for neurasthenia, there lies a
psychoneurosis—hysteria or obsessional neurosis. Hysteria in
especial, which imitates so many organic affections, can easily
assume the appearance of one of the 'actual neuroses' [1] by elev-
ating the latter's symptoms into hysterical ones. Such hysterias
in the form of neurasthenia are not even very rare. Falling back
on psychoneurosis when a case of neurasthenia shows a negative
sexual result, is, however, no cheap way out of the difficulty;
the proof that we are right is to be obtained by the method
which alone unmasks hysteria with certainty—the method of
psycho-analysis, to which we shall refer presently.

There may perhaps be some, however, who are quite willing
to recognize the sexual aetiology in their neurasthenic patients,
but who nevertheless blame it as one-sidedness if they are not
asked to pay attention as well to the other factors which are
always mentioned by the authorities as causes of neurasthenia.
Now it would never occur to me to substitute a sexual aetiology
in neuroses for every other aetiology, and so to assert that the
latter have no operative force. This would be a misunderstanding. What I think is rather that in addition to all the
familiar aetiological factors which have been recognized—and
probably correctly so—by the authorities as leading to neurasthenia, the sexual factors, which have not hitherto been sufficiently appreciated, should also be taken into account. In my

---

[1] ['*Aktuelle Neurose*', literally 'present-day neurosis'. The term appears
for the first time in its usual later form of '*Aktualneurose*' on p. 279 below,
where there is further comment.]

opinion, however, these sexual factors deserve to be given a special place in the aetiological series.[1] For they alone are never absent in any case of neurasthenia, they alone are capable of producing the neurosis without any further assistance, so that those other factors seem to be reduced to the role of an auxiliary and supplementary aetiology, and they alone allow the physician to recognize firm relations between their manifold nature and the multiplicity of the clinical pictures. If, on the other hand, I group together all the patients who have ostensibly become neurasthenic from overwork, emotional agitation, as an after-effect of typhoid fever, and so on, they show me nothing in common in their symptoms. The nature of their aetiology gives me no idea of what kind of symptoms to expect, any more than, conversely, does the clinical picture they present enable me to infer what aetiology is at work in them.

The sexual causes, too, are the ones which most readily offer the physician a foothold for his therapeutic influence. Heredity is no doubt an important factor, when it is present; it enables a strong pathological effect to come about where otherwise only a very slight one would have resulted. But heredity is inaccessible to the physician's influence; everyone is born with his own hereditary tendencies to illness, and we can do nothing to change them. Nor should we forget that it is precisely in regard to the aetiology of the neurasthenias that we must necessarily deny the first place to heredity. Neurasthenia (in both its forms) is one of those affections which anyone may easily acquire without having any hereditary taint. If it were otherwise, the enormous increase in neurasthenia, of which all the authorities complain, would be unthinkable. In what concerns civilization, among whose sins people so often include responsibility for neurasthenia, these authorities may indeed be right (although the way in which this comes about is probably quite different from what they imagine).[2] Yet the state of our civilization is, once again, something that is unalterable for the individual. Moreover this factor, being common to all the members of the same society, can never explain the fact of selectivity in the incidence of the illness. The physician who is not neurasthenic is exposed to the same influence of an allegedly detrimental civilization as the

[1] [For this and what follows see the second paper on anxiety neurosis (1895f), p. 135 above.]   [2] [See p. 278 below.]

neurasthenic patient whom he has to treat.[1] Subject to these
limitations, the factors of exhaustion retain their significance.
But the element of 'overwork', which physicians are so fond of
producing to their patients as the cause of their neurosis, is too
often unduly misused. It is quite true that anyone who, owing
to sexual noxae, has made himself disposed to neurasthenia,
tolerates intellectual work and the psychical exigencies of life
badly; but no one ever becomes neurotic through work or
excitement alone. Intellectual work is rather a protection
against falling ill of neurasthenia; it is precisely the most un-
remitting intellectual workers who remain exempt from neurasthenia, and what neurasthenics complain of as 'overwork that
is making them ill' does not as a rule deserve to be called
'intellectual work' at all, either in its quality or quantity.
Physicians will have to become accustomed to explaining to an
office-worker who has been 'overworked' at his desk or to a
housewife for whom her domestic activities have become too
heavy, that they have fallen ill, not because they have tried to
carry out duties which are in fact easily performed by a civilized
brain, but because all the while they have been grossly neglect-
ing and damaging their sexual life.[2]

Furthermore, it is only the sexual aetiology which makes it
possible for us to understand all the details of the clinical history
of neurasthenics, the mysterious improvements in the middle of
the course of the illness and the equally incomprehensible
deteriorations, both of which are usually related by doctors and
patients to whatever treatment has been adopted. In my re-
cords, which include more than two hundred cases, there is,
for instance, the story of a man who, when the treatment pre-
scribed by his family physician had done him no good, went to
Pastor Kneipp[3] and for a year after being treated by him

[1] [Cf. the much fuller discussions of this question in the paper on
' "Civilized" Sexual Morality and Modern Nervous Illness' (1908d)
and in *Civilization and its Discontents* (1930a). Further references will be
found in the Editor's Notes to these works, *Standard Ed.*, **9**, 179, and
21, 60 ff.]
[2] [Some remarks on 'overwork' occur in the second of the *Three
Essays* (1905d), *Standard Ed.*, **7**, 204, and in a footnote to Section III of
the late technical paper on 'Analysis Terminable and Interminable'
(1937c).]
[3] [Sebastian Kneipp (1821–97), of Bad Wörishofen in Swabia, was

showed an extraordinary improvement in the middle of his illness. But when, a year later, his symptoms grew worse once more and he again went to Wörishofen for help, the second treatment was unsuccessful. A glance into the patient's family record solved the double riddle. Six and a half months after his first return from Wörishofen his wife bore him a child. This meant that he had left her at the beginning of a pregnancy of which he was not yet aware; after his return he was able to practise *natural* intercourse with her. At the close of this period, which had a curative effect on him, his neurosis was started up afresh by his once more resorting to coitus interruptus; the second treatment was bound to prove a failure, since this pregnancy of his wife's remained her last.

There was a similar case, in which, once again, the treatment had an unexpected effect which called for an explanation. This case turned out to be still more instructive, for it exhibited a puzzling alternation in the symptoms of the neurosis. A young neurotic patient had been sent by his physician to a reputable hydropathic establishment on account of a typical neurasthenia. There his condition steadily improved at first, so that there was every prospect that he would be discharged as a grateful disciple of hydrotherapy. But in the sixth week a complete change occurred; the patient 'could no longer tolerate the water', became more and more nervous, and finally left the establishment after two more weeks, uncured and dissatisfied. When he complained to me about this therapeutic fraud I asked him a few questions about the symptoms which had overtaken him in the middle of the treatment. Curiously enough, a complete change had come over them. He had *entered* the sanatorium with intracranial pressure, fatigue and dyspepsia; what had troubled him *during* the treatment were excitement, attacks of dypsnoea, vertigo in walking, and disturbances of sleep. I was now able to say to him: 'You are doing hydrotherapy an injustice. As you yourself very well knew, you fell ill as a result of long-continued masturbation. In the sanatorium you gave up this form of satisfaction, and therefore you quickly recovered.

famous for his cold-water and 'nature cure'. Part of his treatment consisted in walking barefoot through wet grass. The present case had been referred to more briefly by Freud in his first paper on anxiety (1895*b*), p. 104 above.]

When you felt well, however, you unwisely sought to have relations with a lady—a fellow-patient, let us suppose—which could only lead to excitement without normal satisfaction. The beautiful walks in the neighbourhood of the establishment gave you ample opportunity for this. It was this relationship, not a sudden inability to tolerate hydrotherapy, which caused you to fall ill once more. Moreover, your present state of health leads me to conclude that you are continuing this relationship here in town as well.' I can assure my readers that the patient confirmed what I said, point by point.

The present treatment of neurasthenia—which is, perhaps, carried out most successfully in hydropathic establishments— has as its aim the amelioration of the nervous condition by means of two factors: shielding the patient and strengthening him. I have nothing to say against such a method of treatment, except that it takes no account of the circumstances of the patient's sexual life. According to my experience, it is highly desirable that the medical directors of such establishments should become properly aware that they are dealing, not with victims of civilization or heredity, but—*sit venia verbo*—with people who are crippled in sexuality. They would then, on the one hand, be more easily able to account for their successes as well as their failures; and, on the other, they would achieve new successes which, till now, have been at the mercy of chance or of the patient's unguided behaviour. If we take a neurasthenic woman, suffering from anxiety, away from her home and send her to a hydropathic establishment, and if there, freed from all duties, she is made to bathe and take exercise and eat plenty of food, we shall certainly be inclined to think that the improve- ment—often a brilliant one—which is achieved in a few weeks or months is due to the rest which she has enjoyed and to the invigorating effects of hydrotherapy. That may be so: but we are overlooking the fact that her removal from home also entails an interruption of marital intercourse, and that it is only the temporary elimination of this pathogenic cause which makes it possible for her to recover under favourable treatment. Neglect of this aetiological point of view brings its subsequent revenge, when what seemed such a gratifying cure turns out to be a very transitory one. Soon after the patient has returned to ordinary life the symptoms of the complaint appear once more and oblige him either to spend a part of his existence unproductively from time to time in establishments of this kind or to direct his hopes of recovery elsewhere. It is therefore clear that with neurasthenia the therapeutic problems must be attacked, not in hydropathic institutions but within the framework of the patient's life.

In other cases our aetiological theory can help the physician in charge of the institution by throwing light on the source of failures which occur in the institution itself, and can suggest to him means of avoiding them. Masturbation is far commoner among grown-up girls and mature men than is generally supposed, and it has a harmful effect not only by producing neurasthenic symptoms, but also because it keeps the patients under the weight of what they feel to be a disgraceful secret. Physicians who are not accustomed to translate neurasthenia into masturbation account for the patient's pathological state by referring it to some catchword like anaemia, under-nourishment, overwork, etc., and then expect to cure him by applying a therapy devised against those conditions. To their astonishment, however, periods of improvement in him alternate with periods in which all his symptoms grow worse and are accompanied by severe depression. The outcome of such a treatment is, in general, doubtful. If physicians knew that all the while the patient was struggling against his sexual habit and that he was in despair because he had once more been obliged to give way to it, if they understood how to win his secret from him, to make it less serious in his eyes and to support him in his fight against the habit, then the success of their therapeutic efforts might in this way well be assured.

To break the patient of the habit of masturbating is only one of the new therapeutic tasks which are imposed on the physician who takes the sexual aetiology of the neurosis into account; and it seems that precisely this task, like the cure of any other addiction, can only be carried out in an institution and under medical supervision. Left to himself, the masturbator is accustomed, whenever something happens that depresses him, to return to his convenient form of satisfaction. Medical treatment, in this instance, can have no other aim than to lead the neurasthenic, who has now recovered his strength, back to normal sexual intercourse. For sexual need, when once it has been aroused and

has been satisfied for any length of time, can no longer be
silenced; it can only be displaced along another path. Incidentally, the same thing applies to all treatments for breaking an
addiction. Their success will only be an apparent one, so long
as the physician contents himself with withdrawing the nar-
cotic substance from his patients, without troubling about the
source from which their imperative need for it springs. 'Habit' is
a mere form of words, without any explanatory value. Not
everyone who has occasion to take morphia, cocaine, chloral-
hydrate, and so on, for a period, acquires in this way an 'addiction' to them. Closer enquiry usually shows that these narcotics
are meant to serve—directly or indirectly—as a substitute for a
lack of sexual satisfaction; and whenever normal sexual life can
no longer be re-established, we can count with certainty on the
patient's relapse.[1]

Another task is set to the physician by the aetiology of
anxiety neurosis. It consists in inducing the patient to give up
all detrimental forms of sexual intercourse and to adopt normal
sexual relations. This duty, it will be understood, falls primarily
on the patient's trusted physician—his family doctor; and he
will do his patient a serious injury if he regards himself as too
respectable to intervene in this field.

Since in these instances it is most often a question of a married
couple, the physician's efforts at once encounter Malthusian
plans for limiting the number of conceptions in marriage. There
seems to me no doubt that such proposals are gaining ground
more and more among our middle classes. I have come across
some couples who have already begun practising methods for
preventing conception as soon as they have had their first
child, and others whose sexual intercourse was from their
wedding-night designed to comply with that purpose. The
problem of Malthusianism is far-reaching and complicated,
and I have no intention of handling it here in the exhaustive
manner which would actually be necessary for the treatment of

[1] [References to masturbation as the source of neurasthenia occur
many times in the Fliess letters. See, for instance, Draft B of February 8,
1893 (Freud 1950a). Freud's fullest later remarks on masturbation were
made in his contribution to a discussion of the subject in the Vienna
Psycho-Analytical Society (1912f) which showed very little alteration
in his views from these earlier ones. Further references will be found
in the Editor's Note to this (*Standard Ed.*, 12, 241 ff.).]

neuroses. I shall only consider what attitude a physician who recognizes the sexual aetiology of the neuroses had best take up towards the problem.

The worst thing he can do is obviously—under whatever pretext—to try to ignore it. Nothing that is necessary can be beneath my dignity as a doctor; and it is necessary to give a married couple who contemplate limiting the number of their offspring the assistance of one's medical advice if one does not want to expose one or both of them to a neurosis. It cannot be denied that in any marriage Malthusian preventive measures will become necessary at some time or other; and, from a theoretical point of view, it would be one of the greatest triumphs of humanity, one of the most tangible liberations from the constraints of nature to which mankind is subject, if we could succeed in raising the responsible act of procreating children to the level of a deliberate and intentional activity and in freeing it from its entanglement with the necessary satisfaction of a natural need.

A perspicacious physician will therefore take it upon himself to decide under what conditions the use of measures for preventing conception are justified, and, among those measures, he will have to separate the harmful from the harmless ones. Everything is harmful that hinders the occurrence of satisfaction. But, as we know, we possess at present no method of preventing conception which fulfils every legitimate requirement—that is, which is certain and convenient, which does not diminish the sensation of pleasure during coitus and which does not wound the woman's sensibilities. This sets physicians a practical task to the solution of which they could bend their energies with rewarding results. Whoever fills in this lacuna in our medical technique will have preserved the enjoyment of life and maintained the health of numberless people; though, it is true, he will also have paved the way for a drastic change in our social conditions.[1]

This does not exhaust the possibilities which flow from a

[1] [Freud returned to the problem of the use of contraceptives in his paper on ' "Civilized" Sexual Morality' (1908d), *Standard Ed.*, **9**, 194. He had already discussed it several times in his letters to Fliess, going back at least as early as one dated February 8, 1893 (Freud, 1950a, Draft B).]

recognition of the sexual aetiology of the neuroses. The main benefit which we obtain from it for neurasthenics lies in the sphere of prophylaxis. If masturbation is the cause of neurasthenia in youth, and if, later on, it acquires aetiological significance for anxiety neurosis as well, by reason of the reduction of potency which it brings about, then the prevention of masturbation in both sexes is a task that deserves more attention than it has hitherto received. When we reflect upon all the injuries, both the grosser and the finer ones, which proceed from neurasthenia—a disorder which we are told is growing more and more prevalent—we see that it is positively a matter of public interest that *men should enter upon sexual relations with full potency.* In matters of prophylaxis, however, the individual is relatively helpless. The whole community must become interested in the matter and give their assent to the creation of generally acceptable regulations. At present we are still far removed from such a state of affairs which would promise relief, and it is for this reason that we may with justice regard civilization, too, as responsible for the spread of neurasthenia.[1] Much would have to be changed. The resistance of a generation of physicians who can no longer remember their own youth must be broken down; the pride of fathers, who are unwilling to descend to the level of humanity in their children's eyes, must be overcome; and the unreasonable prudery of mothers must be combatted—the mothers who at present look upon it as an incomprehensible and undeserved stroke of fate that 'their children should have been the ones to become neurotic'. But above all, a place must be created in public opinion for the discussion of the problems of sexual life. It will have to become possible to talk about these things without being stamped as a trouble-maker or as a person who makes capital out of the lower instincts. And so here, too, there is enough work left to do for the next hundred years—in which our civilization will have to learn to come to terms with the claims of our sexuality.

The value of making a correct diagnostic separation of the psychoneuroses from neurasthenia is also shown by the fact that the psychoneuroses call for a different practical assessment and for special therapeutic measures. They make their appearance as a result of two kinds of determinants, either independently

[1] [See above, p. 271.]

or in the train of the 'actual neuroses' [1] (neurasthenia and anxiety neurosis). In the latter case we are dealing with a new type of neurosis—incidentally, a very frequent one—a mixed neurosis. The aetiology of the 'actual neuroses' has become an auxiliary aetiology of the psychoneuroses. A clinical picture arises in which, let us say, anxiety neurosis predominates but which also contains traits of genuine neurasthenia, hysteria and obsessional neurosis. When confronted with a mixture of this kind, we shall nevertheless not be wise to give up separating out the clinical pictures proper to each neurotic illness; for after all it is not difficult to explain the case to oneself in the following manner. The predominant place taken by the anxiety neurosis shows that the illness has come into being under the aetiological influence of an 'actual' [i.e. present-day] sexual noxa. But the person concerned was, apart from that, disposed to one or more of the psychoneuroses owing to a special aetiology and would at some time or other have fallen ill of a psychoneurosis either spontaneously or with the advent of some other weakening factor. In this way the auxiliary aetiology for the psychoneurosis which is still lacking is supplied by the actual [current] aetiology of the anxiety neurosis. [2]

For such cases it has quite correctly come to be the therapeutic practice to disregard the psychoneurotic components in the clinical picture and to treat the 'actual neurosis' exclusively. In very many cases it is possible to overcome the [psycho-] neurosis as well which it has brought along with it, provided that the neurasthenia is effectively dealt with. But a different view must be taken in those cases of psychoneurosis which either appear spontaneously or remain behind as an independ-

---

[1] [See footnote, p. 270 above. This is the first occurrence of the term, though the concept was an old one. The distinction between the 'actual' neuroses and the psychoneuroses is implied, for instance, in Freud's contribution to Studies on Hysteria (1895d), Standard Ed., 2, 257 ff.; and it is stated more clearly in the second paper on the neuro-psychoses of defence (1896b), p. 167 f. above, where the 'actual' neuroses are termed the 'simple' neuroses. At this period Freud often referred to them as 'the neuroses' without qualification. (Cf. the early lecture (1893h), p. 39 above.) A list of later references to the 'actual' neuroses is given in an Editor's footnote to the paper on ' "Wild" Psycho-Analysis' (1910k), ibid., 11, 224.]

[2] [Freud had pointed this out less fully above, p. 168.]

ent entity after an illness composed of neurasthenia and psychoneurosis has run its course. When I speak of a 'spontaneous'
appearance of a psychoneurosis, I do not mean that anamnestic
investigation shows us no aetiological element whatever. It
may do so, no doubt; but it may also happen that our attention
is directed to some indifferent factor—an emotional state, an
enfeeblement owing to physical illness, and so on. It must,
however, be borne in mind in all these cases that the true
aetiology of the psychoneuroses does not lie in such precipitating
causes, but remains beyond the reach of ordinary anamnestic
examination.

As we know, it is in an attempt to bridge this gap that the
assumption has been made of a special neuropathic disposition
(which, incidentally, if it existed, would not leave much hope
of success for the treatment of such pathological conditions).
The neuropathic disposition itself is regarded as a sign of a
general degeneracy, and thus this convenient technical term
has come to be superabundantly used against the wretched
patients whom the doctors are quite incapable of helping.
Fortunately, the state of affairs is different. The neuropathic
disposition does no doubt exist, but I must deny that it suffices
for the creation of a psychoneurosis. I must further deny that
the conjunction of a neuropathic disposition with precipitating
causes occurring in later life constitutes an adequate aetiology
of the psychoneuroses. In tracing back the vicissitudes of an
individual's illness to the experiences of his ancestors, we have
gone too far; we have forgotten that between his conception
and his maturity there lies a long and important period of life
—his childhood—in which the seeds of later illness may be
acquired. And that is what in fact happens with a psychoneurosis. Its true aetiology is to be found in childhood experiences, and, once again—and exclusively—in impressions concerned with sexual life. We do wrong to ignore the sexual life of
children entirely; in my experience, children are capable of
every psychical sexual activity, and many somatic sexual ones
as well. Just as the whole human sexual apparatus is not com-
prised in the external genitals and the two reproductive glands,
so human sexual life does not begin only with puberty, as on a
rough inspection it may appear to do. Nevertheless it is true
that the organization and evolution of the human species strives

to avoid any great degree of sexual activity during childhood. It seems that in man the sexual instinctual forces are meant to be stored up so that, on their release at puberty, they may serve great cultural ends. (W. Fliess.) Consideration of this sort may make it possible to understand why the sexual experiences of childhood are bound to have a pathogenic effect. But they produce their effect only to a very slight degree at the time at which they occur; what is far more important is their *deferred* effect, which can only take place at later periods of growth. This deferred effect originates—as it can do in no other way— in the psychical traces which have been left behind by infantile sexual experiences. During the interval between the experiences of those impressions and their reproduction (or rather, the reinforcement of the libidinal impulses which proceed from them), not only the somatic sexual apparatus but the psychical apparatus as well has undergone an important development; and thus it is that the influence of these earlier sexual experiences now leads to an abnormal psychical reaction, and psychopathological structures come into existence.

I can do no more in these brief hints than mention the chief factors on which the theory of the psychoneuroses is based: the deferred nature of the effect and the infantile state of the sexual apparatus and of the mental instrument. To reach a true understanding of the mechanism by which the psychoneuroses come about, a more extended exposition would be necessary. Above all, it would be indispensable to put forward as worthy of belief certain hypotheses, which seem to me to be new, about the composition and mode of operation of the psychical apparatus. In a book on the interpretation of dreams on which I am now engaged I shall find occasion to touch upon those fundamental elements of a psychology of the neuroses. For dreams belong to the same set of psychopathological structures as hysterical *idées fixes*, obsessions, and delusions.[1]

Since the manifestations of the psychoneuroses arise from the deferred action of unconscious psychical traces, they are accessible to psychotherapy. But in this case the therapy must pursue paths other than the only one so far followed of suggestion with

---

[1] [Freud's *Interpretation of Dreams* (1900a), published less than two years after this paper, contained in its seventh chapter the first full publication of his views on the structure and function of the mind.]

or without hypnosis. Basing myself on the 'cathartic' method introduced by Josef Breuer, I have in recent years almost completely worked out a therapeutic procedure which I propose to describe as *'psycho-analytic'*. I owe a great number of successes to it, and I hope I may be able further to increase its effectiveness considerably. The first accounts of the technique and scope of this method were given in *Studies on Hysteria*, written jointly with Breuer and published in 1895. Since then a good deal, as I think I may say, has been altered for the better. Whereas at that time we modestly declared that we could undertake only to remove the symptoms of hysteria, not to cure hysteria itself,[1] this distinction has since come to seem to me without substance, so that there is a prospect of a genuine cure of hysteria and obsessions. It is therefore with very lively interest that I have read in the publications of colleagues that 'in this case the ingenious procedure devised by Breuer and Freud has failed', or that 'the method has not performed what it seemed to promise'. This gave me something of the feelings of a man who reads his own obituary in the paper, but who is able to reassure himself by his better knowledge of the facts. For the method is so difficult that it has quite definitely to be learned; and I cannot recall that a single one of my critics has expressed a wish to learn it from me. Nor do I believe that, like me, they have occupied themselves with it intensely enough to have been able to discover it for themselves. The remarks in the *Studies on Hysteria* are totally inadequate to enable a reader to master the technique, nor are they in any way intended to give any such complete instruction.

Psycho-analytic therapy is not at present applicable to all cases. It has, to my knowledge, the following limitations. It demands a certain degree of maturity and understanding in the patient and is therefore not suited for the young or for adults who are feeble-minded or uneducated. It also fails with people who are very advanced in years, because, owing to the accumulation of material in them, it would take up so much time that by the end of the treatment they would have reached a period of life in which value is no longer attached to nervous health. Finally, the treatment is only possible if the patient has a normal

---

[1] [Cf. the closing sentences of Freud's early lecture (1893*h*), p. 39 above.]

psychical state from which the pathological material can be mastered. During a condition of hysterical confusion, or an interpolated mania or melancholia, nothing can be effected by psycho-analytic means. Such cases can nevertheless be treated by analysis after the violent manifestations have been quieted by the usual measures. In actual practice, chronic cases of psychoneurosis are altogether more amenable to the method than cases with acute crises, in which the greatest stress is naturally laid on the speed with which the crises can be dealt with. For this reason, the most favourable field of work for this new therapy is offered by hysterical phobias and the various forms of obsessional neurosis.

That the method is confined within these limits is to a large extent explained by the circumstances in which I had to work it out. My material does in fact consist of chronic nervous cases derived from the more educated classes. I think it very probable that supplementary methods may be devised for treating children and the public who go for assistance to hospitals. I ought also to say that up to the present I have tried my treatment exclusively on *severe* cases of hysteria and obsessional neurosis; I cannot tell how it would turn out with those mild cases which, to all appearance at least, are cured by some unspecific kind of treatment lasting for a few months. It will readily be understood that a new therapy which calls for many sacrifices can only reckon on obtaining patients who have already tried the generally accepted methods without success, or whose condition has justified the inference that they could expect nothing from these supposedly more convenient and shorter therapeutic procedures. Thus it happened that I was obliged to tackle the hardest tasks straightaway with an imperfect instrument. The test has proved all the more convincing.

The main difficulties which still stand in the way of the psycho-analytic method of cure are not due to itself but to the lack of understanding among doctors and laymen of the nature of the psychoneuroses. It is no more than a necessary corollary to this complete ignorance that doctors consider themselves justified in using the most unfounded assurances for the consolation of their patients or in order to induce them to adopt therapeutic measures. 'Come to my sanatorium for six weeks', they will say, 'and you will get rid of your symptoms' (travel anxiety, obsessions, and so on). Sanatoria are, it is true, indispensable for calming acute attacks that may arise in the course of a psychoneurosis by diverting the patient's attention, nursing him and taking care of him. But towards removing chronic conditions they achieve precisely nothing: and the superior sanatoria, which are supposed to be conducted on scientific lines, do no more than the ordinary hydropathic establishments.

It would be more dignified as well as more helpful to the patient—who, after all, has to come to terms with his ailments— for the doctor to tell the truth, as he knows it from his daily practice. The psychoneuroses as a genus are by no means mild illnesses. When hysteria sets in, no one can foretell when it will come to an end. We mostly comfort ourselves with the vain prophecy that 'one day it will suddenly disappear'. Recovery often enough turns out to be merely an agreement to mutual toleration between the sick part of the patient and the healthy part; or it is the result of the transformation of a symptom into a phobia. A girl's hysteria, calmed down with difficulty, revives in her as a wife after the short interruption of young married happiness. The only difference is that another person, the husband, is now driven by his own interests to keep silence about her condition. Even if an illness of this kind leads to no manifest incapacity on the patients' part to carry on their life, it nearly always prevents free unfolding of their mental powers. Obsessions recur throughout their lives; and phobias and other restrictions upon the will have hitherto been unamenable to treatment of any kind. All this is kept from the knowledge of the layman. The father of a hysterical girl is consequently horrified if, for instance, he is asked to agree to her being given a year's treatment, when she has perhaps only been ill for a few months. The layman is, as it were, deeply convinced in himself that all these psychoneuroses are unnecessary; so he has no patience with the processes of the illness and no readiness to make sacrifices for its treatment. If, in face of a case of typhus which lasts three weeks, or of a broken leg which takes six months to mend, he adopts a more understanding attitude, and if, as soon as his child shows the first signs of a curvature of the spine, he finds it reasonable that orthopaedic treatment should be carried on over several years, the difference in his behaviour is due to the better knowledge on the part of the physicians who pass on their knowledge honestly to the layman. Honesty on the part of the physician and willing acquiescence on the part of the layman will be established for the neuroses too, as soon as an insight into the nature of those affections becomes common property in the medical world. Radical treatment of these disorders will no doubt always require special training and will be incompatible with other kinds of medical activity. On the other hand, this class of physicians, which will, I believe, be a large one in the future, has the prospect of achieving noteworthy results and of obtaining a satisfying insight into the mental life of mankind.

THE PSYCHICAL MECHANISM OF FORGETFULNESS

(1898)

ZUM PSYCHISCHEN MECHANISMUS DER VERGESSLICHKEIT

(a) German Editions:

1898   Mschr. Psychiat. Neurol., **4** (6), 436–443. (December.)

1952   G.W., **1**, 519–27.

(b) English Translation:

'The Psychical Mechanism of Forgetfulness'

The present translation, by Alix Strachey, seems to be the first into English.

The episode which is the subject of this paper occurred during Freud's visit to the Adriatic coast in September, 1898. He sent a short account of it to Fliess on his return to Vienna in a letter dated September 22 (Freud, 1950a, Letter 96), and reported a few days later (September 27, ibid., Letter 97) that he had sent this paper off to the journal in which it appeared soon afterwards. This was the first published history of a parapraxis, and Freud made it the basis of the opening chapter of his longer work on the subject three years later (1901b); the Editor's Introduction to this (*Standard Ed.*, **6**) discusses the whole matter more fully. The present paper was only reprinted after Freud's death, more than fifty years after its first publication. It had been generally assumed, on the basis of Freud's remarks at the beginning of the first chapter of *The Psychopathology of Everyday Life*, ibid., **1**, that what was in question was no more than a rough draft of the later version. An actual comparison of the two works now shows that only the main lines of the topic are the same, that the chain of argument is differently arranged here, and that at one or two points the material is amplified.

THE PSYCHICAL MECHANISM
OF FORGETFULNESS

THE phenomenon of forgetfulness, which I should like to describe and then go on to explain in this paper, has doubtless been experienced by everyone in himself or been observed by him in others. It affects in particular the use of proper names—*nomina propria*—and it manifests itself in the following manner. In the middle of carrying on a conversation we find ourselves obliged to confess to the person we are talking to that we cannot hit on a name we wanted to mention at that moment, and we are forced to ask for his—usually ineffectual—help. 'What *is* his name? I know it so well. It's on the tip of my tongue. Just this minute it's escaped me.' An unmistakable feeling of irritation, similar to that which accompanies motor aphasia, now attends our further efforts to find the name, which we feel we had in our head only a moment before. In appropriate instances two accompanying features deserve our notice. First, an energetic deliberate concentration of the function which we call attention proves powerless, however long it is continued, to find the lost name. Secondly, in place of the name we are looking for, another name promptly appears, which we recognize as incorrect and reject, but which persists in coming back. Or else, instead of a substituted name, we find in our memory a single letter or syllable, which we recognize as parts of the name we are in search of. We say, for instance: 'It begins with a "B".' If we finally succeed, in one way or another, in discovering what the name is, we find in the great majority of cases that it does not begin with a 'B' and does not in fact contain the letter 'B' at all.[1]

The best procedure for getting hold of the missing name is, as is generally known, 'not to think of it'—that is, to divert from the task that part of the attention over which one has voluntary control. After a while, the missing name 'shoots' into one's

---

[1] [Freud enlarges a little on this in Chapter V of *The Psychopathology of Everyday Life* (1901b), *Standard Ed.*, **6**, 55.]

mind; one cannot prevent oneself from calling it out aloud—to the great astonishment of one's companion, who has already forgotten the episode and who has in any case only taken very little interest in the speaker's efforts. 'Really,' he is apt to say, 'it makes no difference *what* the man is called; only go on with your story.' The whole of the time until the matter is cleared up, and even after the intentional diversion [of one's attention], one feels preoccupied to a degree which cannot in fact be explained by the amount of interest possessed by the whole affair.[1]

In a few cases which I have myself experienced of forgetting names in this way, I have succeeded, by means of psychical analysis, in accounting to myself for the chain of events; and I shall now describe in detail the simplest and clearest case of this kind.

During my summer holidays I once went for a carriage-drive from the lovely city of Ragusa[2] to a town nearby in Herzegovina. Conversation with my companion centred, as was natural, round the condition of the two countries (Bosnia and Herzegovina)[3] and the character of their inhabitants. I talked about the various peculiarities of the Turks living there, as I had heard them described years before by a friend and colleague who had lived among them as a doctor for many years. A little later, our conversation turned to the subject of Italy and of pictures, and I had occasion to recommend my companion strongly to visit Orvieto some time, in order to see the frescoes there of the end of the world and the Last Judgement, with which one of the chapels in the cathedral had been decorated by a great artist. But the artist's name escaped me and I could not recall it. I exerted my powers of recollection, made all the details of the day I spent in Orvieto pass before my memory and convinced myself that not the smallest part of it had been obliterated or become indistinct. On the contrary, I was able to conjure up the pictures with greater sensory vividness than is

[1] Nor by any feeling of unpleasure one may have at being inhibited in a psychical act.

[2] [On the Dalmatian coast of the Adriatic, now known as Dubrovnik. Freud's companion on the drive was a Berlin lawyer named Freyhau (Freud, 1950a, Letter 96).]

[3] [Provinces adjoining Dalmatia and forming part of the Austro-Hungarian Empire before 1914.]

usual with me.[1] I saw before my eyes with especial sharpness the artist's self-portrait—with a serious face and folded hands—which he has put in a corner of one of the pictures, next to the portrait of his predecessor in the work, Fra Angelico da Fiesole; but the artist's name, ordinarily so familiar to me, remained obstinately in hiding, nor could my travelling companion help me out. My continued efforts met with no success beyond bringing up the names of two other artists, who I knew could not be the right ones. These were *Botticelli* and, in the second place, *Boltraffio*.[2] The repetition of the sound 'Bo' in the two substitutive names might perhaps have led a novice to suppose that it belonged to the missing name as well, but I took good care to steer clear of that expectation.

Since I had no access to any reference books on my journey, I had for several days to put up with this lapse of memory and with the inner torment associated with it which recurred at frequent intervals each day, until I fell in with a cultivated Italian who freed me from it by telling me the name: *Signorelli*. I was myself able to add the artist's *first* name, *Luca*. Soon my ultra-clear memory of the master's features, as depicted in his portrait, faded away.

What influences had led me to forget the name *Signorelli*, which was so familiar to me and which is so easily impressed on the memory? And what paths had led to its replacement by the names *Botticelli* and *Boltraffio*? A short excursion back into

---

[1] [Freud is here drawing attention to an observation that, when a memory is repressed, there often emerges into consciousness *with unusual vividness* an image of something which is not the repressed memory itself but which, though unimportant and irrelevant, is closely related to the repressed memory. Another instance of this is mentioned at the end of the present paper (p. 297 below), and a similar one in the paper on 'Screen Memories' (1899a) which follows this one (p. 312 f.). In a footnote to *The Psychopathology of Everyday Life* (1901b), where the present instance reappears (*Standard Ed.*, **6**, 13), Freud suggests an explanation of this phenomenon; and other examples appear in the same volume (ibid., 267 and 41), added to the work in 1907 and 1920 respectively. In one of his very last papers, on 'Constructions in Analysis' (1937d, Section III), Freud once again takes up the question and relates it to the general problem of hallucinations. In all of these examples he uses the German word '*überdeutlich*', which is here translated 'ultra-clear'.]

[2] The first of these names was very familiar to me; the second, on the other hand, I hardly knew.

the circumstances in which the forgetting had taken place sufficed to throw a light on both questions.

Shortly before I had come to the subject of the frescoes in the cathedral at Orvieto, I had been telling my travelling-companion something I had heard from my colleague years ago about the Turks in Bosnia. They treat doctors with special respect and they show, in marked contrast to our own people, an attitude of resignation towards the dispensations of fate. If the doctor has to inform the father of a family that one of his relatives is about to die, his reply is: '*Herr* [Sir], what is there to be said? If he could be saved, I know you would help him.' Another recollection lay in my memory close to this story. The same colleague had told me what overriding importance these Bosnians attached to sexual enjoyments. One of his patients said to him once: '*Herr*, you must know, that if *that* comes to an end then life is of no value.' At the time, it seemed to the doctor and me that the two character-traits of the Bosnian people illustrated by this could be assumed to be intimately connected with each other. But when I remembered these stories on my drive into Herzegovina, I suppressed the second one, in which the subject of sexuality was touched on. It was soon after this that the name *Signorelli* escaped me and that the names *Botticelli* and *Boltraffio* appeared as substitutes.

The influence which had made the name *Signorelli* inaccessible to memory, or, as I am accustomed to say, had 'repressed' it, could only proceed from the story I had suppressed about the value set on death and sexual enjoyment. If that was so, we ought to be able to discover the intermediate ideas which had served to connect the two themes. The affinity between their *content*—in the one case, the Last Judgement, 'Doomsday', and in the other, death and sexuality—seems to be very slight; and since the matter concerned the repression from memory of a *name*, it was on the face of it probable that the connection was between one name and another. Now, '*Signor*' means '*Herr* [Sir]', and the '*Herr*' is also present in the name '*Herzegovina*'. Moreover it was certainly not without relevance that both the patients' remarks which I was to recall contained a '*Herr*' as a form of address to the doctor. The translation of '*Signor*' into '*Herr*' was therefore the means by which the story that I had suppressed had drawn after it into repression the name I was looking for. The whole process was clearly made easier by the fact that during the last few days in Ragusa I had been speaking Italian continually—that is, that I had become accustomed to translating German into Italian in my head.[1]

When I tried to recover the name of the artist, to bring it back out of repression, the influence of the tic which the name had entered into in the meantime inevitably made itself felt. I did find an artist's name, but not the right one. It was a displaced name, and the line of displacement was laid down by the names that were contained in the repressed topic. 'Botticelli' contains the same final syllables as 'Signorelli'; the final syllables —which, unlike the first part of the word, 'Signor', could not make a direct connection with the name 'Herzegovina'—had therefore returned; but the influence of the name 'Bosnia', which is regularly associated with the name 'Herzegovina',[2] had shown itself by directing the substitution to two artists' names which began with the same syllable 'Bo': 'Botticelli' and then 'Boltraffio'. The finding of the name 'Signorelli' is thus seen to have been interfered with by the topic which lay behind it, in which the names 'Bosnia' and 'Herzegovina' appear.

For this topic to have been able to produce such effects it is not enough that I should have suppressed it once in conversation—an event brought about by chance motives. We must assume rather that the topic itself was also intimately bound up with trains of thought which were in a state of repression in me—that is, with trains of thought which, in spite of the intensity of the interest taken in them, were meeting with a resistance that was keeping them from being worked over by a particular psychical agency and thus from becoming conscious.

[1] 'A far-fetched, forced explanation', it will be said. This impression is bound to arise because the suppressed topic struggles by every possible means to establish a connection with what is not suppressed; and for this purpose it does not scorn even the path of external association. There is the same 'forced' situation when rhymes have to be made. [The stress under which rhyming verse has to be constructed was described by Freud in Section D of Chapter VI of *The Interpretation of Dreams* (1900a), *Standard Ed.*, 5, 340.—By an 'external association' is meant a superficial one, e.g. by similarity of sound without any connection of meaning.]

[2] [The two provinces were constantly mentioned together owing to their geographical and historical links.]

That this was really true at that time of the topic of 'death and sexuality' I have plenty of evidence, which I need not bring up here, derived from my own self-investigation. But I may draw attention to one consequence of these repressed thoughts. Experience has taught me to require that every psychical product shall be fully elucidated and even overdetermined. Accordingly, it seemed to me that the second substitutive name, 'Boltraffio', called for a further determination; for so far only its initial letters had been accounted for, by their assonance with 'Bosnia'. I now recollected that these repressed thoughts had never engrossed me more than they had a few weeks before, after I had received a certain piece of news.[1] The place where the news reached me was called '*Trafoi*' and this name is too much like the second half of the name 'Boltraffio' not to have had a determining effect on my choice of the latter. In the following small schematic diagram [Fig. 1], I have attempted to reproduce the relations which have now been brought to light.

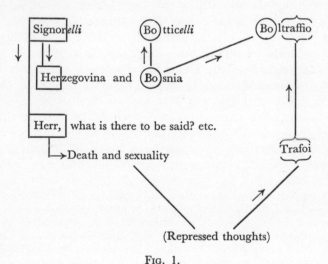

FIG. 1.

It is perhaps not without interest for its own sake to be able to

---

[1] [The news of the suicide of one of his patients 'on account of an incurable sexual complaint'. See *The Psychopathology of Everyday Life*, *Standard Ed.*, **6**, 3. Trafoi is a village in the Tyrol.]

see into the history of a psychical event of this kind, which is among the most trivial disturbances that can affect the control of the psychical apparatus and which is compatible with an otherwise untroubled state of psychical health. But the example elucidated here receives an immensely added interest when we learn that it may serve as nothing more nor less than a model for the pathological processes to which the psychical symptoms of the psychoneuroses—hysteria, obsessions and paranoia—owe their origin. In both cases we find the same elements and the same play of forces between those elements. In the same manner as here and by means of similar superficial associations, a repressed train of thought takes possession in neuroses of an innocent recent impression and draws it down with itself into repression. The same mechanism which causes the substitute names 'Botticelli' and 'Boltraffio' to emerge from 'Signorelli' (a substitution by means of intermediate or compromise ideas) also governs the formation of obsessional thoughts and paranoic paramnesias. Again, we have seen that such cases of forgetfulness have the characteristic of liberating continuous unpleasure till the moment the problem is solved—a characteristic which is unintelligible apart from this, and something which [in the instance I have quoted] was in fact unintelligible to the person I was talking to [p. 290]; but there is a complete analogy to it in the way in which collections of repressed thoughts attach their capacity for producing affect to some symptom whose psychical content seems to our judgement totally unsuited to such a liberation of affect. Finally, the resolution of the whole tension by a communication of the correct name from an external quarter is itself a good example of the efficacy of psychoanalytic therapy, which aims at correcting the repressions and displacements and which removes the symptoms by re-instating the genuine psychical object.[1]

Among the various factors, therefore, which contribute to a failure in recollection or a loss of memory, the part played by repression must not be overlooked; and it can be demonstrated not only in neurotics but (in a manner that is qualitatively the same) in normal people as well. It may be asserted quite

---

[1] [The comparison between the mechanism of parapraxes and of neurotic symptoms had been very briefly indicated in a letter from Freud to Fliess of August 26, 1898 (Freud 1950a, Letter 94).]

generally that the ease (and ultimately the faithfulness, too) with which a given impression is awakened in the memory depends not only on the psychical constitution of the individual, the strength of the impression when it was fresh, the interest directed towards it at the time, the psychical constellation at the present time, the interest that is *now* devoted to its awakening, the connections into which the impression has been drawn, and so on—not only on such things but also on the favourable or unfavourable attitude of a particular psychical factor which refuses to reproduce anything that might liberate unpleasure, or that might subsequently lead to the liberation of unpleasure. Thus the function of memory, which we like to regard as an archive open to anyone who is curious, is in this way subjected to restriction by a trend of the will, just as is any part of our activity directed to the external world. Half the secret of hysterical amnesia is uncovered when we say that hysterical people do not know what they do not *want* to know; and psycho-analytic treatment, which endeavours to fill up such gaps of memory in the course of its work, leads us to the discovery that the bringing back of those lost memories is opposed by a certain resistance which has to be counterbalanced by work proportionate to its magnitude. In the case of psychical processes which are on the whole normal, it cannot, of course, be claimed that the influence of this one-sided factor in the revival of memories in any way regularly overcomes all the other factors that must be taken into account.[1]

In connection with the tendentious nature of our remembering and forgetting, I not long ago experienced an instructive example—instructive because of what it betrayed—of which I

---

[1] It would be a mistake to believe that the mechanism which I have brought to light in these pages only operates in rare cases. It is, on the contrary, a very common one. On one occasion, for instance, when I was meaning to describe the same small incident to a colleague of mine, the name of my authority for the stories about Bosnia suddenly escaped me. The reason for this was as follows. Just before, I had been playing cards. My [Bosnian] authority was called Pick. Now '*Pick*' and '*Herz*' ['Spades' and 'Hearts'] are two of the four suits in the pack. Moreover the two words were connected by an anecdote in which this same person pointed to himself and said: 'I'm not called "*Herz*", but "*Pick*".' '*Herz*' appears in the name '*Herzegovina*' and the heart itself, as a sick bodily organ, played a part in the thoughts I have described as having been repressed.

should like to add an account here. I was intending to pay a twenty-four-hour visit to a friend of mine who unfortunately lives very far away, and I was full of the things I was going to tell him. But before this I felt under an obligation to call on a family of my acquaintance in Vienna, one of whose members had moved to the town in question, so as to take their greetings and messages with me to the absent relative. They told me the name of the *pension* in which he lived, and also the name of the street and the number of the house, and, in view of my bad memory, wrote the address on a card, which I put in my wallet. The next day, when I had arrived at my friend's, I began: 'I've only one duty to carry out that may interfere with our being together; it's a call, and it shall be the first thing I do. The address is in my wallet.' To my astonishment, however, it was not to be found there. So now I had to fall back on my memory, after all. My memory for names is not particularly good, but it is incomparably better than for figures and numbers. I may have been paying medical visits at a certain house for a year on end, and yet, if I should have to be driven there by a cab-driver, I should have difficulty in remembering the number of the house. But in this case I had taken special note of the house-number; it was ultra-clear,[1] as if to jeer at me—for no trace remained in my recollection of the name of the *pension* or the street. I had forgotten all the data in the address which might have served as a starting-point for discovering the *pension*; and, quite against my usual habit, I had retained the number of the house, which was useless for the purpose. In consequence, I was unable to make the call. I was consoled remarkably quickly, and I devoted myself entirely to my friend. When I was back again in Vienna and standing in front of my writing desk, I knew without a moment's hesitation where it was that, in my 'absent-mindedness', I had put the card with the address on it. In my unconscious hiding of the thing the same intention had been operative as in my curiously modified act of forgetting.[2]

[1] [See footnote 1, p. 291 above.]
[2] [This anecdote is told much more shortly in a footnote to Chapter II of *The Psychopathology of Everyday Life, Standard Ed.*, 6, 13.]

SCREEN MEMORIES

(1899)

EDITOR'S NOTE

ÜBER DECKERINNERUNGEN

(a) GERMAN EDITIONS:

1899   *Mschr. Psychiat. Neurol.*, **6** (3), 215–30. (September.)
1925   *G.S.*, **1**, 465–88.
1952   *G.W.*, **1**, 531–54.

(b) ENGLISH TRANSLATION:
                    'Screen Memories'
1950   *C.P.*, **5**, 47–69. (Tr. James Strachey.)

The present translation is a slightly revised reprint of that published in 1950.

An unpublished letter of Freud's to Fliess of May 25, 1899, tells him that on that date this paper was sent in to the editor of the periodical in which it appeared later in the year. He adds that he was immensely pleased by it during its production, which he takes as a bad omen for its future fate.

The concept of 'screen memories' was here introduced by Freud for the first time. It was no doubt brought into focus by his consideration of the particular instance which occupies the major part of the paper and which had been alluded to in a letter to Fliess of January 3, 1899 (Letter 101). Nevertheless the topic was closely related to several others which had been occupying his mind for many months previously—in fact ever since he had embarked on his self-analysis in the summer of 1897—problems concerning the operation of memory and its distortions, the importance and *raison d'être* of phantasies, the amnesia covering our early years, and, behind all this, infantile sexuality. Readers of the Fliess letters will find many approaches to the present discussion. See, for instance, the remarks on phantasies in Draft M of May 25, 1897 and in Letter 66 of July 7, 1897. The screen memories analysed by Freud at the end of

301

Chapter IV of the 1907 edition of *The Psychopathology of Everyday Life* (1901*b*) go back to this same summer of 1897.

It is a curious thing that the type of screen memory mainly considered in the present paper—one in which an early memory is used as a screen for a later event—almost disappears from later literature. What has since come to be regarded as the regular type—one in which an early event is screened by a later memory—is only barely alluded to here, though it was already the one almost exclusively dealt with by Freud only two years later, in the chapter of *The Psychopathology of Everyday Life* just mentioned. (See also footnote, p. 322.)

The intrinsic interest of this paper has been rather undeservedly overshadowed by an extraneous fact. It was not difficult to guess that the incident described in it was in fact an autobiographical one, and this became a certainty after the appearance of the Fliess correspondence. Many of the details, however, can be traced in Freud's published writings. Thus the children in the screen memory were in fact his nephew John and his niece Pauline, who appear at several points in *The Interpretation of Dreams* (1900*a*). (Cf., for instance, *Standard Ed.*, **5**, 424–5, 483 and 486.) These were the children of his much older half-brother, who is mentioned in Chapter X of *The Psychopathology of Everyday Life* (1901*b*), ibid., **6**, 227. This brother, after the break-up of the family at Freiberg when Freud was three, had settled in Manchester, where Freud visited him at the age of nineteen—not twenty, as is implied here (p. 314)—a visit alluded to in the same passage in *The Psychopathology of Everyday Life* and also in *The Interpretation of Dreams* (ibid., **5**, 519). His age at the time of his first return to Freiberg was also a year less than is represented here. He was sixteen, as he tells us in 'Letter to the Burgomaster of Příbor' (1931*e*), ibid., **21**, 259. We learn from this source too that the family with whom he stayed was named Fluss, and it was one of the daughters of this family, Gisela, who was the central figure of the present anecdote. The episode is fully described in the first volume of Ernest Jones's biography (1953, 27–9 and 35–7).[1]

[1] The name of Gisela Fluss makes an unexpected and quite unimportant appearance in Freud's notes on the 'Rat Man' analysis (1955*a*), *Standard Ed.*, **10**, 280.

SCREEN MEMORIES

In the course of my psycho-analytic treatment of cases of hysteria, obsessional neurosis, etc., I have often had to deal with fragmentary recollections which have remained in the patient's memory from the earliest years of his childhood. As I have shown elsewhere,[1] great pathogenic importance must be attributed to the impressions of that time of life. But the subject of childhood memories is in any case bound to be of psychological interest, for they bring into striking relief a fundamental difference between the psychical functioning of children and of adults. No one calls in question the fact that the experiences of the earliest years of our childhood leave ineradicable traces in the depths of our minds. If, however, we seek in our *memories* to ascertain what were the impressions that were destined to influence us to the end of our lives, the outcome is either nothing at all or a relatively small number of isolated recollections which are often of dubious or enigmatic importance. It is only from the sixth or seventh year onwards—in many cases only after the tenth year—that our lives can be reproduced in memory as a connected chain of events. From that time on, however, there is also a direct relation between the psychical significance of an experience and its retention in the memory. Whatever seems important on account of its immediate or directly subsequent effects is recollected; whatever is judged to be inessential is forgotten. If I can remember an event for a long time after its occurrence, I regard the fact of having retained it in my memory as evidence of its having made a deep impression on me at the time. I feel surprised at forgetting something important; and I feel even more surprised, perhaps, at remembering something apparently indifferent.

It is only in certain pathological mental conditions that the relation holding in normal adults between the psychical significance of an event and its retention in memory once more ceases to apply. For instance, a hysteric habitually shows amnesia for some or all of the experiences which led to the onset

[1] [Cf., for instance, 'The Aetiology of Hysteria' (1896), p. 202 f. above.]

303

of his illness and which from that very fact have become important to him and, apart from that fact, may have been important on their own account. The analogy between pathological amnesia of this kind and the normal amnesia affecting our early years seems to me to give a valuable hint at the intimate connection that exists between the psychical content of neuroses and our infantile life.

We are so much accustomed to this lack of memory of the impressions of childhood that we are apt to overlook the problem underlying it and are inclined to explain it as a self-evident consequence of the rudimentary character of the mental activities of children. Actually, however, a normally developed child of three or four already exhibits an enormous amount of highly organized mental functioning in the comparisons and inferences which he makes and in the expression of his feelings; and there is no obvious reason why amnesia should overtake these psychical acts, which carry no less weight than those of a later age.

Before dealing with the psychological problems attaching to the earliest memories of childhood, it would of course be essential to make a collection of material by circularizing a fairly large number of normal adults and discovering what kind of recollections they are able to produce from these early years. A first step in this direction was taken in 1895 by V. and C. Henri, who sent round a paper of questions drawn up by them. The highly suggestive results of their questionnaire, which brought in replies from 123 persons, were published by the two authors in 1897. I have no intention at present of discussing the subject as a whole, and I shall therefore content myself with emphasizing the few points which will enable me to introduce the notion of what I have termed 'screen memories'.

The age to which the content of the earliest memories of childhood is usually referred back is the period between the ages of two and four. (This is the case with 88 persons in the series observed by the Henris.) There are some, however, whose memory reaches back further—even to the time before the completion of their first year; and, on the other hand, there are some whose earliest recollections go back only to their sixth, seventh, or even eighth year. There is nothing at the moment to show what else is related to these individual differences; but it is to be noticed, say the Henris, that a person whose earliest recollection goes back to a very tender age—to the first year of his life, perhaps—will also have at his disposal further detached memories from the following years, and that he will be able to reproduce his experiences as a continuous chain from an earlier point of time—from about his fifth year—than is possible for other people, whose first recollection dates from a later time. Thus not only the date of the appearance of the first recollection but the whole function of memory may, in the case of some people, be advanced or retarded.

Quite special interest attaches to the question of what is the usual *content* of these earliest memories of childhood. The psychology of adults would necessarily lead us to expect that those experiences would be selected as worth remembering which had aroused some powerful emotion or which, owing to their consequences, had been recognized as important soon after their occurrence. And some indeed of the observations collected by the Henris appear to fulfil this expectation. They report that the most frequent content of the first memories of childhood are on the one hand occasions of fear, shame, physical pain, etc., and on the other hand important events such as illnesses, deaths, fires, births of brothers and sisters, etc. We might therefore be inclined to assume that the principle governing the choice of memories is the same in the case of children as in that of adults. It is intelligible—though the fact deserves to be explicitly mentioned—that the memories retained from childhood should necessarily show evidence of the difference between what attracts the interest of a child and of an adult. This easily explains why, for instance, one woman reports that she remembers a number of accidents that occurred to her dolls when she was two years old but has no recollection of the serious and tragic events she might have observed at the same period.

Now, however, we are met by a fact that is diametrically opposed to our expectations and cannot fail to astonish us. We hear that there are some people whose earliest recollections of childhood are concerned with everyday and indifferent events which could not produce any emotional effect even in children, but which are recollected (*too* clearly, one is inclined to say)[1] in

[1] [Cf. footnote 1, p. 291 above. The point appears again below on pp. 312 and 313.]

every detail, while approximately contemporary events, even if, on the evidence of their parents, they moved them intensely at the time, have not been retained in their memory. Thus the Henris mention a professor of philology whose earliest memory, dating back to between the ages of three and four, showed him a table laid for a meal and on it a basin of ice. At the same period there occurred the death of his grandmother which, according to his parents, was a severe blow to the child. But the professor of philology, as he now is, has no recollection of this bereavement; all that he remembers of those days is the basin of ice. Another man reports that his earliest memory is an episode upon a walk in which he broke off a branch from a tree. He thinks he can still identify the spot where this happened. There were several other people present, and one of them helped him.

The Henris describe such cases as rare. In my experience, based for the most part, it is true, on neurotics, they are quite frequent. One of the subjects of the Henris' investigation made an attempt at explaining the occurrence of these mnemic images, whose innocence makes them so mysterious, and his explanation seems to me very much to the point. He thinks that in such cases the relevant scene may perhaps have been only *incompletely* retained in the memory, and that that may be why it seems so unenlightening: the parts that have been forgotten probably contained everything that made the experience noteworthy. I am able to confirm the truth of this view, though I should prefer to speak of these elements of the experience being *omitted* rather than forgotten. I have often succeeded, by means of psycho-analytic treatment, in uncovering the missing portions of a childhood experience and in thus proving that when the impression, of which no more than a torso was retained in the memory, had been restored to completeness, it did in fact agree with the presumption that it is the most important things that are recollected. This, however, provides no explanation of the remarkable choice which memory has made among the elements of the experience. We must first enquire why it should be that precisely what is important is suppressed and what is indifferent retained; and we shall not find an explanation of this until we have investigated the mechanism of these processes more deeply. We shall then form a notion that two psychical forces are concerned in bringing about memories of this sort.

One of these forces takes the importance of the experience as a motive for seeking to remember it, while the other—a resistance —tries to prevent any such preference from being shown. These two opposing forces do not cancel each other out, nor does one of them (whether with or without loss to itself) overpower the other. Instead, a compromise is brought about, somewhat on the analogy of the resultant in a parallelogram of forces. And the compromise is this. What is recorded as a mnemic image is not the relevant experience itself—in this respect the resistance gets its way; what is recorded is another psychical element closely associated with the objectionable one—and in this respect the *first* principle shows its strength, the principle which endeavours to fix important impressions by establishing reproducible mnemic images. The result of the conflict is therefore that, instead of the mnemic image which would have been justified by the original event, another is produced which has been to some degree associatively *displaced* from the former one. And since the elements of the experience which aroused objection were precisely the important ones, the substituted memory will necessarily lack those important elements and will in consequence most probably strike us as trivial. It will seem incomprehensible to us because we are inclined to look for the reason for its retention in its own content, whereas in fact that retention is due to the relation holding between its own content and a different one which has been suppressed. There is a common saying among us about shams, that they are not made of gold themselves but have lain beside something that *is* made of gold.[1] The same simile might well be applied to some of the experiences of childhood which have been retained in the memory.

There are numerous possible types of case in which one psychical content is substituted for another, and these come about in a variety of psychological constellations. One of the simplest of these cases is obviously that occurring in the childhood memories with which we are here concerned—the case, that is, where the essential elements of an experience are represented in memory by the inessential elements of the same experience. It is a case of displacement on to something associated by continuity; or, looking at the process as a whole, a case

[1] [The simile reappears in Chapter VII of Freud's book on jokes (1905c), *Standard Ed.*, **8**, 184.]

of repression accompanied by the substitution of something in the neighbourhood (whether in space or time). I have elsewhere[1] had occasion to describe a very similar instance of substitution which occurred in the analysis of a patient suffering from paranoia. The woman in question hallucinated voices, which used to repeat long passages from Otto Ludwig's novel *Die Heiterethei* to her. But the passages they chose were the most trifling and irrelevant in the book. The analysis showed, however, that there were other passages in the same work which had stirred up the most distressing thoughts in the patient. The distressing affect was a motive for putting up a defence against them, but the motives in favour of pursuing them further were not to be suppressed. The result was a compromise by which the innocent passages emerged in the patient's memory with pathological strength and clarity. The process which we here see at work—conflict, repression, substitution involving a compromise—returns in all psychoneurotic symptoms and gives us the key to understanding their formation. Thus it is not without importance if we are able to show the same process operating in the mental life of normal individuals, and the fact that what it influences in normal people is precisely their choice of childhood memories seems to afford one more indication of the intimate relations which have already been insisted upon between the mental life of children and the psychical material of the neuroses.

The processes of normal and pathological defence and the displacements in which they result are clearly of great importance. But to the best of my knowledge no study whatever has hitherto been made of them by psychologists; and it remains to be ascertained in what strata of psychical activity and under what conditions they come into operation. The reason for this neglect may well be that our mental life, so far as it is the object of our *conscious* internal perception, shows nothing of these processes, apart from instances which we classify as 'faulty reasoning' and some mental operations which aim at producing a comic effect. The assertion that a psychical intensity[2] can be displaced from one presentation (which is then abandoned) on to another (which thenceforward plays the psychological part of the

---

[1] 'Further Remarks on the Neuro-Psychoses of Defence' (1896b). [See above, p. 181.]   [2] [Cf. p. 67 above.]

former one) is as bewildering to us as certain features of Greek mythology—as, for instance, when the gods are said to clothe someone with beauty as though it were with a veil, whereas *we* think only of a face transfigured by a change of expression.

Further investigation of these indifferent childhood memories has taught me that they can originate in other ways as well and that an unsuspected wealth of meaning lies concealed behind their apparent innocence. But on this point I shall not content myself with a mere assertion but shall give a detailed report of one particular instance which seems to me the most instructive out of a considerable number of similar ones. Its value is certainly increased by the fact that it relates to someone who is not at all or only very slightly neurotic.

The subject of this observation is a man of university education, aged thirty-eight.[1] Though his own profession lies in a very different field, he has taken an interest in psychological questions ever since I was able to relieve him of a slight phobia by means of psycho-analysis. Last year he drew my attention to his childhood memories, which had already played some part in his analysis. After studying the investigation made by V. and C. Henri, he gave me the following summarized account of his own experience.

'I have at my disposal a fair number of early memories of childhood which I can date with great certainty. For at the age of three I left the small place where I was born and moved to a large town; and all these memories of mine relate to my birthplace and therefore date from my second and third years. They are mostly short scenes, but they are very well preserved and furnished with every detail of sense-perception, in complete contrast to my memories of adult years, which are entirely lacking in the visual element. From my third year onwards my recollections grow scantier and less clear; there are gaps in them which must cover more than a year; and it is not, I believe, until my sixth or seventh year that the stream of my memories becomes continuous. My memories up to the time of my leaving

[1] [There can be no doubt that what follows is autobiographical material only thinly disguised. See Editor's Note, p. 302 above. At the date at which this paper was sent in for publication in May 1899, Freud was in fact just forty-three years old.]

my first place of residence fall into three groups. The first group consists of scenes which my parents have repeatedly since described to me. As regards these, I feel uncertain whether I have had the mnemic image from the beginning or whether I only construed it after hearing one of these descriptions. I may remark, however, that there are also events of which I have no mnemic image in spite of their having been frequently retailed by my parents. I attach more importance to the second group. It comprises scenes which have not (so far as I know) been described to me and some of which, indeed, *could* not have been described to me, as I have not met the other participants in them (my nurse and playmates) since their occurrence. I shall come to the third group presently. As regards the content of these scenes and their consequent claim to being recollected, I should like to say that I am not entirely at sea. I cannot maintain, indeed, that what I have retained are memories of the most important events of the period, or what I should to-day judge to be the most important. I have no knowledge of the birth of a sister, who is two and a half years younger than I am; my departure, my first sight of the railway and the long carriage-drive before it—none of these has left a trace in my memory. On the other hand, I can remember two small occurrences during the railway-journey; these, as you will recollect, came up in the analysis of my phobia. But what should have made most impression on me was an injury to my face which caused a considerable loss of blood and for which I had to have some stitches put in by a surgeon. I can still feel the scar resulting from this accident, but I know of no recollection which points to it, either directly or indirectly.[1] It is true that I may perhaps have been under two years old at the time.

'It follows from this that I feel no surprise at the pictures and scenes of these first two groups. No doubt they are displaced memories from which the essential element has for the most part been omitted. But in a few of them it is at least hinted at, and in others it is easy for me to complete them by following certain pointers. By doing so I can establish a sound connec-

[1] [This accident is referred to twice in *The Interpretation of Dreams* (1900*a*), *Standard Ed.*, **4**, 17 and footnote, and **5**, 560; also, indirectly, in a letter to Fliess of October 15, 1897 (Freud 1950*a*, Letter 71) and near the beginning of Lecture XIII of the *Introductory Lectures* (1916–17).]

tion between the separate fragments of memories and arrive at a clear understanding of what the childish interest was that recommended these particular occurrences to my memory. This does not apply, however, to the content of the third group, which I have not so far discussed. There I am met by material—one rather long scene and several smaller pictures—with which I can make no headway at all. The scene appears to me fairly indifferent and I cannot understand why it should have become fixed in my memory. Let me describe it to you. I see a rectangular, rather steeply sloping piece of meadow-land, green and thickly grown; in the green there are a great number of yellow flowers—evidently common dandelions. At the top end of the meadow there is a cottage and in front of the cottage door two women are standing chatting busily, a peasant-woman with a handkerchief on her head and a children's nurse. Three children are playing in the grass. One of them is myself (between the age of two and three); the two others are my boy cousin, who is a year older than me, and his sister, who is almost exactly the same age as I am. We are picking the yellow flowers and each of us is holding a bunch of flowers we have already picked. The little girl has the best bunch; and, as though by mutual agreement, we—the two boys—fall on her and snatch away her flowers. She runs up the meadow in tears and as a consolation the peasant-woman gives her a big piece of black bread. Hardly have we seen this than we throw the flowers away, hurry to the cottage and ask to be given some bread too. And we are in fact given some; the peasant-woman cuts the loaf with a long knife. In my memory the bread tastes quite delicious—and at that point the scene breaks off.

'Now what is there in this occurrence to justify the expenditure of memory which it has occasioned me? I have racked my brains in vain over it. Does the emphasis lie on our disagreeable behaviour to the little girl? Did the yellow colour of the dandelions—a flower which I am, of course, far from admiring to-day—so greatly please me? Or, as a result of my careering round the grass, did the bread taste so much nicer than usual that it made an unforgettable impression on me? Nor can I find any connection between this scene and the interest which (as I was able to discover without any difficulty) bound together the other scenes from my childhood. Altogether, there seems to me something not quite right about this scene. The yellow of the flowers is a disproportionately prominent element in the situation as a whole, and the nice taste of the bread seems to me exaggerated in an almost hallucinatory fashion. I cannot help being reminded of some pictures that I once saw in a burlesque exhibition. Certain portions of these pictures, and of course the most inappropriate ones, instead of being painted, were built up in three dimensions—for instance, the ladies' bustles. Well, can you point out any way of finding an explanation or interpretation of this redundant memory of my childhood?'

I thought it advisable to ask him since when he had been occupied with this recollection: whether he was of opinion that it had recurred to his memory periodically since his childhood, or whether it had perhaps emerged at some later time on some occasion that could be recalled. This question was all that it was necessary for me to contribute to the solution of the problem; the rest was found by my collaborator himself, who was no novice at jobs of this kind.

'I have not yet considered that point,' he replied. 'Now that you have raised the question, it seems to me almost a certainty that this childhood memory never occurred to me at all in my earlier years. But I can also recall the occasion which led to my recovering this and many other recollections of my earliest childhood. When I was seventeen and at my secondary school, I returned for the first time to my birthplace for the holidays, to stay with a family who had been our friends ever since that remote date. I know quite well what a wealth of impressions overwhelmed me at that time. But I see now that I shall have to tell you a whole big piece of my history: it belongs here, and you have brought it upon yourself by your question. So listen. I was the child of people who were originally well-to-do and who, I fancy, lived comfortably enough in that little corner of the provinces. When I was about three, the branch of industry in which my father was concerned met with a catastrophe. He lost all his means and we were forced to leave the place and move to a large town. Long and difficult years followed, of which, as it seems to me, nothing was worth remembering. I never felt really comfortable in the town. I believe now that I was never free from a longing for the beautiful woods near our home, in which (as one of my memories from those days tells me) I used to run off from my father, almost before I had learnt to walk. Those holidays, when I was seventeen, were my first holidays in the country, and, as I have said, I stayed with a family with whom we were friends and who had risen greatly in the world since our move. I could compare the comfort reigning there with our own style of living at home in the town. But it is no use evading the subject any longer: I must admit that there was something else that excited me powerfully. I was seventeen, and in the family where I was staying there was a daughter of fifteen, with whom I immediately fell in love. It was my first calf-love and sufficiently intense, but I kept it completely secret. After a few days the girl went off to her school (from which she too was home for the holidays) and it was this separation after such a short acquaintance that brought my longings to a really high pitch. I passed many hours in solitary walks through the lovely woods that I had found once more and spent my time building castles in the air. These, strangely enough, were not concerned with the future but sought to improve the past. If only the smash had not occurred! If only I had stopped at home and grown up in the country and grown as strong as the young men in the house, the brothers of my love! And then if only I had followed my father's profession and if I had finally married her—for I should have known her intimately all those years! I had not the slightest doubt, of course, that in the circumstances created by my imagination I should have loved her just as passionately as I really seemed to then. A strange thing. For when I see her now from time to time—she happens to have married someone here—she is quite exceptionally indifferent to me. Yet I can remember quite well for what a long time afterwards I was affected by the yellow colour of the dress she was wearing when we first met, whenever I saw the same colour anywhere else.'

That sounds very much like your parenthetical remark to the effect that you are no longer fond of the common dandelion. Do you not suspect that there may be a connection between the yellow of the girl's dress and the ultra-clear yellow of the flowers in your childhood scene?[1] [Cf. footnote 1, p. 291.]

---

[1] [This was Freud's regular method of reporting conversations—his interlocutor's remarks in inverted commas and his own without any. Cf., for instance, the dialogue in *The Question of Lay Analysis* (1926*e*).]

'Possibly. But it was not the same yellow. The dress was more of a yellowish brown, more like the colour of wallflowers. However, I can at least let you have an intermediate idea which may serve your purpose. At a later date, while I was in the Alps, I saw how certain flowers which have light colouring in the lowlands take on darker shades at high altitudes. Unless I am greatly mistaken, there is frequently to be found in mountainous regions a flower which is very similar to the dandelion but which is dark yellow and would exactly agree in colour with the dress of the girl I was so fond of. But I have not finished yet. I now come to a second occasion which stirred up in me the impressions of my childhood and which dates from a time not far distant from the first. I was seventeen when I revisited my birthplace. Three years later during my holidays I visited my uncle and met once again the children who had been my first playmates, the same two cousins, the boy a year older than I am and the girl of the same age as myself, who appear in the childhood scene with the dandelions. This family had left my birthplace at the same time as we did and had become prosperous in a far-distant city.'

And did you once more fall in love—with your cousin this time—and indulge in a new set of phantasies?

'No, this time things turned out differently. By then I was at the University and I was a slave to my books. I had nothing left over for my cousin. So far as I know I had no similar phantasies on that occasion. But I believe that my father and my uncle had concocted a plan by which I was to exchange the abstruse subject of my studies for one of more practical value, settle down, after my studies were completed, in the place where my uncle lived, and marry my cousin. No doubt when they saw how absorbed I was in my own intentions the plan was dropped; but I fancy I must certainly have been aware of its existence. It was not until later, when I was a newly-fledged man of science and hard pressed by the exigencies of life and when I had to wait so long before finding a post here, that I must sometimes have reflected that my father had meant well in planning this marriage for me, to make good the loss in which the original catastrophe had involved my whole existence.'

Then I am inclined to believe that the childhood scene we are considering emerged at this time, when you were struggling for your daily bread—provided, that is, that you can confirm my idea that it was during this same period that you first made the acquaintance of the Alps.

'Yes, that is so: mountaineering was the one enjoyment that I allowed myself at that time. But I still cannot grasp your point.'

I am coming to it at once. The element on which you put most stress in your childhood scene was the fact of the country-made bread tasting so delicious. It seems clear that this idea, which amounted almost to a hallucination, corresponded to your phantasy of the comfortable life you would have led if you had stayed at home and married this girl [in the yellow dress]— or, in symbolic language, of how sweet the bread would have tasted for which you had to struggle so hard in your later years. The yellow of the flowers, too, points to the same girl. But there are also elements in the childhood scene which can only be related to the *second* phantasy—of being married to your cousin. Throwing away the flowers in exchange for bread strikes me as not a bad disguise for the scheme your father had for you: you were to give up your unpractical ideals and take on a 'bread-and-butter' occupation, were you not?

'It seems then that I amalgamated the two sets of phantasies of how my life could have been more comfortable—the "yellow" and the "country-made bread" from the one and the throwing-away of the flowers and the actual people concerned from the other.'

Yes. You projected the two phantasies on to one another and made a childhood memory of them. The element about the alpine flowers is as it were a stamp giving the date of manufacture. I can assure you that people often construct such things unconsciously—almost like works of fiction.

'But if that is so, there was *no* childhood memory, but only a phantasy put back into childhood. A feeling tells me, though, that the scene is genuine. How does that fit in?'

There is in general no guarantee of the data produced by our memory. But I am ready to agree with you that the scene is genuine. If so, you selected it from innumerable others of a similar or another kind because, on account of its content (which in itself was indifferent) it was well adapted to represent the two phantasies, which were important enough to you. A recollection of this kind, whose value lies in the fact that it represents in the memory impressions and thoughts of a later date whose content is connected with its own by symbolic or similar links, may appropriately be called a *'screen memory'*. In any case you will cease to feel any surprise that this scene should so often recur to your mind. It can no longer be regarded as an innocent one since, as we have discovered, it is calculated to illustrate the most momentous turning-points in your life, the influence of the two most powerful motive forces—hunger and love.[1]

'Yes, it represented hunger well enough. But what about love?'

In the yellow of the flowers, I mean. But I cannot deny that in this childhood scene of yours love is represented far less prominently than I should have expected from my previous experience.

'No. You are mistaken. The essence of it is its representation of love. Now I understand for the first time. Think for a moment! Taking flowers away from a girl means to deflower her. What a contrast between the boldness of this phantasy and my bashfulness on the first occasion and my indifference on the second.'

I can assure you that youthful bashfulness habitually has as its complement bold phantasies of that sort.

'But in that case the phantasy that has transformed itself into these childhood memories would not be a conscious one that I can remember, but an unconscious one?'

Unconscious thoughts which are a prolongation of conscious ones. You think to yourself 'If I had married so-and-so', and behind the thought there is an impulse to form a picture of what the 'being married' really is.

'I can go on with it now myself. The most seductive part of the whole subject for a young scapegrace is the picture of the marriage night. (What does he care about what comes afterwards?) But that picture cannot venture out into the light of day: the dominating mood of diffidence and of respect towards the girl keeps it suppressed. So it remains unconscious—'

And slips away into a childhood memory. You are quite

[1] [An allusion to a favourite line of Freud's from Schiller's 'Die Weltweisen'.]

right. It is precisely the coarsely sensual element in the phantasy which explains why it does not develop into a *conscious* phantasy but must be content to find its way allusively and under a flowery disguise into a childhood scene.

'But why precisely, into a *childhood* scene, I should like to know?'

For the sake of its innocence, perhaps. Can you imagine a greater contrast to these designs for gross sexual aggression than childish pranks? However, there are more general grounds that have a decisive influence in bringing about the slipping away of repressed thoughts and wishes into childhood memories: for you will find the same thing invariably happening in hysterical patients. It seems, moreover, as though the recollection of the remote past is in itself facilitated by some pleasurable motive: *forsan et haec olim meminisse juvabit.*[1]

'If that is so, I have lost all faith in the genuineness of the dandelion scene. This is how I look at it: On the two occasions in question, and with the support of very comprehensible realistic motives, the thought occurred to me: "If you had married this or that girl, your life would have become much pleasanter." The sensual current in my mind took hold of the thought which is contained in the protasis[2] and repeated it in images of a kind capable of giving that same sensual current satisfaction. This second version of the thought remained unconscious on account of its incompatibility with the dominant sexual disposition; but this very fact of its remaining unconscious enabled it to persist in my mind long after changes in the real situation had quite got rid of the conscious version. In accordance, as you say, with a general law, the clause that had remained unconscious sought to transform itself into a childhood scene which, on account of its innocence, would be able to become conscious. With this end in view it had to undergo a fresh transformation, or rather two fresh transformations. One of these removed the objectionable element from the protasis by expressing it figuratively; the second forced the apodosis into a shape capable of visual representation—using for the purpose

[1] ['Some day, perhaps, it will be a joy to remember even these things.' Virgil, *Aeneid*, I, 203.]

[2] [A protasis is a conditional clause and an apodosis (see below) is a consequential one.]

the intermediary ideas of "bread" and "bread-and-butter occupations". I see that by producing a phantasy like this I was providing, as it were, a fulfilment of the two suppressed wishes—for deflowering a girl and for material comfort. But now that I have given such a complete account of the motives that led to my producing the dandelion phantasy, I cannot help concluding that what I am dealing with is something that never happened at all but has been unjustifiably smuggled in among my childhood memories.'

I see that I must take up the defence of its genuineness. You are going too far. You have accepted my assertion that every suppressed phantasy of this kind tends to slip away into a childhood scene. But suppose now that this cannot occur unless there is a memory-trace the content of which offers the phantasy a point of contact—comes, as it were, half way to meet it. Once a point of contact of this kind has been found—in the present instance it was the deflowering, the taking away of the flowers—the remaining content of the phantasy is remodelled with the help of every legitimate intermediate idea—take the bread as an example—till it can find further points of contact with the content of the childhood scene. It is very possible that in the course of this process the childhood scene itself also undergoes changes; I regard it as certain that falsifications of memory may be brought about in this way too. In your case the childhood scene seems only to have had some of its lines engraved more deeply: think of the over-emphasis on the yellow and the exaggerated niceness of the bread. But the raw material was utilizable. If that had not been so, it would not have been possible for this particular memory, rather than any others, to make its way forward into consciousness. No such scene would have occurred to you as a childhood memory, or perhaps some other one would have—for you know how easily our ingenuity can build connecting bridges from any one point to any other. And apart from your own subjective feeling which I am not inclined to under-estimate, there is another thing that speaks in favour of the genuineness of your dandelion memory. It contains elements which have not been solved by what you have told me and which do not in fact fit in with the sense required by the phantasy. For instance, your boy cousin helping you to rob the little girl of her flowers—can you make any sense of the idea of being helped in deflowering someone? or of the peasant-woman and the nurse in front of the cottage?

'Not that I can see.'

So the phantasy does not coincide completely with the childhood scene. It is only based on it at certain points. That argues in favour of the childhood memory being genuine.

'Do you think an interpretation like this of an apparently innocent childhood memory is often applicable?'

Very often, in my experience. Shall we amuse ourselves by seeing whether the two examples given by the Henris can be interpreted as screen memories concealing subsequent experiences and wishes? I mean the memory of a table laid for a meal with a basin of ice on it, which was supposed to have some connection with the death of the subject's grandmother, and the other memory, of a child breaking off a branch from a tree while he was on a walk and of his being helped to do it by someone.

He reflected for a little and then answered: 'I can make nothing of the first one. It is most probably a case of displacement at work; but the intermediate steps are beyond guessing. As for the second case, I should be prepared to give an interpretation, if only the person concerned had not been a Frenchman.'

I cannot follow you there. What difference would that make?

'A great deal of difference, since what provides the intermediate step between a screen memory and what it conceals is likely to be a verbal expression. In German "to pull one out" is a very common vulgar term for masturbation.[1] The scene would then be putting back into early childhood a seduction to masturbation—someone was helping him to do it—which in fact occurred at a later period. But even so, it does not fit, for in the childhood scene there were a number of other people present.'

Whereas his seduction to masturbate must have occurred in solitude and secrecy. It is just that contrast that inclines me to accept your view: it serves once again to make the scene innocent. Do you know what it means when in a dream we see 'a lot of strangers', as happens so often in dreams of nakedness in which we feel so terribly embarrassed? Nothing more nor less

---

[1] [Cf. *The Interpretation of Dreams* (1900a), *Standard Ed.*, **5**, 348, footnote 2.]

than secrecy, which there again is expressed by its opposite.[1] However, our interpretation remains a jest, since we have no idea whether a Frenchman would recognize an allusion to masturbation in the words *casser une branche d'un arbre* or in some suitably emended phrase.

This analysis, which I have reproduced as accurately as possible, will, I hope, have to some extent clarified the concept of a 'screen memory' as one which owes its value as a memory not to its own content but to the relation existing between that content and some other, that has been suppressed. Different classes of screen memories can be distinguished according to the nature of that relation. We have found examples of two of these classes among what are described as the earliest memories of childhood—that is, if we include under the heading of screen memories the incomplete childhood scenes which are innocent by very reason of their incompleteness. It is to be anticipated that screen memories will also be formed from residues of memories relating to later life as well. Anyone who bears in mind their distinctive feature—namely that they are extremely well remembered but that their content is completely indifferent—will easily recall a number of examples of the sort from his own memory. Some of these screen memories dealing with events later in life owe their importance to a connection with experiences in early youth which have remained suppressed. The connection, that is, is the reverse of the one in the case which I have analysed, where a childhood memory was accounted for by later experiences. A screen memory may be described as 'retrogressive' or as having 'pushed forward' according as the one chronological relation or the other holds between the screen and the thing screened-off.[2] From another point of view, we can distinguish positive screen memories from negative ones (or refractory memories) whose content stands in a contrary relation to the suppressed material. The whole subject deserves a more thorough examination; but I must content myself with pointing out what complicated processes—processes, incidentally, which are altogether analogous to the for-

---

[1] [Cf. ibid., 4, 245-6.]

[2] [I.e. according to whether the displacement has been in a backward or forward direction.]

mation of hysterical symptoms—are involved in the building up of our store of memories.

Our earliest childhood memories will always be a subject of special interest because the problem mentioned at the beginning of this paper (of how it comes about that the impressions which are of most significance for our whole future usually leave no mnemic images behind) leads us to reflect upon the origin of conscious memories in general. We shall no doubt be inclined at first to separate off the screen memories which are the subject of this study as heterogeneous elements among the residues of childhood recollections. As regards the remaining images, we shall probably adopt the simple view that they arise simultaneously with an experience as an immediate consequence of the impression it makes and that thereafter they recur from time to time in accordance with the familiar laws of reproduction. Closer observation, however, reveals certain features which do not tally with this view. Above all, there is the following point. In the majority of significant and in other respects unimpeachable childhood scenes the subject sees himself in the recollection as a child, with the knowledge that this child is himself; he sees this child, however, as an observer from outside the scene would see him. The Henris duly draw attention to the fact that many of those taking part in their investigation expressly emphasized this peculiarity of childhood scenes. Now it is evident that such a picture cannot be an exact repetition of the impression that was originally received. For the subject was then in the middle of the situation and was attending not to himself but to the external world.

Whenever in a memory the subject himself appears in this way as an object among other objects this contrast between the acting and the recollecting ego may be taken as evidence that the original impression has been worked over. It looks as though a memory-trace from childhood had here been translated back into a plastic and visual form at a later date—the date of the memory's arousal. But no reproduction of the original impression has ever entered the subject's consciousness.

There is another fact that affords even more convincing evidence in favour of this second view. Out of a number of childhood memories of significant experiences, all of them of similar distinctness and clarity, there will be some scenes which, when they are tested (for instance by the recollections of adults), turn out to have been falsified. Not that they are complete inventions; they are false in the sense that they have shifted an event to a place where it did not occur—this is the case in one of the instances quoted by the Henris—or that they have merged two people into one or substituted one for the other, or the scenes as a whole give signs of being combinations of two separate experiences. Simple inaccuracy of recollection docs not play any considerable part here, in view of the high degree of sensory intensity possessed by the images and the efficiency of the function of memory in the young; close investigation shows rather that these falsifications of memory are tendentious—that is, that they serve the purposes of the repression and replacement of objectionable or disagreeable impressions. It follows, therefore, that these falsified memories too, must have originated at a period of life when it has become possible for conflicts of this kind and impulsions towards repression to have made a place for themselves in mental life—far later, therefore, than the period to which their content belongs. But in these cases too the falsified memory is the first that we become aware of: the raw material of memory-traces out of which it was forged remains unknown to us in its original form.

The recognition of this fact must diminish the distinction we have drawn between screen memories and other memories derived from our childhood. It may indeed be questioned whether we have any memories at all *from* our childhood: memories *relating to* our childhood may be all that we possess. Our childhood memories show us our earliest years not as they were but as they appeared at the later periods when the memories were aroused. In these periods of arousal, the childhood memories did not, as people are accustomed to say, *emerge*; they were *formed* at that time. And a number of motives, with no concern for historical accuracy, had a part in forming them, as well as in the selection of the memories themselves.[1]

[1] [The type of screen memory considered here is related to the 'retrospective phantasies' often discussed by Freud later; e.g. in the 'Rat Man' analysis (1909*d*), *Standard Ed.*, **10**, 206–8 *n*., in Sections V and VII of the 'Wolf Man' analysis (1918*b*) and in Lectures XXI and XXIII of the *Introductory Lectures* (1916–17).]

AUTOBIOGRAPHICAL NOTE
(1901 [1899])

AUTOBIOGRAPHICAL NOTE

(*a*) GERMAN EDITION:
1901   In J. L. Pagel's *Biographisches Lexicon hervorragender Ärzte
des neunzehnten Jahrhunderts* [Biographical Lexicon of
Eminent Doctors of the Nineteenth Century]. Berlin and
Vienna, Column 545.

It appears that this has never been reprinted and that this
translation, by James Strachey, is the first into English.

Internal evidence shows that this must have been written in
the autumn of 1899. It is of interest as showing the view which
Freud expected to have taken of his activities on the eve of the
publication of the work which was to revolutionize his position
in the scientific world. The numerous abbreviations in the
original have been expanded.

AUTOBIOGRAPHICAL NOTE

Freud, Sigm., Vienna. Born May 6, 1856, at Freiberg in Moravia. Studied in Vienna. Pupil of Brücke, the physiologist. Promotion [M.D. degree], 1881. Pupil of Charcot in Paris, 1885-6. Habilitation [appointment as Privatdozent], 1885. Has worked as physician and Dozent at Vienna University since 1886. Proposed as Professor Extraordinarius, 1897.[1] Earlier, Freud produced writings on histology and cerebral anatomy, and, subsequently, clinical works on neuropathology; translated writings by Charcot and Bernheim. In 1884 'Über Coca' ['On Coca'], a paper which introduced cocaine into medicine. In 1891 *Zur Auffassung der Aphasien* [On the Interpretation of the Aphasias]. In 1891 and 1893 monographs on the cerebral palsies of children, which culminated in 1897 in the volume on the subject in Nothnagel's *Handbuch*. In 1895 *Studien über Hysterie* [Studies on Hysteria] (with Dr. J. Breuer). Since then Freud has turned to the study of the psychoneuroses and especially hysteria, and in a series of shorter works he has stressed the aetiological significance of sexual life for the neuroses. He has also developed a new psychotherapy of hysteria, on which only extremely little has been published. A book, *Die Traumdeutung* [The Interpretation of Dreams], is in the press.

[1] [See Editor's Note to Freud's list of abstracts of his early writings (1897*b*), p. 225 f. above.]

BIBLIOGRAPHY
AND AUTHOR INDEX

[Titles of books and periodicals are in italics; titles of papers are in inverted commas. Abbreviations are in accordance with the *World List of Scientific Periodicals* (London, 1952). Further abbreviations used in this volume will be found in the List at the end of this bibliography. Numerals in thick type refer to volumes; ordinary numerals refer to pages. The figures in round brackets at the end of each entry indicate the page or pages of this volume on which the work in question is mentioned. In the case of the Freud entries, the letters attached to the dates of publication are in accordance with the corresponding entries in the complete bibliography of Freud's writings to be included in the last volume of the *Standard Edition*.

For non-technical authors, and for technical authors where no specific work is mentioned, see the General Index.]

BEARD, G. M. (1881) *American Nervousness, its Causes and Consequences*, New York. (90)
    (1884) *Sexual Neurasthenia (Nervous Exhaustion), its Hygiene, Causes, Symptoms and Treatment*, New York. (90)
BERNHEIM, H. (1886) *De la suggestion et de ses applications à la thérapeutique*, Paris. (23, 54, 63, 257)
    (1891) *Hypnotisme, suggestion et psychothérapie: études nouvelles*, Paris. (257)
BREUER, J. and FREUD, S. (1893) *See* FREUD, S. (1893*a*)
    (1895) *See* FREUD, S. (1895*d*)
BRUN, R. (1936) 'Sigmund Freuds Leistungen auf dem Gebiete der organischen Neurologie', *Schweiz. Arch. Neurol. Psychiat.*, **37**, 200. (226)
CHARCOT, J.-M. (1887) *Leçons sur les maladies du système nerveux*, Vol. III, Paris. (10, 192, 218, 257)
    (1888) *Leçons du mardi, 1887-8*, Paris. (10, 11, 13, 18, 65, 257)
    (1889) *Leçons du mardi, 1888-9*, Paris. (10, 11)
    (1886-90) *Oeuvres complètes* (9 vols.), Paris. (11)
DARKSCHEWITSCH, L. (1886) *See* FREUD, S. (1886*b*)
ERLENMEYER, F. A. (1885) Criticism of Freud's views on Cocaine, *Zbl. Nervenheilk.*, **8.** (233)
    (1886) 'Über Cocainsucht', *Wien med. Pr.*, **27**, Col. 918. (233)
    (1887) *Die Morphiumsucht und ihre Behandlung*, 3rd ed., Berlin, Leipzig and Neuwied. (233)
FISHER, J. (1955) *Bird Recognition III*, Penguin Books. (31)
FLIESS, W. (1892) *Neue Beiträge und Therapie der nasalen Reflexneurose*, Vienna. (90)

327

(1893) 'Die nasale Reflexneurose', *Verhandlungen des Kongresses für innere Medizin*, Wiesbaden, 384. (90)

FREUD, S. (1877a) 'Über den Ursprung der hinteren Nervenwurzeln im Rückenmarke von Ammocoetes (Petromyzon Planeri)', *S.B. Akad. Wiss. Wien* (Math.-Naturwiss. Kl.), III Abt., 75, 15. (227, 228, 230)

(1877b) 'Beobachtungen über Gestaltung und feineren Bau der als Hoden beschriebenen Lappenorgane des Aals', *S.B. Akad. Wiss. Wien* (Math.-Naturwiss. Kl.), I Abt., 75, 419. (227, 228, 230)

(1878a) 'Über Spinalganglien und Rückenmark des Petromyzon', *S.B. Akad. Wiss. Wien* (Math.-Naturwiss. Kl.), III Abt., 78, 81. (228-9, 230)

(1879a) 'Notiz über eine Methode zur anatomischen Präparation des Nervensystems', *Zbl. med. Wiss.*, 17, Nr. 26, 468. (229)

(1882a) 'Über den Bau der Nervenfasern und Nervenzellen beim Flusskrebs', *S.B. Akad. Wiss. Wien* (Math.-Naturwiss. Kl.), III Abt., 85, 9. (230)

(1884a) 'Ein Fall von Hirnblutung mit indirekten basalen Herdsymptomen bei Scorbut', *Wien. med. Wschr.*, 34, Nr. 9, 244, and 10, 276. (232)

(1884b) 'Eine neue Methode zum Studium des Faserverlaufes im Centralnervensystem', *Zbl. med. Wiss.*, 22, Nr. 11, 161. (231)

(1884c) 'A New Histological Method for the Study of Nerve-Tracts in the Brain and Spinal Cord' [in English], *Brain*, 7, 86. (231)

(1884d) 'Eine neue Methode zum Studium des Faserverlaufes im Centralnervensystem', *Arch. Anat. Physiol., Lpz.*, Anat. Abt., 453. (231)

(1884e) 'Über Coca', *Zbl. ges. Ther.*, 2, 289. (233, 325)
[*Trans. (abridged :* 'Coca', *St Louis med. surg. J.*, 47, 502.]

(1884f [1882]) 'Die Struktur der Elemente des Nervensystems', *Jb. Psychiat. Neurol.*, 5, Heft 3, 221. (230)

(1885a) 'Beitrag zur Kenntnis der Cocawirkung', *Wien. med. Wschr.*, 35, Nr. 5, 129. (233, 234)

(1885b) 'Über die Allgemeinwirkung des Cocaïns', *Med.-chir. Zbl.*, 20, Nr. 32, 374. (226, 233)

(1885c) 'Ein Fall von Muskelatrophie mit ausgebreiteten Sensibilitätsstörungen (Syringomyelie)', *Wien. med. Wschr.*, 35, Nr. 13, 389, and 14, 425. (232, 235)

(1885d) 'Zur Kenntnis der Olivenzwischenschicht', *Neurol. Zbl.*, 4, Nr. 12, 268. (234)

(1885e) 'Gutachten über das Parke Cocaïn', in Gutt, 'Über die verschiedenen Cocaïn-Präparate und deren Wirkung', *Wien. med. Pr.*, 26, Nr. 32, 1036. (233)

(1886a) 'Akute multiple Neuritis der spinalen und Hirnnerven', *Wien. med. Wschr.*, 36, Nr. 6, 168. (232, 236)

(1886b) With DARKSCHEWITSCH, L., 'Über die Beziehung des Strickkörpers zum Hinterstrang und Hinterstrangskern nebst Bemerkungen über zwei Felder der Oblongata', *Neurol. Zbl.*, 5, Nr. 6, 121. (234, 237)

(1886c) 'Über den Ursprung des Nervus acusticus', *Mschr. Ohrenheilk.*, Neue Folge **20**, Nr. 8, 245, and 9, 277. (234, 238)

(1886d) 'Beobachtung einer hochgradigen Hemianästhesie bei einem hysterischen Manne (Beiträge zur Kasuistik der Hysterie I)', *Wien. med. Wschr.*, **36**, Nr. 49, 1633. (238)

(1886f) Translation with Preface and Footnotes of J.-M. Charcot's *Leçons sur les maladies du système nerveux*, Vol. III, Paris, 1887, under the title *Neue Vorlesungen über die Krankheiten des Nervensystems insbesondere über Hysterie*, Vienna. (10, 257)
[*Trans.*: Preface and Footnotes to Charcot's *Neue Vorlesungen über die Krankheiten des Nervensystems insbesondere über Hysterie*, Standard Ed., **1.**]

(1887d) 'Bemerkungen über Cocainsucht und Cocainfurcht, mit Beziehung auf einen Vortrag W. A. Hammond's', *Wien. med. Wschr.*, **37**, Nr. 28, 929. (233, 239)

(1888a) 'Über Hemianopsie im frühesten Kindesalter', *Wien. med. Wschr.*, **38**, Nr. 32, 1081, and 33, 1116. (239)

(1888b) 'Aphasie', 'Gehirn', 'Hysterie' and 'Hysteroepilepsie' in Villaret's *Handwörterbuch der gesamten Medizin*, **1**, Stuttgart. (Unsigned, authorship uncertain.) (240)

(1888-9) Translation with Introduction and Notes of H. Bernheim's *De la suggestion et de ses applications à la thérapeutique*, Paris, 1886, under the title *Die Suggestion und ihre Heilwirkung*, Vienna. (23, 54, 63, 257)
[*Trans.*: Introduction to Bernheim's *Die Suggestion und ihre Heilwirkung*, C.P., **5**, 11; Standard Ed., **1.**]

(1891a) With RIE, O., 'Klinische Studie über die halbseitige Cerebrallähmung der Kinder', Heft III of *Beiträge zur Kinderheilkunde*, ed. Kassowitz, Vienna. (14, 239, 241-2, 245, 325)

(1891b) *Zur Auffassung der Aphasien*, Vienna. (240-1, 245, 248, 325)
[*Trans.*: On Aphasia, London and New York, 1953.]

(1892a) Translation of H. Bernheim's *Hypnotisme, suggestion et psychothérapie: études nouvelles*, Paris, 1891, under the title *Neue Studien über Hypnotismus, Suggestion und Psychotherapie*, Vienna. (257)

(1892-3) 'Ein Fall von hypnotischer Heilung nebst Bemerkungen über die Entstehung hysterischer Symptome durch den "Gegenwillen" ', G.S., **1**, 258; G.W., **1**, 3. (32, 242-3)
[*Trans.*: 'A Case of Successful Treatment by Hypnotism', C.P., **5**, 33; Standard Ed., **1.**]

(1892-4) Translation with Preface and Footnotes of J.-M. Charcot's *Leçons du mardi (1887-8)*, Paris, 1888, under the title *Poliklinische Vorträge*, **1**, Vienna. (10, 13, 18, 65, 257)
[*Trans.*: Preface and Footnotes to Charcot's *Poliklinische Vorträge*, **1**, Standard Ed., **1.**]

(1893a) With BREUER, J., 'Über den psychischen Mechanismus hysterischer Phänomene: Vorläufige Mitteilung', G.S., **1**, 7; G.W., **1**, 81. (3, 26, 37, 43, 46, 47, 49, 60-1, 63, 65, 80, 163, 242, 244, 250)

[*Trans.*: 'On the Psychical Mechanism of Hysterical Phenomena: Preliminary Communication', *C.P.*, **1**, 24; *Standard Ed.*, **2**, 3.]

(1893*b*) 'Zur Kenntnis der cerebralen Diplegien des Kindesalters (im Anschluss an die Little'sche Krankheit)', Heft III, Neue Folge, of *Beiträge zur Kinderheilkunde*, ed. Kassowitz, Vienna. (239, 245–7, 325)

(1893*c*) 'Quelques considérations pour une étude comparative des paralysies motrices organiques et hystériques' [in French], *G.S.*, **1**, 273; *G.W.*, **1**, 39. (3, 43, 63, 65, 72, 248)
[*Trans.*: 'Some Points for a Comparative Study of Organic and Hysterical Motor Paralyses', *C.P.*, **1**, 42; *Standard Ed.*, **1**.]

(1893*d*) 'Über familiäre Formen von cerebralen Diplegien', *Neurol. Zbl.*, **12**, Nr. 15, 512, and 16, 542. (239, 247)

(1893*e*) 'Les diplégies cérébrales infantiles' [in French], *Rev. neurol.*, **1**, No. 8, 177. (239, 247)

(1893*f*) 'Charcot', *G.S.*, **1**, 243; *G.W.*, **1**, 21. (4, 5, 43, 81, 242, 243)
[*Trans.*: 'Charcot', *C.P.*, **1**, 9; *Standard Ed.*, **3**, 9.]

(1893*g*) 'Über ein Symptom, das häufig die Enuresis nocturna der Kinder begleitet', *Neurol. Zbl.*, **12**, Nr. 21, 735. (243)

(1893*h*) Vortrag 'Über den psychischen Mechanismus hysterischer Phänomene' [shorthand report revised by lecturer], *Wien. med. Pr.*, **34**, Nr. 4, 121, and 5, 165. (3, 49, 63, 65, 197, 279, 282)
[*Trans.*: Lecture 'On the Psychical Mechanism of Hysterical Phenomena', *Int. J. Psycho-Anal.*, **37**, 8; *Standard Ed.*, **3**, 27.]

(1894*a*) 'Die Abwehr-Neuropsychosen', *G.S.*, **1**, 290; *G.W.*, **1**, 59. (36, 62–6, 71, 72, 73, 75, 76, 77, 83–4, 88, 97, 98, 108, 154, 159–60, 162, 163, 166, 170, 193, 195, 210, 218, 219, 249, 263)
[*Trans.*: 'The Neuro-Psychoses of Defence', *C.P.*, **1**, 59; *Standard Ed.*, **3**, 43.]

(1895*b* [1894]) 'Über die Berechtigung, von der Neurasthenie einen bestimmten Symptomenkomplex als "Angstneurose" abzutrennen', *G.S.*, **1**, 306; *G.W.*, **1**, 315. (63, 71, 81, 83–4, 121, 123–139, 146, 150, 166, 250, 251, 252, 263, 268, 273)
[*Trans.*: 'On the Grounds for Detaching a Particular Syndrome from Neurasthenia under the Description "Anxiety Neurosis" ', *C.P.*, **1**, 76; *Standard Ed.*, **3**, 87.]

(1895*c* [1894]) 'Obsessions et phobies' [in French], *G.S.*, **1**, 334; *G.W.*, **1**, 345. (45, 56, 58, 83–4, 91, 97, 145, 153, 173, 245, 250, 263)
[*Trans.*: 'Obsessions and Phobias', *C.P.*, **1**, 128; *Standard Ed.*, **3**, 71.]

(1895*d*) With BREUER, J., *Studien über Hysterie*, Vienna. *G.S.*, **1**, 3; *G.W.*, **1**, 77 (omitting Breuer's contributions). (3, 5, 26, 29–35, 43, 44, 46, 47, 48, 51, 52, 55, 57, 62, 63, 65, 67, 79, 80, 93, 100, 106, 123, 131, 151, 162, 164, 177, 180, 192–3, 198, 216, 218, 221, 244, 250–1, 279, 282, 325)
[*Trans.*: *Studies on Hysteria*, *Standard Ed.*, **2**. Including Breuer's contributions.]

(1895*e*) 'Über die Bernhardt'sche Sensibilitätsstörung am Oberschenkel', *Neurol. Zbl.*, **14**, Nr. 11, 491. (253)

(1895*f*) 'Zur Kritik der "Angstneurose" ', *G.S.*, **1**, 343; *G.W.*, **1**, 357. (65, 83, 89, 99, 105, 106, 114, 142, 147, 182, 209, 252, 263, 271)
[*Trans.:* 'A Reply to Criticisms of my Paper on Anxiety Neurosis', *C.P.*, **1**, 107; *Standard Ed.*, **3**, 121.]

(1896*a*) 'L'hérédité et l'étiologie des névroses' [in French], *G.S.*, **1**, 388; *G.W.*, **1**, 407. (21, 47, 72–3, 79, 109, 122, 139, 159, 160, 167, 190, 199, 255, 263)
[*Trans.:* 'Heredity and the Aetiology of the Neuroses', *C.P.*, **1**, 138; *Standard Ed.*, **3**, 143.]

(1896*b*) 'Weitere Bemerkungen über die Abwehr-Neuropsychosen', *G.S.*, **1**, 363; *G.W.*, **1**, 379. (53, 100, 142, 152, 154, 155, 156, 190, 197, 199, 204, 208, 212, 219, 253, 263, 279, 308)
[*Trans.:* 'Further Remarks on the Neuro-Psychoses of Defence', *C.P.*, **1**, 155; *Standard Ed.*, **3**, 159.]

(1896*c*) 'Zur Ätiologie der Hysterie', *G.S.*, **1**, 404; *G.W.*, **1**, 425. (103, 160, 163, 167, 254, 261, 263, 303)
[*Trans.:* 'The Aetiology of Hysteria', *C.P.*, **1**, 183; *Standard Ed.*, **3**, 189.]

(1897*a*) *Die infantile Cerebrallähmung*, II Theil, II Abt. of Nothnagel's *Specielle Pathologie und Therapie*, **9**, Vienna. (239, 256, 261–2, 325)

(1897*b*) *Inhaltsangaben der wissenschaftlichen Arbeiten des Privatdozenten Dr. Sigm. Freud (1877–1897)*, Vienna. *G.W.*, **1**, 463. (4, 9, 43, 71, 87, 88, 121, 142, 159, 189, 325)
[*Trans.:* *Abstracts of the Scientific Writings of Dr. Sigm. Freud (1877–1897)*, *Standard Ed.*, **3**, 225.]

(1898*a*) 'Die Sexualität in der Ätiologie der Neurosen', *G.S.*, **1**, 439; *G.W.*, **1**, 491. (83, 104, 105, 109, 150, 167)
[*Trans.:* 'Sexuality in the Aetiology of the Neuroses', *C.P.*, **1**, 220; *Standard Ed.*, **3**, 261.]

(1898*b*) 'Zum psychischen Mechanismus der Vergesslichkeit', *G.W.*, **1**, 519. (3)
[*Trans.:* 'The Psychical Mechanism of Forgetfulness', *Standard Ed.*, **3**, 289.]

(1899*a*) 'Über Deckerinnerungen', *G.S.*, **1**, 465; *G.W.*, **1**, 531. (4, 181, 291)
[*Trans.:* 'Screen Memories', *C.P.*, **5**, 47; *Standard Ed.*, **3**, 301.]

(1900*a*) *Die Traumdeutung*, Vienna. *G.S.*, **2–3**; *G.W.*, **2–3**. (5, 64–6, 130, 132, 225, 262, 281, 293, 302, 310, 319–20, 324, 325)
[*Trans.:* *The Interpretation of Dreams*, London and New York, 1955; *Standard Ed.*, **4–5**.]

(1901*b*) *Zur Psychopathologie des Alltagslebens*, Berlin, 1904. *G.S.*, **4**, 3; *G.W.*, **4**. (5, 10, 37, 288, 289, 291, 294, 297, 302)
[*Trans.:* *The Psychopathology of Everyday Life, Standard Ed.*, **6**.]

(1901c [1899]) Autobiographical Note, in J. L. Pagel's *Biographisches Lexicon hervorragender Ärzte des neunzehnten Jahrhunderts*, Berlin. [*Trans.: Standard Ed.*, **3**, 325.]

(1904a) 'Die Freud'sche psychoanalytische Methode', *G.S.*, **6**, 3; *G.W.*, **5**, 3. (3, 5)
[*Trans.:* 'Freud's Psycho-Analytic Procedure', *C.P.*, **1**, 264; *Standard Ed.*, **7**, 249.]

(1905a) 'Über Psychotherapie', *G.S.*, **6**, 11; *G.W.*, **5**, 13. (3)
[*Trans.:* 'On Psychotherapy', *C.P.*, **1**, 249; *Standard Ed.*, **7**, 257.]

(1905c) *Der Witz und seine Beziehung zum Unbewussten*, Vienna. *G.S.*, **9**, 5; *G.W.*, **6**. (5, 36, 307)
[*Trans.: Jokes and their Relation to the Unconscious, Standard Ed.*, **8**.]

(1905d) *Drei Abhandlungen zur Sexualtheorie*, Vienna. *G.S.*, **5**, 3; *G.W.*, **5**, 29. (5, 108, 122, 160–1, 168, 190, 272)
[*Trans.: Three Essays on the Theory of Sexuality*, London, 1949; *Standard Ed.*, **7**, 125.]

(1905e [1901]) 'Bruchstück einer Hysterie-Analyse', *G.S.*, **8**, 3; *G.W.*, **5**, 163. (5, 13, 111, 198)
[*Trans.:* 'Fragment of an Analysis of a Case of Hysteria', *C.P.*, **3**, 13; *Standard Ed.*, **7**, 3.]

(1906a) 'Meine Ansichten über die Rolle der Sexualität in der Ätiologie der Neurosen', *G.S.*, **5**, 123; *G.W.*, **5**, 149. (3, 5, 52, 122, 160)
[*Trans.:* 'My Views on the Part played by Sexuality in the Aetiology of the Neuroses', *C.P.*, **1**, 272; *Standard Ed.*, **7**, 271.]

(1906b) Preface to Freud's *Sammlung kleiner Schriften zur Neurosenlehre aus den Jahren 1893–1906, G.S.*, **1**, 241; *G.W.*, **1**, 557.
[*Trans.:* Preface to Freud's Shorter Writings 1893–1906, *Standard Ed.*, **3**, 3.]

(1906c) 'Tatbestandsdiagnostik und Psychoanalyse', *G.S.*, **10**, 197; *G.W.*, **7**, 3. (46)
[*Trans.:* 'Psycho-Analysis and the Establishment of the Facts in Legal Proceedings', *C.P.*, **2**, 13; *Standard Ed.*, **9**, 99.]

(1908d) 'Die "kulturelle" Sexualmoral und die moderne Nervosität', *G.S.*, **5**, 143; *G.W.*, **7**, 143. (148, 262, 272, 277)
[*Trans.:* ' "Civilized" Sexual Morality and Modern Nervous Illness', *C.P.*, **2**, 76; *Standard Ed.*, **9**, 179.]

(1909a) 'Allgemeines über den hysterischen Anfall', *G.S.*, **5**, 255; *G.W.*, **7**, 235. (44)
[*Trans.:* 'Some General Remarks on Hysterical Attacks', *C.P.*, **2**, 100; *Standard Ed.*, **9**, 229.]

(1909b) 'Analyse der Phobie eines fünfjährigen Knaben', *G.S.*, **8**, 129; *G.W.*, **7**, 243. (84)
[*Trans.:* 'Analysis of a Phobia in a Five-Year-Old Boy', *C.P.*, **3**, 149; *Standard Ed.*, **10**, 3.]

(1909d) 'Bemerkungen über einen Fall von Zwangsneurose', *G.S.*, **8**, 269; *G.W.*, **7**, 381. (52, 161, 169, 170, 322)

[*Trans.:* 'Notes upon a Case of Obsessional Neurosis', *C.P.*, **3**, 293; *Standard Ed.*, **10**, 155.]

(1910*a* [1909]) *Über Psychoanalyse*, Vienna. *G.S.*, **4**, 349; *G.W.*, **8**, 3. (49)
[*Trans.:* 'Five Lectures on Psycho-Analysis', *Amer. J. Psychol.*, **21** (1910), 181; *Standard Ed.*, **11**, 3.]

(1910*d*) 'Die zukünftigen Chancen der psychoanalytischen Therapie', *G.S.*, **6**, 25; *G.W.*, **8**, 104. (122)
[*Trans.:* 'The Future Prospects of Psycho-Analytic Therapy', *C.P.*, **2**, 285; *Standard Ed.*, **11**, 141.]

(1910*k*) 'Über "wilde" Psychoanalyse', *G.S.*, **6**, 37; *G.W.*, **8**, 118. (279)
[*Trans.:* ' "Wild" Psycho-Analysis', *C.P.*, **2**, 297; *Standard Ed.*, **11**, 221.]

(1911*b*) 'Formulierungen über die zwei Prinzipien des psychischen Geschehens', *G.S.*, **5**, 409; *G.W.*, **8**, 230. (66)
[*Trans.:* 'Formulations on the Two Principles of Mental Functioning', *C.P.*, **4**, 13; *Standard Ed.*, **12**, 215.]

(1912*f*) 'Zur Onanie-Diskussion', *G.S.*, **3**, 324; *G.W.*, **8**, 332. (276)
[*Trans.:* 'Contributions to a Discussion on Masturbation', *Standard Ed.*, **12**, 243.]

(1913*i*) 'Die Disposition zur Zwangsneurose', *G.S.*, **5**, 277; *G.W.*, **8**, 442. (190)
[*Trans.:* 'The Disposition to Obsessional Neurosis', *C.P.*, **2**, 122; *Standard Ed.*, **12**, 313.]

(1914*c*) 'Zur Einführung des Narzissmus', *G.S.*, **6**, 155; *G.W.*, **10**, 138. (93)
[*Trans.:* 'On Narcissism: an Introduction', *C.P.*, **4**, 30; *Standard Ed.*, **14**, 69.]

(1914*d*) 'Zur Geschichte der psychoanalytischen Bewegung', *G.S.*, **4**, 411; *G.W.*, **10**, 44. (10, 49, 62)
[*Trans.:* 'On the History of the Psycho-Analytic Movement', *C.P.*, **1**, 287; *Standard Ed.*, **14**, 3.]

(1915*c*) 'Triebe und Triebschicksale', *G.S.*, **5**, 443; *G.W.*, **10**, 210. (65, 66, 112)
[*Trans.:* 'Instincts and their Vicissitudes', *C.P.*, **4**, 60; *Standard Ed.*, **14**, 111.]

(1915*d*) 'Die Verdrängung', *G.S.*, **5**, 466; *G.W.*, **10**, 248. (52, 54, 67–8, 84)
[*Trans.:* 'Repression', *C.P.*, **4**, 84; *Standard Ed.*, **14**, 143.]

(1915*e*) 'Das Unbewusste', *G.S.*, **5**, 480; *G.W.*, **10**, 264. (66–7, 84, 219)
[*Trans.:* 'The Unconscious', *C.P.*, **4**, 98; *Standard Ed.*, **14**, 161.]

(1916–17) *Vorlesungen zur Einführung in die Psychoanalyse*, Vienna. *G.S.*, **7**; *G.W.*, **11**. (13, 66–8, 116, 121, 122, 173, 228, 234, 310, 322)
[*Trans.: Introductory Lectures on Psycho-Analysis*, revised ed., London,

1929 (*A General Introduction to Psychoanalysis*, New York, 1935); *Standard Ed.*, **15–16.**]

(1918*b* [1914]) 'Aus der Geschichte einer infantilen Neurose', *G.S.*, **8**, 439; *G.W.*, **12**, 29. (84, 168, 322)
[*Trans.*: 'From the History of an Infantile Neurosis', *C.P.*, **3**, 473; *Standard Ed.*, **17**, 3.]

(1920*g*) *Jenseits des Lustprinzips*, Vienna. *G.S.*, **6**, 191; *G.W.*, **13**, 3. (65, 116)
[*Trans.*: *Beyond the Pleasure Principle*, London, 1961; *Standard Ed.*, **18**, 3.]

(1921*c*) *Massenpsychologie und Ich-Analyse*, Vienna. *G.S.*, **6**, 261; *G.W.*, **13**, 73. (23)
[*Trans.*: *Group Psychology and the Analysis of the Ego*, London, 1959; New York, 1960; *Standard Ed.*, **18**, 67.]

(1923*a*) ' "Psychoanalyse" und "LibidoTheorie" ', *G.S.*, **11**, 201; *G.W.*, **13**, 211. (102)
[*Trans.*: 'Two Encyclopaedia Articles', *C.P.*, **5**, 107; *Standard Ed.*, **18**, 235.]

(1923*b*) *Das Ich und das Es*, Vienna. *G.S.*, **6**, 353; *G.W.*, **13**, 237. (55)
[*Trans.*: *The Ego and the Id*, London, 1927; *Standard Ed.*, **19**, 3.]

(1923*c*) 'Bemerkungen zur Theorie und Praxis der Traumdeutung', *G.S.*, **3**, 305; *G.W.*, **13**, 301. (199, 205)
[*Trans.*: 'Remarks on the Theory and Practice of Dream-Interpretation', *C.P.*, **5**, 136; *Standard Ed.*, **19**, 109.]

(1923*d*) 'Eine Teufelsneurose im siebzehnten Jahrhundert', *G.S.*, **10**, 409; *G.W.*, **13**, 317. (20)
[*Trans.*: 'A Seventeenth Century Demonological Neurosis', *C.P.*, **4**, 436; *Standard Ed.*, **19**, 69.]

(1924*a*) Letter [in French] to *Le Disque Vert*, *G.S.*, **11**, 266; *G.W.*, **13**, 446. (12)
[*Trans.*: *Standard Ed.*, **19**, 290.]

(1924*b*) 'Neurose und Psychose', *G.S.*, **5**, 418; *G.W.*, **13**, 387. (59)
[*Trans.*: 'Neurosis and Psychosis', *C.P.*, **2**, 250; *Standard Ed.*, **19**, 149.]

(1924*c*) 'Das ökonomische Problem des Masochismus', *G.S.*, **5**, 374; *G.W.*, **13**, 371. (66)
[*Trans.*: 'The Economic Problem of Masochism', *C.P.*, **2**, 255; *Standard Ed.*, **19**, 157.]

(1924*e*) 'Die Realitätsverlust bei Neurose und Psychose', *G.S.*, **6**, 409; *G.W.*, **13**, 363. (59)
[*Trans.*: 'The Loss of Reality in Neurosis and Psychosis', *C.P.*, **2**, 277; *Standard Ed.*, **19**, 183.]

(1925*d* [1924]) *Selbstdarstellung*, Vienna, 1934. *G.S.*, **11**, 119; *G.W.*, **14**, 33. (10, 13, 59, 234, 236)
[*Trans.*: *An Autobiographical Study*, London, 1935 (*Autobiography*, New York, 1935); *Standard Ed.*, **20**, 3.]

(1926*d*) *Hemmung, Symptom und Angst*, Vienna. *G.S.*, **11**, 23; *G.W.*, **14**, 113. (84, 87, 89, 93, 109, 111, 116–17, 156, 168, 175)

[*Trans.: Inhibitions, Symptoms and Anxiety*, London, 1960 (*The Problem of Anxiety*, New York, 1936); *Standard Ed.*, **20**, 77.]

(1926*e*) *Die Frage der Laienanalyse*, Vienna. *G.S.*, **11**, 307; *G.W.*, **14**, 209. (313)
[*Trans.: The Question of Lay Analysis*, London, 1947; *Standard Ed.*, **20**, 179.]

(1926*f*) An Article in the *Encyclopaedia Britannica* [published as 'Psycho-Analysis: Freudian School'], *Encyclopaedia Britannica*, 13th ed., New Vol. **3**, 253; *Standard Ed.*, **20**, 261. (63)
[*German Text:* 'Psycho-Analysis', *G.S.*, **12**, 372; *G.W.*, **14**, 299. German original first appeared in 1934.]

(1927*e*) 'Fetischismus', *G.S.*, **11**, 395; *G.W.*, **14**, 311. (59, 67)
[*Trans.:* 'Fetishism', *C.P.*, **5**, 198; *Standard Ed.*, **21**, 149.]

(1930*a*) *Das Unbehagen in der Kultur*, Vienna. *G.S.*, **12**, 29; *G.W.*, **14**, 421. (93, 102, 262, 272)
[*Trans.: Civilization and its Discontents*, London and New York, 1930; *Standard Ed.*, **21**, 59.]

(1931*b*) 'Über die weibliche Sexualität', *G.S.*, **12**, 120; *G.W.*, **14**, 517. (130, 161)
[*Trans.:* 'Female Sexuality', *C.P.*, **5**, 252; *Standard Ed.*, **21**, 223.]

(1931*e*) Letter to the Burgomaster of Příbor, *G.S.*, **12**, 414; *G.W.*, **14**, 561. (302)
[*Trans.: Standard Ed.*, **21**, 259.]

(1937*c*) 'Die endliche und die unendliche Analyse', *G.W.*, **16**, 59. (161, 206, 272)
[*Trans.:* 'Analysis Terminable and Interminable', *C.P.*, **5**, 316; *Standard Ed.*, **23**.]

(1937*d*) 'Konstruktionen in der Analyse', *G.W.*, **16**, 43. (291)
[*Trans.:* 'Constructions in Analysis', *C.P.*, **5**, 358; *Standard Ed.*, **23**.]

(1940*d* [1892]) With BREUER, J., 'Zur Theorie des hysterischen Anfalls', *G.W.*, **17**, 9. (49, 63, 65)
[*Trans.:* 'On the Theory of Hysterical Attacks', *C.P.*, **5**, 27; *Standard Ed.*, **1**.]

(1940*e* [1938]) 'Die Ichspaltung im Abwehrvorgang', *G.W.*, **17**, 59. (59)
[*Trans.:* 'Splitting of the Ego in the Process of Defence', *C.P.*, **5**, 372; *Standard Ed.*, **23**.]

(1941*a* [1892]) Letter to Josef Breuer, *G.W.*, **17**, 5. (49, 65, 122, 193)
[*Trans.: C.P.*, **5**, 25; *Standard Ed.*, **1**.]

(1941*b* [1892]) 'Notiz "III" ', *G.W.*, **17**, 17. (122)
[*Trans.:* 'III', *C.P.*, **5**, 31; *Standard Ed.*, **1**.]

(1950*a* [1887–1902]) *Aus den Anfängen der Psychoanalyse*, London. Includes 'Entwurf einer Psychologie' (1895). (37, 51, 55, 56–7, 62, 64–7, 87–8, 90, 91, 97, 100, 102, 105, 106, 108, 110, 111, 121–2, 132, 133, 139, 142, 160, 161, 162–3, 167, 184, 185, 189, 225–6, 243, 245, 261, 262, 276, 277, 288, 290, 295, 301–2, 310)
[*Trans.: The Origins of Psycho-Analysis*, London and New York,

336   BIBLIOGRAPHY

1954. (Partly, including 'A Project for a Scientific Psychology',
in *Standard Ed.*, **1.**)]

(1955*a* [1907–8]) Original Record of the Case of Obsessional
Neurosis (the 'Rat Man'), *Standard Ed.*, **10**, 259. German text
unpublished. (302)

(1956*a* [1886]) 'Report on my Studies in Paris and Berlin, on a
Travelling Bursary Granted from the University Jubilee Fund,
1885–6', *Int. J. Psycho-Anal.*, **37**, 2; *Standard Ed.*, **1.** (10, 12, 17)
[*German Text (unpublished)*: 'Bericht über meine mit Universitäts-
Jubiläums Reisestipendium unternommene Studienreise nach
Paris und Berlin.']

(1960*a*) *Briefe 1873–1939* (ed. E. L. Freud), Berlin. (10, 230)
[*Trans.: Letters 1873–1939* (ed. E. L. Freud) (trans. T. and
J. Stern), New York, 1960; London, 1961.]

GÉLINEAU, J. B. É. (1894) *Des peurs maladives ou phobies*, Paris. (74)

HAMMOND, W. A. (1886) 'Remarks on Cocaine and the so-called
Cocaine Habit', *J. nerv. ment. dis.*, **11**, 754. (239)

HECKER, E. (1893) 'Über larvirte und abortive Angstzustände bei
Neurasthenie', *Zbl. Nervenheilk.*, **16**, 565. (91, 94, 123)

HENRI, V. and C. (1897) 'Enquête sur les premiers souvenirs de
l'enfance', *L'année psychologique*, **3**, 184. (304–6, 309, 321–2)

ICONOGRAPHIE DE LA SALPÊTRIÈRE, 3 (1879–80), Paris. (241–2)

JANET, PIERRE, (1892–4) *État mental des hystériques* (2 vols.), Paris. (46)
(1893) 'Quelques définitions récentes de l'hystérie', *Arch. neurol.*,
25, 417, and **26**, 1. (46, 51)

JONES, E. (1953) *Sigmund Freud: Life and Work*, Vol. 1, London and New
York. (Page references are to the English edition.) (10, 14, 66,
226, 230, 233, 302)
(1955) *Sigmund Freud: Life and Work*, Vol. 2, London and New York.
(Page reference is to the English edition.) (207)

KAAN, H. (1893) *Der neurasthenische Angstaffekt bei Zwangsvorstel-lungen und
der primordiale Grübelzwang*, Vienna. (91)

KASSOWITZ, M. (ed.) (1890 etc.) *Beiträge zur Kinderheilkunde*, Vienna.
(241, 245, 257)

KRAFFT-EBING, R. VON (1867) *Beiträge zur Erkennung und richtigen foren-
sischen Beurteilung krankhafter Gemütszustände für Ärzte, Richter und
Verteidiger*, Erlangen. (72)

LÖWENFELD, L. (1893) *Pathologie und Therapie der Neurasthenie und Hysterie*,
Wiesbaden. (125)
(1895) 'Über die Verknüpfung neurasthenischer und hysterischer
Symptome in Anfallsform nebst Bemerkungen über die Freudsche
Angstneurose', *Münchener med. Wschr.*, **42**, 282. (121–39, 99)
(1904) *Die psychischen Zwangserscheinungen*, Wiesbaden. (3, 5, 72, 91,
97)
(1906) *Sexualleben und Nervenleiden*, 4th ed., Wiesbaden. (3, 5, 52,
160)

MÖBIUS, P. J. (1894) *Neurologische Beiträge*, Vol 2, Leipzig. (98)

MOLL, A. (1898) *Untersuchungen über die Libido sexualis*, Vol. 1, Berlin. (102)

NIEMANN, A. (1860) *Über eine neue organische Basis in den Cocablättern*, Göttingen. (233)

NOTHNAGEL, H. (ed.) (1897) *Specielle Pathologie und Therapie*, Vol. 9, Vienna. (256, 261, 325)

PEYER, A. (1893) 'Die nervösen Affektionen des Darmes bei der Neurasthenie des männlichen Geschlechtes (Darmneurasthenie)', *Vorträge aus der gesamten praktischen Heilkunde*, 1. Vienna. (98)

RIE, O. (1891) *See* FREUD, S. (1891a)

ROSENBERG, L. (1893) *Casuistische Beiträge zur Kenntnis der cerebralen Kinderlähmungen und der Epilepsie*, Heft IV, Neue Folge of *Beiträge zur Kinderheilkunde*, ed. Kassowitz, Vienna. (257)

ROSENTHAL, E. (1892) *Contribution à l'étude des diplégies cérébrales de l'enfance*. Thèse de Lyon. (257)

STEKEL, W. (1895) 'Koitus im Kindesalter', *Wien. med. Bl.*, **18**, 247. (207)

TUKE, D. HACK (1894) 'Imperative Ideas', *Brain*, **17**, 179. (74)

WALDEYER, W. (1891) *Über einige neuere Forschungen im Gebiete der Anatomie des Centralnervensystems*, Leipzig. (230)

WERNICKE, K. (1894) Lecture on Anxiety Psychosis, reported in *Allg. Z. Psychiat.*, **51** (1895), 1020. (91)

LIST OF ABBREVIATIONS

G.S.	=	Freud, *Gesammelte Schriften* (12 vols.), Vienna, 1924–34
G.W.	=	Freud, *Gesammelte Werke* (18 vols.), London, from 1940
C.P.	=	Freud, Collected Papers (5 vols.), London, 1924–50
Standard Ed.	=	Freud, *Standard Edition* (24 vols.), London, from 1953
S.K.S.N.	=	Freud, *Sammlung kleiner Schriften zur Neurosenlehre* (5 vols.), Vienna, 1906–22
S.P.H.	=	Freud, *Selected Papers on Hysteria and Other Psychoneuroses*, New York, 1909–20

GENERAL INDEX

This index includes the names of non-technical authors. It also includes the names of technical authors where no reference is made in the text to specific works. For references to specific technical works, the Bibliography should be consulted.—The compilation of the index was undertaken by Angela Richards.

Abreaction, 37–9, 47, 60, 63, 244

Abstinence, sexual, 81, 101, 102, 109–10, 111, 113–14, 124, 132, 150, 251, 268

Absurdity of obsessions, 55, 75, 77

'Actual' neuroses (*see also* Aetiology, sexual; Anxiety attacks; Anxiety neurosis; Hypochondria; Neurasthenia), 44, 64, 83, 84, 142, 167 *n.*, 270 and *n.*, 279 and *n.* 1
distinguished from psychoneuroses, 266–70, 278–80
no psychical mechanism in, 58, 81, 107–8, 114–15, 124, 125–6

Addictions related to masturbation, 276

Adolescent anxiety, 99–100

Adriatic, the, 288, 290 *n.* 2

Aeneid, 317 and *n.* 1

Aetiological
equation, 121–2, 122 *n.*, 135–8
series, 122, 210, 271

Aetiology (*see also* Heredity, role of, in aetiology of the neuroses)
different classes of causes in, 34–5, 106, 135–9, 146–7, 209–10, 252
of anxiety neurosis, 81, 99–139, 150–1, 251–2, 276–9
of hysteria, 27–39, 46–51, 80, 151–6, 163–8, 189–221, 244, 249, 250–1, 253–4
of 'mixed' neuroses (*see* 'Mixed' neuroses)
of neurasthenia, 109, 123, 150–1, 268, 275–6
of obsessional neurosis, 51–8, 74–80, 151, 155–6, 168–74, 249, 250, 253
of phthisis pulmonum, 136–7
of psychoneuroses, 278–85
of smallpox, 209

of tuberculosis, 209
specific factor in, 103, 106, 123, 127, 130, 131, 135–8, 145–50, 156, 163–8, 209, 210, 252, 253, 271
'stock' factors in, 99, 103, 105–6, 127, 128, 130–1, 133, 137, 148–9
summation in, 103, 106, 130

Aetiology, sexual
of 'actual' neuroses and psychoneuroses, 149–56, 263–85, 325
of anxiety neurosis, 99–112, 123–39, 167–8, 251–2, 268–9
of hysteria, 47–8, 151–5, 160, 163–8, 199–221, 253
of neurasthenia, 123, 167–8, 267–72
of obsessional neurosis, 52–7, 75–7, 155–6, 160, 168–74, 219, 253
of paranoia, 160, 161, 174–85, 219, 253
of phobias, 81, 133–4

Aetiology, traumatic, of neuroses, 27–39, 47–50, 151–6, 163–9, 172, 192–7, 253
revision of theory, 168 *n.* 1, 203 *n.* 1, 204 *n.*
theory abandoned, 262

Affect
abreaction of, 37
displacement of, 52 and *n.* 1, 53–8, 60, 75–80
distinguished from excitation, 66–8
essential element of obsessions, 74, 250
expressed by hysterical symptoms, 19–20, 51 *n.* 1
justified in obsessions, 75, 77, 171, 250

341

auto-, 38
theory of, 22–3
unnecessary in treating obsessions and phobias, 54–5
used by *Breuer* and *Freud*, 30, 32–5, 39, 59, 242 and *n.* 2
used by *Charcot*, 22, 28, 244
Hypochondria, 78, 93 and *n.* 1, 97, 102, 171
Hysteria (*see also* Aetiology; Aetiology, sexual; Defence, neuropsychoses of; 'Mixed' neuroses; Psychoneuroses)
acquired, 45, 47, 107
and anxiety neurosis compared, 114–15, 125
and malingering, 19, 27
and obsessional neurosis compared, 146
and paranoia compared, 180, 184
Charcot's contribution to study of, 19–23, 27
conversion, 44 *n.* 1, 249
cure of, prospects of, 39, 282–3
defence, 47
disposition to, 50, 166
hypnoid, 47
male, 21–3, 163, 201, 207, 210, 238 and *n.* 2
mechanism of, 26–39
mental 'sensitivity' in, 217–18
occurrence in lower classes, 207, 210, 211
ousted by psychosis, 59
precedes 'congenital' anxiety neurosis, 129
preference of females for, 156 and *n.* 1, 163
reaction apparently exaggerated in, 216–18
retention, 47
sexual, 115
splitting of consciousness in, 20, 45–8, 49–51, 51 *n.* 3, 249
traumatic, 28–9, 30–1, 107
Hysterical
aura, 28
confusion, 283
conversion, 44 *n.* 1, 49, 50, 54, 58, 175
counterwill, 32, 242–3
deliria, 38
paralyses, 20, 22, 27–9, 43, 244, 248
Hysterical attacks, 50, 218

major, 20–1
minor, 21
Hysterical symptoms, 19–21, 28–9, 34, 80 and *n.*, 193, 201, 211–14, 254
overdetermined, 216
Hystero-neurasthenia, 266
Hysterogenic
points, 218 and *n.* 1
zones, 21, 34, 218 *n.* 1

Ideas (*see also* Association; Incompatible ideas; Obsessions; Repressed ideas)
antithetic, 242
vicissitude of, under repression, distinct from that of affect, 52 *n.* 1, 67 and *n.* 2
Idées fixes, hysterical, 281
Illness, physical, in aetiology of neuroses, 148–9, 252, 271, 280
Incompatible ideas, 47–54, 58–9, 72, 75, 77, 79–80, 111, 163, 210–11, 213, 249, 250
translation of term, 51 *n.* 4, 72
Infantile
factors in aetiology of neuroses, 152–6, 161–2, 163–9, 183, 190, 203–15, 219–20, 253–4, 280–1
factors in aetiology of paranoia, 178–83, 253
sexuality, spontaneous, 160–1, 168 *n.* 1, 262, 301
sexuality, polymorphously perverse, 190, 214–15
Inheritance, 'dissimilar' and 'similar' (*see also* Heredity), 255
Innervations
motor, included in affects, 67
somatic, in conversion, 49, 50, 54, 175, 249
Insanity (*see also* Psychosis), 145
Instincts, psychical representatives of, 67
Instinctual
energy (*see* Energy)
forces, sexual, serve cultural ends (*Fliess*), 281
Intensity, psychical (*see also* Energy, psychical), 67, 130, 174, 308
Interpretation of Dreams, The (*Freud*), 262, 281 and *n.*, 324, 325
Intoxication in aetiology of neuroses, 148

Multiple sclerosis, 14
Myopathies, 145
Mysophobia, 79 and *n.* 2

Nasal reflex neurosis (*Fliess*), 90
Nasal sinus, infected, 269–70
Nausea in anxiety neurosis, 97
Nervous system
  anatomical preparations of, 229, 231
  structure of, 227–30, 230 *n.*
Neuralgia
  facial, 143, 255
  hysterical, 34
Neurasthenia (*see also* 'Actual' neuroses; Aetiology; Aetiology, sexual; 'Mixed' neuroses), 39, 44, 58, 74, 81, 87–8, 90–3, 144, 148, 250, 267–76
  anxiety neurosis distinguished from, 87–139, 146, 150–1, 251, 268
  cerebral, 105 *n.* 3, 128
  hysteria distinguished from, 115, 125
  masturbation as cause of, 102, 109, 111, 113, 150, 251, 268, 275–8
  periodic, 171
  pseudo-, 90
  symptoms of, 90, 91 *n.* 2, 150, 268, 273
  treatment of, 274–6
Neurological basis of psychology, 64–5, 88, 216
Neurology
  Freud's interest shifts from, to psychology, 9, 43, 64, 190, 203, 234 *n.* 2, 238 *n.* 2, 245 *n.* 1, 325
  Freud's work on, 225–43, 245–47, 253, 256–7, 325
Neurone theory, 64, 230 *n.*
'Neuronic inertia', principle of, 65
Neuro-psychoses of defence, 43–61, 159–85
Neuropathology
  Charcot's contribution to, 11, 13–16, 18–19
  science of, undeveloped in mid-nineteenth century, 11
Neuroses (*see also* Anxiety neurosis; Defence, neuro-psychoses of; Hysteria; Obsessional neurosis; Neurasthenia; Traumatic neuroses)
  s.f. III—z*

and organic nervous affections, 23
major, 146, 149, 162–3 *n.*
theory of, *Freud*'s preface to shorter writings on, 5–6
Neurosis, choice of, 156, 166–7 *n.*, 168–9, 190, 219–20, 255
'major' (*see also* Hysteria), 27, 143
nasal reflex (*Fliess*), 90
Neurotic symptoms (*see* Symptoms)
Newly-married women, anxiety in, 100, 103, 110
Nirvana principle, 65
Nodal points, 198 and *n.*, 199
Nothnagel, H. (*see also* Bibliography), 225, 256 *n.*
Notre Dame de Paris, 9
Nuns, hysterical deliria of, 38

Obsessional actions, 77–9, 172–4
  as protective procedures, 77, 82, 97, 172–3
  replace incompatible ideas, 77
Obsessional neurosis (*see also* Aetiology; Aetiology, sexual; Defence, neuro-psychoses of; 'Mixed' neuroses; Psychoneuroses), 44 *n.* 1, 51–8, 74–80, 142, 146, 168–74, 249, 253
  affect displaced in, 52–8, 75–80, 171–2, 175
  affect justified in, 75, 171, 250
  and hysteria compared, 146
  and paranoia compared, 183–5
  cure of, prospects of, 282–3
  first use of term, 96, 97 *n.* 1
  hysterical substratum of, 155–6, 168 and *n.* 2, 219
  ideas distorted in, 170–1, 175
  mechanisms of, 51–8, 96–7, 161, 168–74, 183–4
  preference of males for, 156 and *n.* 1, 168, 220
  translation of German term, 72
Obsessions, 44, 45, 48, 52, 54–5, 57–8, 71–2, 74–84, 250, 281, 284
  absurdity of, 55, 75, 171
  as compromises between repressed and repressing forces, 161, 170–2
  as self-reproaches, 155, 161, 169–71, 174, 178, 184, 220, 253
  as substitutes for incompatible ideas, 53–4, 75, 77, 79–80, 97, 249